HOW I BECAME
A SUSHI CHEF

FROM APPRENTICE TO TEACHER

STACY
THANK YOU FOR
"ROLLING"
WITH ME!
KAZ
9. 12. '21

KAZ MATSUNE

I have changed some of the names of individuals, restaurants, and establishments in this story to protect their privacy.

CONTENTS

I hope that in this year to come, you make mistakes. Because if you are making mistakes, then you are making new things, trying new things, learning, living, pushing yourself, changes your world. You're doing things you've never done before, and more importantly, you're doing something.

—Neil Gaiman

PROLOGUE

May 2000. Tokyo.

"One *Kara-Age Bento*. Ready," the woman shouted. Three men were waiting for an order. No one came forward.

"Sir, your Bento is ready," she said again, waving the plastic bag in my direction.

"Oh, yes. I am sorry, I didn't hear you." I turned around, grabbed the bag, and said, "Thank you."

As I walked back to my 300 square foot apartment, I rented only four months before, I contemplated what to do, stay in Tokyo, or go back to Los Angeles. The last time I lived in Tokyo was over 25 years ago when I was in kindergarten. A lot had changed since then. The city changed. I changed. I tried to remember those younger days in Tokyo, but none of my memories made me feel nostalgic.

I think I want to go back to L.A., I said to myself.

For the past year, I worked in Tokyo as a film producer. My job, however, didn't go as well as expected, so I quit. It felt like taking the producer job had been a big mistake. I thought I could do my job really well, but in the end, I couldn't.

It was my fourth, fifth, or maybe my sixth career. I didn't know because I never really counted. When I graduated from Art College ten years earlier, I was a Graphic Designer. I worked full-time for a year and then became a freelance designer. For the five or six years that followed, I designed Hollywood movie posters, newspaper and billboard ads, and video packaging. In the beginning, it was exciting to see my designs displayed on billboards and at video stores; but my excitement slowly started to dissipate. It was the same old, same old formula for "success," according to the movie studio executives: guns, explosions, and boobs. I'm sure you've seen them: Blockbuster movie posters, featuring action heroes, such as Arnold Schwarzenegger and Bruce Willis. Yep, violence,

1

action, and sex sell, and the more, the better. What I designed ignored all the principles I learned in school. The money was good, but the work was painful.

I didn't know this when I first started; in fact, I never dreamed of designing movie posters. It just so happened that the first company I worked for was an ad agency in Beverly Hills, specializing in movie posters. That was the beginning of my graphic design career.

I graduated from one of the most Avant-garde, experimental graphic design programs in the country. Yet, I wound up working for a company designing generic, mass-produced posters. It was like I lived in Hawaii all of my life, and now someone asked me to live in Alaska.

Eventually, I started drifting away from the movie poster design world. I started doing small jobs here and there, like working as a Production Assistant on video shoots and for corporate events, set design, creating slide presentations for corporate meetings, editing infomercials (the ones you see on TV at two in the morning), and just about any media design-related job I could pick up. I had a lot of jobs, but I didn't have a career. I didn't really know what I wanted to do.

I had ideas. I knew I wanted to start my own business, so I tried to start my own design firm, but that didn't work out. When the Internet came around, I tried a website called *classifiedonline.com*, but it never took off. I attended business seminars and talked to consultants. I even tried business ventures with friends: exporting beer to Japan and a cookie business in China. They all failed.

I knew one day I would make something happen, but I didn't know what it would be or when. The only thing I had to go on was my strong gut feeling.

That's when I met Kaneda-san, owner of a small film production company in Tokyo. In the beginning, I did small jobs for him, and one day he asked me to work in his office in Tokyo.

I was excited. I thought this might be it. This job would give me a chance to go back to Japan, and possibly work in both Tokyo and L.A., something I had always dreamed about. But soon, I was at a loss again.

MY DECISION

INTERVIEW, TOKYO

I always wanted to work in a restaurant. For a while, I also thought it would be fun to work as a bartender on the weekends. I enjoyed being with a crowd, watching people, and serving drinks. I thought I would enjoy working at a bar a lot more than being a customer, using my hard-earned cash to get drunk.

I went to the local bookstore and found a magazine with listings of available restaurant jobs in Tokyo. I bought several publications with tons of job listings and went back to my apartment.

There were a lot more Chef positions available than I thought there would be. I saw openings for both part- and full-time jobs, and almost every one of them required me to work in the evening. I never worked a night job before, but since it was a restaurant, I figured it would be okay.

A lot of listings also had age restrictions like "Restaurant server, age 24-35." I was 30 years old then. I almost forgot that age restrictions are common for restaurant workers in Japan. Most Japanese men my age would think twice about applying for a job like this. It never occurred to me that I might have difficulty finding a job because of my age, jobs in the US never listed such age restrictions.

I made several calls and lined up some interviews. Each restaurant asked me to bring my resume. I rushed out to the nearest office supply store and bought the standard, formatted resume paper. It looked like a form from City Hall, or when I got my driver's license. I carefully prepared five sets of resumes, all handwritten, with photos, and put them in my briefcase for the interviews. It had been over ten years since I filled out a resume form; it felt strange.

My first interview was at an *izakaya* restaurant in Shinjuku. I got on the Yūrakuchō Line subway and headed from Ikebukuro to Shinjuku. When I arrived, I looked at the menu and saw many appetizers, beers and wine, and pictures. I peeked through the window, but it was too dark to see the inside. I could barely see the bar full of liquor, the dark wood chairs, and tables. Business hours said they were open from 5 PM until 3 AM.

I stood outside by the front door, feeling nervous. I wasn't worried about the interview, but nervous because I had never faced such an interview in Japan.

A man appeared from the back of the restaurant. He opened the door and invited me to come in. "I believe you're here for the interview. You are Matsune-san, yes?" he said.

"Yes, I am Matsune," I said, slightly nodding my head down to acknowledge and show respect.

"My name is Tanaka. I am the restaurant manager. Nice to meet you," the man in his mid-thirties said, with a polite tone.

"Nice to meet you, too," I said.

"Please come inside," Tanaka-san said.

"Thank you." I followed him.

As he looked at my resume, Tanaka-san began to explain the restaurant operation, menu, my job duties, and pay. I could tell he wasn't really interested in my resume because I had no experience related to restaurant work. He saw that I felt embarrassed, but he reminded me, "You have to start somewhere, so there is nothing to be ashamed of."

"Do you have *any* previous experience?" Tanaka-san looked up.

I knew he was going to ask me that question, I looked straight into his eyes and replied, "No, nothing at all."

"Okay! You understand that most of the workers here are younger than you. Do you think it's going to be a problem?"

"Uh, no, not at all. Why could it be a problem?" I asked.

Culturally, as well as traditionally, in Japan, a younger person must pay respect to the elders. However, in the workplace, a junior employee must pay respect to the senior employee, so age didn't matter. Therefore, in my case, it might be an issue among senior employees who were younger than me.

Even if I didn't have a problem using respectful Japanese words, the other employees might feel awkward because of my age. Perhaps they would feel the need to address me with respect, and therefore not be able to command or ask me to perform any tasks.

During my ten years in the U.S., this was not a problem, but for the Japanese, it was.

"I'll let you talk to the kitchen manager," Tanaka-san said. He went into the kitchen and returned with the kitchen manager.

"My name is Suzuki," the kitchen manager introduced himself.

I stood up from my chair and bowed slightly to show respect. No handshake.

"Nice to meet you, Suzuki-san," I responded.

"So, I hear you have no previous experience..." he began.

"Yes, that is correct. I have never worked in a restaurant before."

"Do you know how to cook?" Suzuki-san asked me, looking into my eyes.

"Yes, I always cook for myself. I can cook *Osechi*."

"All right, that is good," he said in a way that sounded as if it didn't matter.

The kitchen manager seemed reluctant, showing very little interest and enthusiasm when talking to me. It made me uncomfortable.

"Why are you looking for a job?" he asked, curious.

"I was in L.A. for a while, but I have been in Tokyo since last year. I was working as a film producer, but now I want to change my career and focus on cooking."

"Okay. Do you have any questions for me?"

"No," I replied.

"Okay, thank you. The manager will call you and let you know about the result," Suzuki-san said.

"Thank you," I said to both Suzuki-san and Tanaka-san.

That was the end of my short, ten-minute interview.

A few days later, the restaurant manager called and said that they had decided not to hire me.

"The kitchen manager said it would be difficult for him to work with someone older than himself. I am sorry."

"Okay, thank you," I said.

I applied for positions at two other restaurants, but they both said the same thing: I was too old to work with their younger staff.

That was the moment I realized I needed to return to L.A. to work in a restaurant. After spending almost ten years working in the U.S., I now had different work ethics. Tokyo was no longer the place for me to feel at home or to work. Despite my love for Japan, I knew I didn't belong there. I headed back to L.A.

Kaz Matsune

SUSHI TRAINING

INTERVIEW, L.A.

I moved out of my L.A. apartment back in January, before moving to Tokyo and put everything I owned into a storage facility in Marina Del Rey. When I arrived back in the area, I stayed with a friend in Santa Monica.

I picked up a local Japanese newspaper, the *Nikkan Sun*, which listed their job openings in Japanese. I noticed there were tons of "Sushi Chef Wanted" ads, with a few even mentioning, "No experience necessary. We will train you."

While reading the ads, I realized I never thought about becoming a Sushi Chef in my whole life, not even once. Since they were in high demand, I also realized that becoming a Sushi Chef was the best way for me to start, or rather, *restart* my career.

Circling just three of the vacancies, I called them immediately. One was for Rock'n Hollywood Sushi, which was the very first restaurant interview I had in L.A.

I can't say that I was filled with hope. But I was so excited that I never even thought I wouldn't get the job, even with my lack of experience. Instead, I was confident that I would start working at a restaurant sooner or later.

I drove from Santa Monica through the infamous Sunset Strip, past the Whisky a Go-Go, Rainbow Room, The House of Blues, and so on. I found Rock'n Hollywood Sushi located at the east end of Sunset Strip.

The Strip was a place for aspiring actors, where some Hollywood stars partied, but usually only once a year after the Academy Awards.

The rest of the time, the crowd was filled with regular people and so-called "wannabees." There was no Hollywood. The whole town had been built up as an image, an illusion created by writers, producers, directors, actors, and movie studio executives. The general public, ordinary people like us, who watched those movies, simply believed what we saw actually existed in a place called Hollywood. It did not. Its image was a kind of magic trick and a good one at that. When tourists visit Hollywood, they quickly find out that there is only Grauman's Chinese Theater, with its Hollywood Walk of Fame, and souvenir stores.

Unlike the 1930s and 40s, or the so-called "Golden Years," Hollywood Stars didn't live in Hollywood anymore. The only "movie studio" left in Hollywood is Paramount Studios. Still it's at least a fifteen-minute drive from the famous Chinese Theater found in a place where no tourist would actually venture. Most Los Angelenos know this. One can see the Hollywood Sign on the top of the hill, but it's not where the movie magic happens. Harrison Ford isn't standing by the sign, welcoming you to Hollywood Land. Instead, he lives in Wyoming and only visits Hollywood to work. As I was driving through these world-famous streets, however, I never dreamed that I was about to start my sushi career right here on Sunset Boulevard.

As I parked my car in the lot at 4 P.M., the sky was still a bright, sunny, 78°F, a typically Southern California day.

The outside of the building looked nothing like a sushi restaurant. It looked a lot like a giant treehouse, sitting on a steep hill overlooking West Hollywood and Beverly Hills. A long staircase led to the back door, which looked old, beat up, and a bit scary. As I started to climb the stairs, they made a heavy squeaky noise each time I placed my foot down. Nervously, I wondered if the stairs were strong enough. As I opened the door to the kitchen, I realized I was also nervous about the interview.

It was the very first time I entered the kitchen of a restaurant and seen what was there. There was a large sink, with some dishes and leftover sushi from the night before. All the way in the back, there was a large six-burner stove, oven, and many large pots placed on shelving. The kitchen felt old. Even though it wasn't dirty, it felt creepy. It was also hot, basking in the Southern California sun. I started to wonder if I had made the right choice coming here for an interview.

I walked through the kitchen to the front of the restaurant, where the owner was already waiting for me. He stood up from his seat at the Sushi Bar and greeted me.

"Hi. My name is Saito. I am the owner of the restaurant," he said, opening the window. "It's getting hot here."

The man reached out his right hand, so I reached out mine and shook his hand.

"Hello, my name is Kaz. Nice to meet you," I greeted him with a smile.

"So, you want to work here, right? Do you have any experience?"

"Yes and no, I mean... yes, I want to work here. And no, I don't have any experience. The ad said it was alright to have no experience. So, I thought I'd give it a try. I will do anything; that's why I came here today."

"Alright, that sounds good. Let me introduce you to the Head Chef, Toshi," Saito-san said. I was surprised that he didn't seem to care if I had experience or not. I was also surprised that he didn't ask me one other question.

Mr. Saito went back into the kitchen and brought another Japanese person, who appeared to be almost my age.

"Hello, I am Toshi," he greeted me. Without waiting for my response, he shot another question, "So, you have no experience?" he said bluntly.

"Yes—I mean no experience," I said, looking at Toshi.

"Have you done any cooking before?" Toshi asked.

"A little. I cook my own meals," I replied.

"Have you ever worked in a restaurant?" Toshi followed up.

"No. The only food-related experience I have is working food service in my college cafeteria," I answered.

"Okay," Toshi said.

Toshi seemed to be a quiet person, not grumpy exactly, but he didn't give off a pleasant feeling at first glance. Toshi had medium-long hair worn in a ponytail, and looked as if he hadn't shaved in three days. He appeared to be sweating a little, his skin looked oily.

"What do you think, Toshi-chan?" the owner asked him.

Chan is a Japanese word for juveniles, but adults use it with sincerity when naming someone close.

"Why not? I think it's a go," Toshi said.

"Sounds good," Mr. Saito said. Turning around and looking at me he said,

"Why don't you start tomorrow?"

I was shocked. I never expected the interview to be so easy or to be hired on the spot.

I had two more interviews lined up, so I hesitantly asked, "Um, how about two days later, on Wednesday? I have a few things to take care of today and tomorrow."

"Wednesday it is. What time should Kaz come, Toshi?"

"Three o'clock in the afternoon," Toshi answered.

Much as my very first restaurant interview in Tokyo, this one also took only ten minutes, but this time, I was hired. People often ask me how I became a Sushi Chef, and this is how. I became a Sushi Chef with absolutely no training and zero experience.

I had no idea what was ahead of me, but I was excited. One quality I've always had is that I never worry too much about whether or not I am going to make it. I believe the most important thing is my determination. I hardly knew anything about being a professional chef, let alone had any traditional training on sushi techniques. However, I was open and willing to take whatever was placed on my plate, like ordering *Omakase* at a Sushi Bar. I was leaving myself in the hands of the chef.

I enjoyed cooking at home, and I enjoyed eating. That was my practice. I also enjoyed dining out, visiting new restaurants, and trying new dishes. When traveling, I always try "local" fares, like a Po'boy Sandwich or Seafood Gumbo in New Orleans. I tried the Papaya Salad at the Market in Bangkok, grilled lamb in fresh olive oil on the island of Santorini, in Greece, Shoyu Ramen in Tokyo, and freshly caught *Uni* in

Sapporo. I've practiced eating all of my life, so I knew I was ready to learn how to work in a professional kitchen.

THE FIRST DAY

Is there anything I should bring to work? I wondered. It was my first day as a Sushi Chef. And it was my first day working at a restaurant, ever. I had no idea how to prepare for work. How should I dress? I forgot to ask if I needed a uniform. I forgot to ask if I should bring in any utensils. I had no idea.

I was nervous again. But then I realized that since neither Saito-san nor Toshi-san had said anything, I could just show up, and everything would be okay.

My shift was from 3 PM to 2 AM, an eleven-hour shift with a short break in the middle. I never worked at night before except for overtime. I wasn't just changing my career; I was changing my daily routine.

Around 2 PM, I got in my car and drove to Hollywood from Santa Monica. The drive was about forty minutes, so I decided to leave early.

I drove through Sunset Strip to Rock'n Hollywood Sushi. Right across the street was the once-famous club, Roxy. When Roxy closed, it became a huge sushi and Japanese restaurant, Miyagi's. It was supposedly named after Mr. Miyagi from the original *Karate Kid* movie, played by Pat Morita. Miyagi's was more of a club than a restaurant. It had three dance floors and dining areas with Sushi Bars on each floor. Some of the bars were round instead of the traditional straight, long counter bar.

*****

I pulled my car into the parking lot next to the strip club, Body Shop. During my first visit, I hadn't noticed that Rock'n Hollywood Sushi was right next door to a strip club. I felt a rise in my male testosterone, as I started to fantasize about good-looking dancers coming to visit me while I worked. It was so close and convenient; they must come in often, which made me think that I would have a good chance of getting to know them, and they would fulfill all my sexual fantasies.

This is a good start, I said to myself, but then I shook my head, *how silly am I to even think that would happen.* It was similar to the fantasy I had had about sitting next to a young, attractive female on the flight from L.A. to N.Y.C.; it never happens. Only a fantasy. Just an illusion. Like this city called Hollywood. Hollywood does not exist in Hollywood or at a Chinese Theater. No movie stars live in Hollywood. They all live somewhere else. Hollywood exists only in the movies. Harrison Ford lives in Wyoming.

*****

I walked into the kitchen and greeted the Sushi Chef, Jun.

He replied, "Good morning."

"Good morning?" I mumbled. I was confused.

"Yes, Good Morning," he smiled, "because we are seeing each other for the first time today, and this is the start of our shift. Ordinary workers' shifts start in the morning, so that's why we say good morning, even if it's three in the afternoon."

It felt weird to greet my coworker with "Good Morning" at 3 PM. Though I was still confused, I just nodded in agreement. It took me a while to get used to this custom.

Later I learned that, in Japan, this is the correct practice at restaurants and hospitality businesses, as well as in the entertainment industry. I suppose it was an agreeable practice so that employees would feel "normal," even though they started work late in the afternoons or evenings. Perhaps it did give them a sense of starting work in the morning?

"Here is your uniform." Jun handed me a white Japanese-style Sushi Chef uniform.

The fabric was thin, almost see-through. It was different from what I imagined, but then again, I didn't really have a vivid picture in my head. I never dreamed about becoming a Sushi Chef, so I never really thought about it.

"Oh, thank you," I replied with a smile hiding my disappointment and complaints. "Well, it was not Jun's fault that the uniform is thin," I muttered.

"We change upstairs," Jun said.

"Where should I put my personal belongings?" I asked Jun.

"Oh, yes, that. Since we have no lockers, everyone puts them in here, with the cleaning supplies," Jun said. Jun showed me a small door to a storage space under the stairs where they stored some cleaning supplies.

"Really, this is where we put our clothes?" my jaw almost dropped.

"Yes. If you don't like it, you can put your clothes in your car."

"Great." *That's fancy*, I thought and nodded again.

I took the stairs to the second floor, where it was even hotter and mustier than downstairs. The restaurant was red with black leather booths and could hold about thirty people. The carpet was dark, with a smell of soy sauce and something else that I couldn't figure out. The room gave me the creeps.

It didn't look like the kind of sushi restaurant I was hoping for. It looked more like a lounge at a fraternity house with a bunch of beanbags on the floor.

I changed into my new uniform and looked at myself in the mirror. I hated it. I looked like an Asian actor from a cheap B-Hollywood movie. One that people never heard of, but probably watched at 2 AM on a cable movie channel when they had nothing else to do. Jun also gave me a cheap-looking white hat to wear. I hated wearing a hat but didn't say anything. I had no choice but to wear it. Besides, I was the one who wanted to be a Sushi Chef.

As soon as I returned to the Sushi Bar, Jun explained: "The first thing we do is to make rice, but before we do that, we need to turn the switch on."

"What switch?" I asked.

"It's for the fish refrigerator, the Sushi *Neta* Case on the Sushi Bar. It gets pretty hot inside the restaurant, so it takes a while for it to get cold.

We need to turn it on now before we start putting the fish in."

"Ah, that makes sense," I said, looking at the refrigerator. I never worked in an environment where I had to prioritize my tasks. This was a great lesson.

The Sushi *Neta* Case looked old. It wasn't exactly dirty, but it wasn't the cleanest thing I had ever seen, either. I'd seen these before at other sushi restaurants, but until that moment, I never paid any attention.

Jun reached for the switch under the Sushi Bar and turned it on.

We returned to the back kitchen, and Jun picked up a large stainless-steel bowl from the shelf, about twenty inches in diameter. He removed a lid from a large gray plastic trash bucket. Using a measuring cup, Jun scooped out uncooked rice and poured it into the bowl. He did that three times, scooping out at least thirty cups.

He then took the bowl to the sink and rinsed the rice in water. After draining the water he pressed the rice firmly with his right hand a couple of times, as he rotated the whole bowl, and then rinsed again. He repeated the same process a couple more times until the water was less milky. Once the water drained, he transferred the rice into a large rice cooker.

I was already familiar with the whole washing and rinsing process. I learned to do it by watching my mom, other Japanese chefs on TV, and I also read about it in cookbooks. What Jun was doing looked no different from what I already knew.

No problem, I thought.

"This is a gas rice cooker, which can make almost fifty cups. We need to let the rice sit in water at least fifteen minutes before we hit the start switch," Jun said.

"Why fifteen minutes?" I asked Jun as I continued to observe him.

"That way, rice tastes better," he smiled, and continued, "Glucose in the rice is in the core of the grain. So, by soaking the rice in water for fifteen-to-thirty minutes, it helps to bring out more sweetness from the rice."

I nodded and watched Jun as he placed his left hand on the rice and checked the water level with his wrist before putting the lid on the rice cooker.

I had seen Japanese chefs do this before but didn't understand the method. It never made any sense to me how they measured the water using their wrist. *What are you looking for? You've already measured the water, so why bother?* This time, however, I didn't ask.

Jun opened the door of the walk-in refrigerator and grabbed ten English cucumbers, each individually wrapped with plastic. English cucumbers are longer and thinner than American cucumbers.

"Okay, now we can go back to the Sushi Bar and do some prep work."

We went into the Sushi Bar, which was much warmer than the kitchen.

"The sushi refrigerator has been on for about fifteen minutes. Now, we can start arranging the fish. First, place these white plates... like this." He started placing them as he continued explaining, "You can put seven plates on each side like this."

I noticed the white plates had holes in the bottom.

"How come there are holes in these plates?" I asked Jun.

"To let water drip," Jun said.

"What water?" I asked again.

"Water from the fish. When fish gets old, water starts to drip, so we need to let it drain," Jun said.

"The older fish goes on the left side of the *Neta* Case, and there is always an order. First, Octopus and Squid, then *Saba*, Whitefish like *Tai* or *Hirame*, *Hamachi*, Salmon, Tuna, and Shrimp. They need to be in this order all the time. Otherwise, everyone gets confused. The older fish is *Aniki*, the older brother. The fresher fish is *Otòto*, younger brother," Jun explained.

"I see," I nodded; however, I did not fully understand the reason why they must be in that order every time. It took me a while to learn to realize the importance of the Japanese way of *mise en place* or things in order.

After laying out all of the fish, Jun picked up four Plexiglas sliding doors, placed them on the case, and closed the doors to seal in the cold air.

"We use Snow Crab pack," Jun said, after looking at a small refrigerator inside the Sushi Bar. "This is where we keep everything that doesn't fit in the sushi refrigerator. We have *Ume* Plum paste, *Tsukemono* pickles, *Mirugai*, giant clams, extra crab and mixes, and *Amaebi* (Sweet Shrimp)," Jun said, pointing at the refrigerator.

I looked inside and saw a lot more than he mentioned. I felt like I was looking in someone's home refrigerator. I also felt like I shouldn't touch anything.

Jun walked to the back kitchen, returning with a package of frozen solid Snow Crab, the size of a thick cookbook, such as *The Joy of Cooking*.

"Oh, I forgot to tell you that right next to the walk-in is the freezer," Jun said.

"That's where we keep all the frozen stuff like crab and *Unagi*," Jun added.

"Wait, what's a walk-in?" I asked.

"A refrigerator in the kitchen. It's called walk-in because you can walk-in, you know," Jun said.

Jun placed the frozen Crab Pack in a sink and let the water run slowly to thaw.

"This Snow Crab is called 'sandwich' because the lump leg meat is on the top and the bottom. The flakes are between them. After thawing, we'll mix this with mayo, but not the lump meat. We'll use the lump meat for *nigiri* or *Sashimi*."

Jun took out some crab meat from the small side refrigerator. It was separated, just as he had said.

"On weeknights, we typically go through half of the pack, so we can mix half for tonight and leave the unmixed crab in the side fridge. It takes a good hour or two before the whole thing melts. We need to check the crab early during the prep because it's our responsibility to make sure we have enough Crab Mix ready before the restaurant opens."

That was the moment I realized that every chef has a set of tasks that they have to take care of before the restaurant opens. If he forgets to do one thing, it could cause a problem for everyone. Therefore, it was both an individual and a team effort at the same time.

Not only does everyone focus on their own work, but they also keep an eye on each other at the same time in the kitchen. I suppose it's similar to playing baseball. I remember what my Junior League coach used to tell us, "One error equal one run to the other team."

One simple mistake during prep can lead to a delay or an unhappy customer in the restaurant. Every step in prep is important, I made a note to myself.

After it thawed, Jun showed me how to make the Crab Mix. It looked simple, except I had to remember the quantity of mayo because there wasn't a recipe. Jun was just guessing, eyeballing how much mayo to put in. It looked like he was making the mix based on how it tasted. So, I figured I should do the same.

"Do we have a recipe written down somewhere?"

"Nope, no recipe whatsoever," Jun grinned.

*****

"We are going to use these for all the rolls like California Roll and Spicy Tuna," Jun told me. He placed the English cucumbers on the counter. Using his knife, I watched him cut off one cucumber end and peel off the plastic. He put it on the cutting board and began showing me how to cut it.

"We are going to cut them into three pieces each," he explained.

Using his left hand, Jun measured a cucumber before he cut it.

"Four fingers, or the length of your palm, this is how we measure things at the Sushi Bar."

"Four fingers?"

"Yes, that's right. Four left fingers, like this."

Jun placed his left hand on the cucumber, then put his knife just to the right of his palm and sliced the cucumber.

I started cutting the tips of the rest of the cucumbers, while Jun did the same. I quickly learned how to unwrap the cucumbers. It took fifteen seconds each, but when you have twelve of them, multiply that thirty seconds by twelve, and it will take three minutes. Then we started to cut cucumbers at the four-finger width. I tried the same technique and cut some cucumbers into five- or six-inch pieces.

After cutting all the cucumbers, Jun asked me, "Can you do *katsuramuki*?"

"No, I've never tried," I said. I felt good knowing what *katsuramuki* was.

"Do it like this," Jun explained, as he showed me at the same time.

Katsuramuki, also known as pillar peeling, is a technique used to peel vegetables paper-thin. It's like peeling the skin of an apple. Imagine holding a cucumber in your left hand and a knife in your right. Move the knife up and down as you turn the cucumber and peel off the skin. You will go around it a couple of times before you reach the core of the cucumber.

If you've never seen a chef do this, you'll probably think it's an accident waiting to happen, with his left-hand right in front of the knife. And that's exactly what happened to me. I cut my finger as I was peeling my second cucumber. My knife just slid through and cut my left index finger.

"Oh, no!" I shouted. Blood started to come out of my finger. "I cut my finger. Where is the Band-Aid? "I asked Jun.

"There is a First Aid kit in the kitchen," Jun told me.

What a terrible start. I had already cut my finger, and it was only the first hour of my first day on the job.

*****

At 4 PM, Toshi, the Head Chef, arrived. His main task was to fillet and prep fish.

"You are still working on cucumbers?" Toshi asked as he came to the

Sushi Bar to check on us.

"*Ohayo Gozaimasu*," Jun said to Toshi.

I immediately followed Jun and said, "*Ohayo Gozaimasu*." I paused and added, "Um, yes," as I still had five more cucumbers left to *katsuramuki*.

"Well, do it fast," Toshi said.

Toshi had an unfriendly look. He had dark black hair, and when not ponytailed, he reminded me of a rock singer from a dark, smoky dive bar in Hollywood.

One of the fish Toshi prepped was Tuna. Tuna came in quarter cuts called, *shibuichi*, in Japanese. A whole Yellowfin Tuna weighs around eighty pounds. A *shibuichi*, or "one-fourth" of the whole Tuna, is approximately twelve- to- fifteen pounds, after the head and the bones are removed.

"Here you go, Jun-chan," Toshi handed him a small block of Tuna, two to three pounds, about the size of a football.

Jun immediately picked up his spoon and started scraping the block of Tuna.

"What are you doing, and what's this for?" I asked Jun.

"It's for Spicy Tuna. This is the tail of Tuna. These parts are no good for *nigiri* or *Sashimi* because it's too chewy."

"Chewy?"

"You see the white lines? These are tendons and too tough because they are just fiber. The only way we can use the meat around is to scrape it with the spoon. Here you can try, too," Jun said, as he cut the block, handing me half.

"You scrape the same direction as the tendon is running, then you can separate the meat easily," Jun said.

"We need to make sure only red part, not white tendons, in scraped meat," Jun said.

This was tedious work. I applied a good amount of pressure to my spoon and scraped for nearly twenty minutes. My hands stunk of fish, and scraps of Tuna were dried between my fingers and skin. I couldn't say I was enjoying this scraping prep work.

"You add mayo, House-Made Chili Oil, *Masago* (fish egg), and *shichimi* peppers," Jun explained as he mixed the scraped Tuna with the other ingredients in a large stainless-steel bowl. There were more Tuna scrapes than I had ever seen in my life. It must have been at least six pounds of Spicy Tuna mix.

"And, the recipe?" I asked.

"Of course not. No recipe. We all remember the taste, and you just taste it," Jun said.

Jun transferred the mix into three smaller containers, placed two in the Sushi *Neta* Case, and the last one in the side refrigerator.

I had to remember both the ingredients and how it tasted, too, just like the Crab Mix for California Rolls. I never knew I was supposed to write down all the recipes in the kitchen since I learned by doing. I felt there was no need to write them down. I kept asking for recipes and where things were, which sort of drove some people crazy. It took me a while to learn.

After the Tuna, Toshi brought some fresh cut *Hamachi*, *Tai*, and *Hirame* to the front Sushi Bar. Jun placed all *Aniki* fish to the left side of the *Neta* Case, which is where Toshi stood, the Head Chef's side.

"How are we doing on *Ebi*?" Toshi asked Jun.

"I think we are okay for today, and maybe we prep tomorrow?"

It took only five minutes to place all the "old" fish, but we needed Toshi's fresh-cut fish to complete the *Neta* Case. Now the sushi refrigerator looked complete, with all the fish beautifully laid out and ready for business. I felt fresh and ready to get started on my very first evening at the Sushi Bar.

Jun walked to the back kitchen and brought one of the stainless rice warmers out to the Sushi Bar and placed it on a small stool.

"Wait, where is the parsley for the Sushi *Neta* Case?" Toshi asked.

"Shoot, I forgot. Sorry." Jun took out a bunch of parsley from the side refrigerator.

"Why is there parsley inside of the *Neta* Case in front of the fish?" I asked

"Green looks good in contrast with fish," Jun said.

"Oh, I forgot to bring the oranges, too," Jun added.

"Oranges?" I asked.

"Yes, I need this," Jun said, grabbing a tall white bucket, heading towards the walk-in. I followed him and saw him fill the bucket with oranges and some ice.

"We serve oranges to the customers at the Sushi Bar. Half an orange per customer. Only Sushi Bar customers get oranges, not all tables. It's a special service."

After the oranges, Jun told me that we were done prepping for the day. I sighed in relief.

*****

Around 4:30 PM, the first waitress came in to start her shift. "Hello. You must be the new chef. The manager told me you were starting today. My name is Emma."

"I'm Kaz," I greeted her back.

"Kaz, nice to meet you," she smiled.

Emma was a petite, outgoing, energetic, Asian American girl. Everyone liked her, and she made good tips. She was living in an apartment close to the restaurant with her boyfriend, who wanted to become an actor. We heard Emma also tried a few auditions but didn't even get selected for a small part. I never figured out why Emma wanted to be an actress; she didn't look like the typical Hollywood wannabee-actress-waitress-type.

After she greeted the others, Emma wasted no time and started setting up the tables with chopsticks and napkins. Of course, I had no idea what her job duties were, but it looked like she knew what she was doing, and she was performing each task in a very efficient way. I could tell she was a good worker. It must be her Asian heritage.

"So, have you worked at a restaurant before, Kaz?" she asked me, while still setting up the tables.

"No, I haven't," I replied.

"Oh, okay. Well, you look like a quick learner. Everyone here is nice, especially the Sushi Chefs, Toshi, Kai, Jun and Juan. I'm sure you will be fine," Emma reassured me with a pleasant smile.

No, that smile didn't belong to someone who wanted to be an actress. She was too nice to be in Hollywood, I thought. It was only a few minutes since I met her, but I could sense that she was a nice person already.

"We do get lots of young kids on the weekends. You know, it's Sunset Strip, so all the kids come here and party. And they love it here. They come here to get drunk on *sake* and beer. But, it's Tuesday tonight, so it won't be that bad," Emma explained.

After a brief conversation with Emma, I had nothing else to do.

"What should I do next?" I asked Toshi. It was only five o'clock.

"Why don't you take a break and have some dinner."

"Dinner? Where can I get dinner? Is there *makanai*, the employee meal?"

"Well, here, no *makanai*. Everyone eats on his own, and you can make your dinner or order something from the kitchen."

"Okay, thanks," I said to Toshi and walked towards the back kitchen.

Since it was my first day, and I was still very nervous, I figured it was safer to order something from the kitchen, instead of making something for myself. I had no idea where all the cooking tools were or what kind of ingredients they had in the walk-in.

In the back kitchen, I met Alejandro, a short Mexican man in his fifties with a mustache. I asked Alejandro to make me some Tempura. I put rice, Miso Soup, and Tempura sauce in the bowl while I waited for Alejandro to finish.

Two hours of prep time went so fast, it seemed. I still had eight more hours to go until 2 AM.

Alejandro handed me a plate of shrimp, Japanese yam, carrots, and *kabocha* squash.

"Thanks," I said and went upstairs to eat my Tempura *makanai*.

My stomach was full. Suddenly, I felt exhausted due to anxiety. After all, I was working in a professional kitchen for the very first time. I wasn't physically tired, but emotionally overwhelmed and excited all at the same time. I wondered what the rest of the day would hold. For the first time in my life, I would be standing at a Sushi Bar, working as a Sushi Chef. I laid down on the black sofa and looked up the ceiling. I felt the warm air in the room. I held my bandaged finger up in the soft summer Southern California sunshine coming through the window.

THE FIRST NIGHT

After my thirty-minute dinner break, I returned to the Sushi Bar. It was almost 6 PM. There were a few customers in the restaurant.

"I finished my break. What should I do now?" I asked Toshi.

"Why don't you stand behind us and keep an eye on what we do. You can look at this sushi menu and learn about our rolls, *nigiri*, and *Sashimi*. If you have any questions, just let us know," Toshi said, with no facial expression.

Gosh, he is so unfriendly, I thought. *Really? This is it? That's all I do for the rest of the evening? Just stand here and do nothing but watch you guys work?* The words remained at the tip of my tongue, as I almost yelled it in my mind, but I chose to say nothing to Toshi. I wanted to say, "I can try making a roll. I am sure it won't be great, but how can I improve unless I try?" Oh well, it was just wishful thinking.

The orders came in through a printer that was on the back shelf of the Sushi Bar. That was also where they kept all the plates, so each time they got an order, they turned around and grabbed a plate or two. Every time the printer spat out a ticket, it made a loud grinding noise, like an old computer printer back in the 80s.

Jun reached out, grabbed the ticket, and placed it on top of the *Neta* Case. Toshi and Jun both looked at the ticket for a second, then Toshi said, "Well, Jun-chan, you can do this order by yourself."

Jun nodded, quickly turned, and grabbed a medium-sized plate from the shelf and placed it on the top of the Sushi Case.

He picked up a sheet of *nori* and grabbed the stainless rice warmer lid. He then wet his hands and picked up some of the Sushi Rice he had prepped in the afternoon. He quickly spread the rice over the *nori*, sprinkled some sesame seeds, flipped it over, and placed some Crab Mix, cucumber, and avocado on top. He reached for a *makisu*, a bamboo rolling mat, and gave it a gentle squeeze after placing it over the California Roll. Then, he removed the mat and cut the roll into six pieces with his knife.

It was my first time watching someone make a California Roll, so I was paying close attention to how Jun worked.

The whole process didn't seem very complicated. It took Jun less than a minute to make one roll.

Just like the California Roll, Jun made another roll, Spicy Tuna. A Spicy Tuna only had cucumber, no avocado. The only other difference between the California Roll and the Spicy Tuna Roll was the mix, and the rest was the same. Grab the rice, spread it, shake some sesame, flip, place the fillings, roll, and cut. That was the whole process.

Even though Jun had been there for three months, he appeared relaxed. He looked to me as if he was quite good at what he was doing.

Jun finished the order, picked up the plate with his ticket, and placed the plate on top of the small counter behind the wall by the Sushi Bar. Once the plate was ready, the waitress came to pick it up. Jun did not ring the bell or yell, "Order ready!" as I heard in some Japanese restaurants.

"Don't you say anything?" I asked Jun slowly.

"No, there's no need to say anything. Once we finish the order, all we have to do is put the plate along with the ticket on top, so waitresses can see it," Jun said. "But the ticket is very important. That is the only thing they will see and check to make sure we have every order on the plate. If not, they are supposed to tell us.

"I see," I nodded.

"So, always double-check the order. Half the time, waitresses don't remember their orders and don't notice if something is missing. They always come back and tell us to make the missing item, as if it was our fault. Emma is not like that; she is good, but others are not," Jun said.

I was starting to get a sense that this was not a typical restaurant. But then, what really is typical? It was not as if I had worked at another restaurant before and knew the ins-and-outs of the operation. I just thought it sounded strange.

*****

I stood there feeling disappointed, wondering why they had asked me just to watch, instead of giving me something to do. I had to stand there for another six hours, and that was my job. Was Toshi being mean, or testing me to see if I could think of some task while standing there? What was there to watch? Wouldn't it be better if they taught me how to make their Special Rolls now? I just wanted to work, and I wanted to work as a Sushi Chef. It was only my first day, and I already had storms of disappointment in my mind.

They say, "rice cooking three years" in Japan, referring to a sushi apprentice's training, but at that moment in my life, that wasn't what I had in my mind. "We are not in Japan, but in L.A.," I wanted to say. I wanted to get things rolling ASAP. I was eager and didn't want to waste any time. *Gee, how long would I have to train to be a Sushi Chef?* I thought that the light at the end of the tunnel had just disappeared. Maybe it was because, as it seemed, the tunnel was never-ending.

Looking back now, what else was there to do, anyway? At the time, I didn't know how to make a California Roll. I had never made one before. I never sliced fish for sushi. I never made *nigiri* before. Above all, I was unable to tell the difference between *Hamachi* and *Tai*. If I were in Japan, I probably wouldn't be allowed to enter a Sushi Bar. I would be washing dishes or just bussing tables. So, even though it seemed like a slow start, I can say it was still a good, if not great, start.

*****

The Sushi Bar was quite small—only three people could stand side-by-side, with a little room in the back for just one more person to stand. I guessed the room was only about eight feet long.

For the first hour, the restaurant was slow. There was nothing much to do, nothing much to watch, either. I was beginning to feel bored. I tried to search for questions that I could ask Toshi, but at the moment, I had nothing to ask.

Toshi looked as if he had something on his mind. He was not unfriendly, as I saw him talking to Jun, but I sensed Toshi was wrapped in this invisible shield. I started thinking about how to phrase my questions so that he would answer me. I thought my first question should be something simple, easy to answer, like hitting on a girl at a bar a "Do-you-come-here-often?" type question.

"Is Tuesday always like this?" I asked Toshi in a polite Japanese tone.

"Usually, it's not that busy. Sometimes, it gets busy, though. Monday and Sundays are the slowest nights here," Toshi replied. He did not say more.

For a few minutes, we all stood at the Sushi Bar. I picked up a menu and studied the rolls. I knew some of them—Philadelphia, Caterpillar, and Spider Roll. But now I was expected to make them, and I had no idea what was in a Philadelphia Roll. I then remembered the Japanese saying: "Steal with your eyes." Yes, Picasso had said the same thing, too: "Good artists copy. Great artists steal." That was the moment I decided not just to watch but to pay attention to everything I could. Until they ask me to do something else, that became my job. I realized that maybe the tunnel was not so long after all. It was certainly one way to see the light faster. For me, it was all about "watching and stealing" all the techniques from Toshi and Jun.

Once I finally realized what I needed to do, I became busy. I was busy learning, copying, and stealing everything I saw. I soon realized there was a lot I could learn.

I watched how they held the *Yanagiba* knife, placing their index finger on the top edge of the blade and thumb just by the wood handle. Both Toshi and Jun moved their knives really fast when they cut the rolls, quickly moving forward and back. Toshi only moved once to cut his rolls. Toshi was a lot faster than Jun, especially when he made *nigiri*. I noticed that they wet their hands before touching the *shari* Sushi Rice, and then made it into a small ball. When they did, it looked like the rice was coming out of their hands, like a magician making a handkerchief appear. I watched how they sliced fish for *nigiri*: it looked as if they were slicing a block of fish differently, depending on the type of fish. Toshi angled his knife almost flat against the Salmon block, while, for Tuna, it was angled practically straight up, ninety degrees vertical to the *saku* block. I later learned that, for some fish, you need to cut against the grain. *Sashimi* looked easier than *nigiri*. *Sashimi* was just slicing the fish. *How difficult could it be*, I thought. I was dead wrong; it is one of the most challenging skills to master.

Both Toshi and Jun used their towels frequently to wash off the cutting board and the knife. They kept the cutting board clean, free of any fish and rice debris, continually washing the towel in the sink.

I noticed how they greeted the customers, saying, "*Irasshaymase*," meaning "Welcome" in Japanese. I realized I could follow along and say *Irasshaymase* with them, so I waited for the next customer to walk in and shouted, "*Irasshaymase*." It felt good, unifying my voice with them.

My observation continued. I began to take mental notes on how they took orders from the customers at the Sushi Bar. I watched how they interacted with customers, too. It looked simple to me at that time, only because I had never done it. *I wonder if I could do it the same way*, I thought.

Now my attention shifted back to the preparation. I watched the quantities of rice they would use for a roll and *nigiri*. I observed Toshi most of all. I watched how he made *nigiri*, finding it a bit harder to follow his movements. His hands moved too fast, like the sword of a Samurai, swift and agile. Everything around me was a bit blurry: I was only watching his hands. That was, indeed, magic.

Once, he grabbed a slice of fish in one hand, and with the other, he quickly grabbed some *shari* . Within a few seconds, both of his hands were moving too fast to follow. Once he slowed down, I saw a bite-sized *nigiri*. There it was... rice in the bottom with the fish, slightly arched, and on top. Later, they put *wasabi* and *gari* on the plate. Once again, my mind registered the quantity they used, as I continued to watch how they picked up the remaining fish, placing it back in the fridge.

I stood and watched until midnight, when Toshi said, "I think you can go home now, Kaz."

"Ok, thank you. I will see you tomorrow. Goodnight," I said to both Toshi and Jun.

The restaurant was almost empty, just a few customers still downstairs. Upstairs was closed, so I went up and changed into my clothes. My legs felt heavy. My entire body felt heavy, like a water-soaked sponge. I felt like I just crossed a finish line of a full marathon; however, I had only finished my first day.

THE SECOND DAY

It was ten in the morning in Santa Monica.

"We still can make it to 10:45 Yoga class," my friend said, looking at me. I was sleeping on a yoga mat on the floor.

"No, thanks. I'm going to rest until it's time for work," I said.

It wasn't long since I left Tokyo, and I didn't have any place to stay on my own. I was staying at a friend's apartment, which is why I was sleeping on the floor. I got up and immediately felt tired again, in spite of decent sleep. My back was hurting, not because I slept on a floor, but because at work last night, I was on my feet for fourteen hours. I had never spent that long working on my feet. This was a first. My legs were still heavy and stiff, like an overcooked chicken, dry, running out of juice. I could move my legs, but only half the distance of what I intended.

Every inch of my body felt pounded like tenderized meat, as I tried to stay on my feet with immense effort, almost falling. I was soon down on the floor again, sitting on my knees. After what it felt like an eternity, I put my arms on my knees, forcing my body to get back up and move away from the yoga mat. My body did not cooperate with me.

"Thank God I still have five hours to go," I sighed. I looked out the window, and the sun was perhaps teasing me. That morning it was unusually brighter than normal. The clock moved too fast, and soon after that, it was already 2 PM.

*****

When I parked my car in the back parking lot, I noticed Jun's car was already there. I walked with a limp to the back stairs, entering the restaurant from the employee entrance in the kitchen. As I walked in, it was hot, and there was an unpleasant smell of food.

"*Ohayo Gozaimasu*," I wished Jun, trying to hide all the uneasiness.

"*Ohayo Gozaimasu*," Jun replied with a simple nod.

I grabbed my uniform from the cleaning-supply-storage-employee-locker and walked upstairs to change. After I switched to my uniform, I quickly ran downstairs to the Sushi Bar.

"Let's place the fish in the Sushi *Neta* Case," Jun told me. I walked up to the Sushi Bar and turned on the refrigerator, just like the day before.

As the Southern California sun hit directly through the window, the inside of the dining room became hot and musty. The Sushi Bar and dining room had old carpet and smelled like soy sauce. *Just like yesterday*, I sighed and tried to avoid deep breaths. I couldn't stand the smell of the old carpet and soy sauce, like the rug absorbed ten years' worth of odors. I opened a window to let some fresh air in.

It must have been several years since they put in that carpet, and I'm sure that hundreds of customers spilled their soy sauce, sake, and beer on it. I smiled at my guesses.

Just like the previous day, I took out the long cutting board first and then the white towels that were soaked overnight in a bucket full of soap and bleach. I wondered why they didn't use a new towel every day or use a linen service. I took the bucket from the back kitchen, washed all the towels, and took them back to the Sushi Bar for the other chefs. After washing the towels, my hands smelled like bleach. Someone must want to kill the smell of fish on the towels really badly, I thought.

I forgot to grab the white trays – the ones with holes - for the Neta Case. I noticed that they are also perfectly-sized for the *Neta* Case. I walked to the back kitchen and looked at the plates in the dishwashing area. I grabbed all of them and walked back into the Sushi Bar.

My whole body ached. I still had the lingering fatigue from the previous night. But knowing it was just my second day, I couldn't allow fatigue to stop me from working. So, I continued. After laying out the plates, I quickly put on the plastic doors to seal the cold air coming out from the compressor in the *Neta* Case.

Since it was always really hot inside the restaurant, it was important to make sure the inside of the *Neta* Case was cold enough before laying out the fish. I remembered to place the old fish to the left, but I couldn't remember the order. I stopped and tried to recall for a couple of minutes, but I couldn't remember. I finally gave up and decided to ask Jun. I felt embarrassed, so I grabbed a piece of paper and a pencil and asked Jun to tell me one more time.

"I'm sorry, I forgot...," I said to Jun.

"It's not a problem," Jun said. "From left, *Taco, Hirame, Tai, Ebi, Sake, Hamachi,* and *Maguro,*" Jun replied. This time, I wrote it down. I thanked him and quickly went back to the Sushi Bar to lay out the fish.

"What should I do next?"

"We can do *katsuramuki.*"

"Again? We did some yesterday," I asked.

"We need more cucumbers. We used almost all of them from yesterday," Jun replied.

At Rock'n Hollywood Sushi, we put julienned cucumber in almost every roll. On an average night, we made three hundred rolls altogether. We made enough julienned cucumber for twenty rolls from just one whole European cucumber. This meant we had to peel and cut at least fifteen cucumbers each day. Since running out of cucumbers was not an option during a busy evening, we always made sure to have extra.

Jun brought out six or seven English cucumbers from the walk-in and started to peel the plastic off. Just like the day before, I picked one up and started to slide my knife up and down. I looked at the Band-Aid on my left finger and reminded myself not to cut my finger today. The cucumber was rotating on my left hand. Surprisingly, I felt I was improving. It was less awkward than the day before. Still challenging, but I was feeling comfortable with the *Sashimi* knife. I felt confident but remained calm to avoid making another mistake and cutting myself again.

I didn't know anything about the *Yanagiba*, the *Sashimi* knife; it was long, 272 millimeters, narrow-shaped, light, and the blade felt gawky. Because it's designed to slice fish, not vegetables, doing *katsuramuki* was something that required even more experience. I wished I had a *Nakiri*, a vegetable knife. That would make things much easier, smoother, and faster.

*****

My second day was going well so far. The most challenging part of *katsuramuki* was keeping the same thickness top and bottom. As I rotated the cucumber, my knife tilted, causing an uneven thickness.

Toshi arrived at four, which was the beginning of his shift.

"*Ohayo Gozaimasu,*" Jun and I wished Toshi.

"*Ohayo Gozaimasu,*" Toshi replied.

"Are you still working on the cucumbers?"

"Yes, sorry," Jun said before I said anything to Toshi.

After Toshi went to the back kitchen, Jun told me that we had to make some *tsuma*, or garnish. This consisted of a thinly-shredded *daikon* radish for *Sashimi*. We used a tool called *benriner*, a Japanese mandoline slicer. It looks like a miniature guillotine, except the blade doesn't move; instead, you move your hands to slice the *daikon*.

"You need to be really careful using this. So many times, I've cut my fingers. In case you cut your fingers, it'll take a long time to heal because you also lose part of your skin," Jun warned me.

I peeled the skin off the *daikon* and cut it into three-inch pieces. I started to slide the radish on the mandoline slicer, hoping, yet again, not to cut my fingers.

*****

Toshi carried a large sheet-pan full of freshly cut blocks of fish— *Maguro*, *Hamachi*, Salmon, *Tai*, and *Hirame* into the Sushi Bar. I was excited to see all the fish, like a child seeing a mound of chocolate in the bakery. Like a soldier who was handed a gun full of ammunition, I was ready to go to a battlefield. Looking at these fresh ingredients, we were about to play our game, turning these fish into sushi. Jun placed them on the right side of the refrigerator case. I observed the placement of each fish, comparing with my notes.

After my dinner break, I was told to stand behind the Sushi Bar, just like the previous night, and to watch Toshi and Jun while they worked.

The printer kept expelling out order tickets. Toshi and Jun started making rolls first, cutting the fish, and making *nigiri*. All I could do was watch them make sushi. I noticed something that I didn't see the previous night—the plates. For a small order of *Sashimi*, they used a small rectangular plate. The plates were perfect for five pieces of fish with *tsuma*. Toshi always put a handful of *tsuma* first, then a sheet of *shiso* leaf, and then placed the plate on top of the *Neta* case. Later, he picked up the block of fish, sliced five pieces, plated, and placed *wasabi* on the right side at the end of the plate.

"Does one order of *Sashimi* always have five pieces?" I asked Toshi.

"Yes, that is right," Toshi replied.

"How come it's five, not four, or even numbers?" I asked.

"I don't know, actually," Toshi said. "There are multiple theories, but I heard those odd numbers create juxtaposition."

"Juxtaposition?" I asked him back.

"Yes, that's exactly what I mean. Four pieces sound better than five, we tend to think. So, someone decided to make it five slices. It was intentional. It was playfulness. It makes you wonder why," Toshi explained. "That's why Japanese China always come in sets of five, not six like Western China sets."

"Oh, that's right. I wondered why Japanese China is always a set of five," I said.

"Another interesting thing about five pieces is that it's symmetric," Toshi said.

"How could five be symmetric?" I asked Toshi.

"The third slice of *Sashimi* is the center of the five-piece *Sashimi*, which makes the two slices on left and right symmetric," Toshi said. "It creates a central focal point."

I looked at the plate of *Sashimi* Jun had made and understood what Toshi just told me. He was right. It *was* symmetric.

"Ah, very interesting," I said.

"So, then, what if the customer wants only three pieces?" I said.

"Easy. You calculate the price for one piece and multiply it by three. We use the price of *nigiri* to figure this out," Toshi said.

"*Nigiri* comes in two pieces. Tuna *Nigiri* is $5, so a piece of Tuna *Sashimi* is $2.50. If someone wanted three-piece *Sashimi*, it would be $7.50." I ran the calculations in my mind while listening to Toshi. I picked up a menu and looked at the price of each *nigiri* so that I would remember and be able to calculate the cost of *Sashimi*, if and when I am asked to make a special three-piece order.

There were five types of plates stacked behind the Sushi Bar. The small rectangular ones were used for one order of *Nigiri* Rolls or *Sashimi*. There was a medium 10-inch round plate that was good for placing a couple of rolls and *nigiri*, and the biggest round plate was about 15 inches made to hold five or six rolls.

"Never put *Sashimi* on the same plate as *nigiri* and rolls. Always plate *Sashimi* separately and serve them first," Toshi said.

That day and most of the evening, I stood behind Toshi and Jun and continued watching them work. My back and my feet began to hurt again. So, I moved my legs and shook them at regular intervals to keep the blood flowing.

Along with the pain and lightly lingering fatigue, boredom started to take over again. I thought to reach for the order tickets and hand them to Toshi. If he was busy, I stuck them up in the center of *Neta* Case and made sure to place the newest tickets on the bottom of the pile. Neither Toshi, nor Jun, told me much or gave me any instructions, so I just kept paying attention to what they were doing.

I recalled the order of the fish in the *Neta* Case. There was a small refrigerator next to the Sushi Bar, that stored extra fish and other items—*Mirugai* (Giant Clam), *Amaebi* (Sweet Shrimp), *ume* (salty plum paste), *daikon tsuma* (radish garnish), and sometimes *natto* (fermented soybeans) for the occasional Japanese customers. Rock'n Hollywood Sushi catered mainly to non-Japanese. So, it was rare to see Japanese customers come in. When they did, however, they would order sushi. Most of the time, I heard them say, "Hmmm, this is interesting."

MY FIRST CALIFORNIA ROLL

It had only been one week since I started working as a Sushi Chef. My back was still hurting from standing on my feet for fourteen hours a day, so I bought a back support belt from Home Depot. When Toshi noticed me wearing one, he sounded pessimistic, "Well, that is an interesting use of the support belt."

My legs felt like they were ten pounds heavier than they were two weeks ago, and they seemed to get heavier every day. All of the other chefs were fine standing for such a long time, so I knew it wouldn't be long before my body would get used to it too.

Day after day, I'd watch Toshi, Kai, Jun, and Juan make sushi, and I was getting used to the set-up and prep routine. I cut cucumbers faster and could cook the rice and mix it with sushi vinegar. Unfortunately, "slicing" the rice was still very hard. I was getting used to using the *Yanagiba* knife, but I had already cut my finger twice in one week.

It was a Tuesday night at 6 PM. One couple was sitting at table #1, a party of four at Table #3, and another couple at table #1. Typically, Tuesday was not a busy night because the Valley Boys and Girls didn't come out to Sunset Strip until Thursday or Friday.

Toshi glanced at the clock, looked back at me, and said, "Well, I don't think it's going to be busy tonight. Since we are not busy right now, let me show you how to make a roll."

"Really?" I had been anxiously waiting for this moment. It had only taken Toshi one week, and I wished he had shown me earlier.

"Let's start with California Roll because it's the most popular roll we have," Toshi said.

"You've been looking at the menu, so you know what's in a California Roll, right?" Toshi asked.

"Umm, crab, cucumber, and avocado?" I said.

"Good, that's correct," Toshi said.

"Now, the most important part of making a roll is to keep the *shari* fluffy. When you apply too much pressure to spread *shari* on the *nori*, you will smash it and make it mushy," Toshi explained. "Texture of *shari* is what you need to be careful. Ideally, the *shari* should spread apart inside of your mouth when you put the roll in your mouth."

Oh, shari, that's right, not rice. it's Sushi rice, so it's shari. I've got to get used to saying that.

Toshi picked up a piece of *nori* and showed it to me.

"Place *nori* on the cutting board, inside up. The rough side is inside; you know that, right?"

"Yes, I do," I nodded. Actually, I vaguely knew there was a shiny side and a rough side to *nori*, but I didn't realize that the *shari* should go on the rough inside, until now.

"Okay. First, wet your hands in *temizu* before you touch the *shari*," Toshi said.

Temizu? Hand water? I panicked, unsure what Toshi meant. I refrained from asking him what *temizu* was, thinking I would look stupid. Seeing Toshi dipping his hands in the bowl of water, I figured he was referring to the water.

"Now, grab some *shari*... about this size." Toshi showed me a rice ball that was the size of a tennis ball. It was more *shari* than I expected.

"Gee, that much *shari*... for just one roll?" I asked.

"Yup, it's a lot of *shari* and lots of sugar from sushi vinegar," Toshi replied. "But, never mention it to the customers, especially the female customers, because they freak out when they find out how much sugar is in one roll."

He placed the rice ball on the top left corner of the *nori*.

"Now, start spreading the *shari*, using the left hand only, like this."

Toshi began to press and spread the *shari* from left to right as if it were soft bread dough.

"At the same time, make 'U' shape with your right hand to guide the *shari*. You should cover only the top half of the *nori*."

His hands flew from left to right, and his left fingers made a wave-like motion. It took him just three seconds to spread the *shari* on the top half of the *nori*. The whole movement was smooth, like a deck of playing cards popping out from a magician's hand. Toshi made it look simple and easy, but I knew it would not be that easy for me.

He was explaining and demonstrating faster than I could remember, and I quickly got confused. *I wish I had a notepad and a pencil with me.* It would be too embarrassing to ask him to stop and show me again, so I decided to concentrate on not missing a single word or a single movement.

"Your right hand is more important. I mean, both of your hands are important. In the beginning, many people think it's the left hand that is doing all the work and forget to move the right hand," Toshi explained. "So, you must remember to use both hands at the same time. It's a little bit like playing the piano."

Now, the top half of the *nori* was covered with *shari*.

"From here, spread the *shari* down to cover the bottom half," Toshi explained, as he moved his hands smoothly and rhythmically.

"After you are finished spreading the *shari*, sprinkle some sesame seeds and turn it over so that the *shari* is down and the *nori* is up."

"I remember that part because I have seen it enough for the past week," I told Toshi.

He didn't say anything, just looked at me and continued, "Place some Crab Mix right in the center. Put the filling here below the center. It's easier to roll that way. Then some cucumber strips and avocado slices."

Toshi put all the ingredients neatly across the *nori*, horizontally.

"Why below the center?" I asked Toshi.

"Because it's easier to roll, and when you do so, the filling ends up being in the center when you rolled it up," Toshi explained.

"I see," I nodded.

"Now, we are ready to roll it up."

Toshi grabbed the bottom end of *nori* with both hands, started to roll, and tucked in the top end before sealing the roll. He then turned the roll ninety degrees, so the seam was facing in, not towards the customer.

"Pick up the *makisu* and place it over the roll."

When I picked it up, I wondered why the *makisu* had a plastic wrap. I had never seen this in Japan.

"How come it's in plastic wrap?" I asked Toshi.

"That's because, without it, *shari* will stick to *makisu*. We are making Uramaki," Toshi said. "When *shari* is out, it will stick to *makisu*, and we have to wash it every time we make a roll, which is a waste of time. So, we wrap it in plastic to keep *makisu* rice-free."

"I see."

I also noticed everyone had two *makisu*—one in plastic and one without.

"Is that one without plastic used to make traditional *nori*-out rolls?" I asked Toshi.

"Yes, that is correct. We also use it for Rainbow and Caterpillar Rolls," Toshi said.

"Rainbow?" I asked. I wanted to learn the Rainbow Roll. "How?"

"I will explain to you later when I show you how to make a Rainbow Roll," Toshi said.

He continued with the demonstration.

"Just squeeze over the *makisu*, applying pressure from the side of the roll, but not from the top, so that the top side of the roll stays round," Toshi said.

"Slide your hands left and right like this," Toshi said, moving his hands a couple of times. When he removed the *makisu*, there was a beautiful, long, inside-out roll sitting on the cutting board. He picked up his *Yanagiba*, wiping the blade with his towel.

"Make sure your knife is wet and clean before you cut a roll," Toshi said. "A wet knife makes cutting easier."

"Now, cutting will be difficult," Toshi looked at me with his knife in his right hand. Suddenly, he was more intense, more focused. I sensed it was because he had a knife in his hand.

"Before I explain about cutting, let me talk something about a knife," Toshi paused, removing his left hand from the California Roll.

"When handling your knife at the Sushi Bar, you need to be very careful of your surroundings, co-workers, and objects around you," Toshi said. "We have to be careful not to cause an accident. The worst thing you can do is to cause injury, so when handling your knife, make sure to move it slowly, and no one is within reach of your knife," Toshi said.

"No sudden movement. No swinging your knife around. No reaching for something with your knife in your hand. When you walk around with a knife in the kitchen, say, 'knife' and hold it behind your back so that you don't hurt someone by accident," Toshi explained.

"I understand," I said.

"Good."

"Now, let's get back to the cutting," Toshi continued. "You can move the knife forward and back like a saw. An experienced chef can do this with a single stroke like this," he quickly moved the knife forward, pulling it back only once, and the roll was cut. He repeated this twice again, and the roll was cut into six pieces.

"Forcing your knife down will smash the roll like this," Toshi pressed down his knife without sliding it back and forth. The knife did not cut through the roll. Instead, it made a dent on the top.

"During the cutting, the surface of your knife may get ricey. When that happens, make sure to wipe with your towel. When wiping with a towel, make sure to do so with the blade facing out, not toward your palm, so that you don't cut your finger by accident," Toshi said. "Never place the knife into the bowl of water to wet it because that is dangerous unless you have your own bowl. When we get busy; you may accidentally cut someone's hand. Now, you try it."

Toshi moved away from the cutting board, inviting me to stand in his spot. I was nervous and excited all at the same time, remembering only some of what he just explained. I picked up a sheet of *nori* and put it on the cutting board. I wet my hands in the bowl of water and grabbed some rice from the rice warmer, unsure whether I had the right amount or not. I rolled the *shari* in my hand to form a small ball, and my hands were already sticky, with rice sticking to the palm of my hand. I put the ball of rice down on the *nori* and washed my hands in the sink.

I started to spread the *shari* with my left hand, but it didn't spread at all. Instead, the *shari* was spread unevenly and mushed on my sheet of *nori*. I noticed some black spots too. By this time, my hands were glued with rice again.

Not good, not good, I said to myself, silently. It wasn't perfect, but at least I managed to cover the entire surface of *nori*.

"Now, flip this over?" I said, nervously, looking at Toshi.

"Yes…" Toshi said, squinting his eyes. "But, some sesame seeds before you flip."

"Oh, that's right," I said with relief.

I sprinkled on some sesame seeds and tried to pick it up to flip. It was stuck on the cutting board, and the *nori* was soggy from the *shari*.

"Oh, no, what happened?" I exclaimed.

"You spent too long spreading the *shari*. Moisture from the *shari* makes *nori* wet," Toshi said. "That one is no good. *Nori* will tear apart when you roll it up. You should start again."

I threw away my first attempt and picked up a new sheet of *nori*. I wet my hands, grabbed some *shari*, placed it on the *nori*, and started spreading as Toshi told me. This time, it was a little better. I felt like I had more control over the *shari*. Still, my hands got pretty sticky, which forced me to wash them a couple of times. When I picked up the rice-spread *nori*, it wasn't as soggy as the first one, and I could now add some fillings. I placed some Crab Mix, cucumber, and avocado on the *nori* and rolled it up. I then picked up the makusi, applied some pressure, and formed a roll. I finally cut it into six pieces, just as Toshi had shown me. He was right, cutting was difficult.

"Practice, practice, practice," Toshi said, looking at my roll.

The small printer behind the Sushi Bar spat out a table order. Toshi picked it up and looked at me, "That's it. We got to work. Let's switch places," he said to me.

I looked at my sad California Roll on the cutting board, looking nothing like the one Toshi had made. His California Roll was round, fluffy, cut evenly, the same height when turned, and had the same amount of fillings in each piece. Mine? The rice was unevenly spread on the *nori* so that each piece came in a different size. One section had more Crab Mix than the other, and the end pieces had cucumber sticking out. One of the pieces even fell apart when I cut because I did not seal it tight enough. It was worse than I anticipated.

My very first California Roll looked awful, but I wasn't sad. I knew I had a long way to go, but this was just another step toward becoming a Sushi Chef. I'd get there someday. All I needed now was, as Toshi would say, "Practice, practice, practice."

RAINBOW & INSIDE-OUT ROLLS

Once I got the hang of making California Rolls, Spicy Tuna was a breeze. It was like knowing the secret to a magic trick. Now, I could see the steps from a different angle. Before I was in the audience and now, I was watching backstage. I could see all of the small details I didn't notice before. Keep your hands wet all the time, but not too wet. Use your towel like it's your best friend. Don't touch the *shari* too much. Spicy Tuna Mix is easier to spread than the Crab Mix. Spicy Tuna rolls don't have avocado, only cucumber - I liked that a lot better. Now, I knew how to make two kinds of rolls, and I was ready to tackle the third, and most popular roll in the house, Rainbow.

I observed Toshi and Kai make Rainbow Roll, it seemed simple. Once they made a California Roll, they just added thinly sliced fish—Maguro, Salmon, Ebi, Tai, and avocado—on top of the roll, placed plastic wrap on top, cut it into eight pieces, and voila. It was done. Simple, but not easy.

"Which fish do we put on Rainbow?" I asked Toshi.

"Usually, it's *Maguro*, Salmon, Ebi, and Tai. **Not** *Hamachi* because it's expensive."

"What if we run out of some fish?"

"Then, use whatever we have to make it colorful," Toshi grinned.

"Is Rainbow more difficult than California?"

"I say it's more complicated. The difficult part for you is slicing the fish," Toshi said. "You are not yet ready to slice the fish, so we need to make the slices for you until you can. But let me show you how to make Rainbow."

"Rainbow? Great,"

"First, you cut the fish. One piece of Tuna, two pieces of Tai, two Salmon, and one shrimp," Toshi explained to me.

He grabbed each block of fish and made his slices using his *Yanagiba*.

I watched him anxiously. I wanted to try slicing fish, but I knew he wouldn't let me.

"Slicing fish would be the most difficult part," Toshi said.

I was thinking, *how hard could it be? It's only slicing. All I have to do is to move my knife, right?*

Toshi continued. "You need to pull your knife backward when slicing the fish and never press down the knife too hard. When you apply too much pressure, you will break the soft flesh of the fish and its tissue."

"Okay," I responded, not fully understanding what he meant. *Why does the tissue matter?* I asked myself.

"You have to be gentle, using as little force as possible. Let the knife run is what they say," Toshi said.

"Run?" I asked.

"Yes, run the knife. Let the knife do the work. Use the sharpness, weight, and length of the knife. Make only one stroke when slicing fish, never pulling and pushing back and forth. One stroke. That's why *Yanagiba* is long," Toshi pointed at his knife.

His knife was longer than my $60 stainless-steel knife. It also had a nice wooden handle.

"That looks like a nice knife," I said.

"Thanks. It's made by Masamoto," he told me.

"Masamoto?"

"Yup, it's one of the most popular chef knife makers in Japan. This one cost me about $600," Toshi said. "Actually, it's a gift from my mom," Toshi said.

Toshi quickly made a California Roll and then started to place the sliced fish on top of the roll.

"Place the fish diagonally because you use less fish to cover the outside. Use more avocado instead of fish, that way, you can save the food cost," Toshi whispered. He placed the fish one piece at a time, alternating.

"Finally, plastic wrap," Toshi grabbed a piece of plastic wrap, placed it over the roll, and cut it into eight pieces.

"All Special Rolls are cut into eight, not six. That way, it looks like more food, though it's the same size *nori*. You can use more rice for the Special Rolls, so that they look bigger, too. We charge more for the Special Rolls, so we need to make it look like they are getting more food," Toshi explained.

Toshi didn't let me try making a Rainbow Roll, which was disappointing. But, at least now, I knew how to make it. I decided to keep concentrating on observing Toshi, Kai, and Jun make sushi. When the time came to make my first Rainbow Roll, I knew I would be successful.

Needless to say, I was wrong

*****

"By the way, do you know who invented the California Roll?" Toshi asked.

"I dunno," I said.

"A chef in Little Tokyo, Los Angeles, at a restaurant called Tokyo Kaikan," he said.

"Really?"

"Yes. It's an American invention. I heard Americans did not like the taste of seaweed, so the chef decided to make 'inside-out' so that they don't taste the seaweed," Toshi said, amusingly.

"Unlike California Roll, no one seems to know who invented the Rainbow Roll. But there is Niji-Maki in Japan, which looks close to American Rainbow Roll," Toshi said.

"I think some Sushi Chef invented Rainbow Roll because he saw some unwanted pieces of fish lying inside of Sushi *Neta* Case," Toshi explained.

"That's how you were using those small bits of pieces lying around," I mentioned.

"When you have too many of those pieces, you can put all of them in one roll and call it an Everything Roll and serve it as a special to the customers at the Sushi Bar. They'll love it!" Toshi exclaimed.

"The downside of an Inside-Out Roll is that you can't taste the fish that is inside of a roll. All you taste is the rice, not fish," Toshi explained.

"Is that true?" I did not quite understand.

"Try it and see it for yourself," he handed me a plate with two pieces of California Roll on it.

I put one in my mouth and started chewing. I could taste the *shari* first, *nori* second, then some avocado and mayo, and lastly crab.

"Wow, you are right. Very little flavor of crab, and by the time I could taste the crab, I am almost done eating," I said. "I like Tekka Maki lot better because you can taste the seaweed, rice, and Tuna inside."

"Yes, Tekka, I must say, is my favorite. The rice and Tuna are perfectly balanced, and the aroma of seaweed is great. Inside-Out rolls use too much rice, I think. *Nori*-Out uses less, and I think they taste better that way," Toshi said.

"How do you make *Nori*-Out Rolls?" I asked Toshi.

"Wait," Toshi looked up at the order paper, glanced at Kai, and said, "This one is small, so you can do it yourself, right?"

"Yes, no problem," Kai said.

Toshi turned his attention back to me, "Let me show you, Tekka Maki," he said, taking a makusi without plastic wrap from the top of the *Neta* Case.

"You use the one without the plastic for *Nori*-Out Rolls," Toshi said.

"First, you need to cut Tuna, about one centimeter in diameter, the same length as your *nori*." Toshi picked up a Tuna *saku* block and cut one side of it exactly the same length as a sheet of *nori*. Then, he took some *shari* and made a small ball in his hand. This ball looked a lot smaller than the one he used for a California Roll.

"You only need half as much rice," Toshi explained, as he spread the rice on the *nori*. He left one-centimeter blank on the top and bottom of the *nori*.

"You need to keep the top and bottom empty— not too much rice on the *nori*. Too much rice, you cannot seal the roll," he told me.

Using the tip of his right index finger, Toshi then picked up a small amount of *wasabi* with his index finger and slid his finger across the *shari*. There was now a thin green line of *wasabi* on the white *shari*.

"*Wasabi* goes well with Tuna. All the *Nori*-Out Rolls have *wasabi*, and you can spread it using your index finger," Toshi said.

Then, he lifted the *nori* with one hand and picked up the *makisu* with the other. He placed the *makisu* onto the cutting board and slowly put the *nori* down on top of it.

"You roll the whole thing, grabbing the bottom of the bamboo mat," Toshi moved his hands quickly, sealed the roll, rolled it halfway forward, and then applied some pressure with his fingers.

"Like California roll, we cut it into six pieces," Toshi grabbed his knife and moved it back and forth on top of the black roll.

All the six pieces came out exactly the same height.

"That's how you make Tekka. Kappa is the same. You can practice *Nori*-Out Rolls with cucumber later," Toshi said.

YANAGIBA

A dull knife is more dangerous than a sharp one. A Sushi Chef must own his knives. Sharpen your knife before your shift, never during the shift. It's not about how good a knife is, it's how you sharpen it. These are some of the new concepts I had to get used to.

*****

It was my third day as a Sushi Chef at Rock'n Hollywood Sushi. I was slicing avocados at the Sushi Bar. I was using one of many beat up *Yanagiba*s someone had left in a box by the Sushi Bar because I couldn't afford to buy a new knife. The wood handle was dark. The blade was worn out. It felt awkward, like wearing someone else's shoes.

"Kaz, I think we need to get you a knife," Toshi said, seeing me squinting my eyes as I cut avocados.

"If you want to be a real Sushi Chef, you must own your own."

Why? I immediately thought. Couldn't I just use this knife? The restaurant supplied the uniform, so why not the knife?

"One of the Japanese food distributors carries lots of *Yanagiba*. I think the cheapest one is $60. It's the same one Jun is using right now," Toshi said, looking over at Jun.

"It's not the greatest knife, but it's good enough for now. Besides, you need it right away. It'll do the job. When you get more practice, you can buy a nicer one."

Before I could say anything, Toshi was on the phone, placing an order for my new *Yanagiba*. Unfortunately, $60 was something I didn't have to spare at the moment. The cost of that knife was equivalent to twenty days of living expenses for me. I couldn't even afford to buy a single pack of gum. But, I was too ashamed to tell him that.

"They will bring it tomorrow," Toshi said and walked back to the kitchen.

I wasn't upset, but I was stunned. In fact, I felt a little relieved. For what? I had no idea.

"It feels cheap and hard to use," Jun whispered to me.

"Really?" I said.

"Toshi ordered for me, too. I am thinking of getting another one, but I don't have any money right now," Jun sighed.

I wished Jun had said something before Toshi ordered my knife, but it was too late to cancel now.

*****

The following day, my *Yanagiba* arrived. It was left on the cutting board along with an invoice.

"I don't have the money right now," I told Toshi. "Can I pay from my next pay?"

"Yes, that's not a problem. We already paid it for you," Toshi said. I was relieved.

I couldn't say it was the most beautiful knife I'd ever seen, but it looked better than I expected. Compared to Toshi's $600 carbon steel *Yanagiba*, well, there was no comparison. At least, my *Yanagiba* came with a nice *saya* or wood blade cover. I pulled off the *saya* and saw the thin, narrow stainless blade. It was shiny and sharp. When I tried to feel the sharpness of the blade with my index finger, Toshi stopped me, "No. Never place your finger on the blade. Do like this." He put the blade on top of his thumb's fingernail.

"Apply slight pressure to the side. If the knife sticks to your thumb, then it's sharp. If it slides, then you need to sharpen it," Toshi said.

I placed my knife on the fingernail of my thumb, just like Toshi showed me and applied a little pressure from the side. My knife slid off of my thumb.

"I am not sure if I felt anything," I said to Toshi.

"When you get used to it, you will feel the blade sticking to your fingernail," Toshi said.

"Now you got your own, you need to learn how to sharpen it," Toshi said. "You need to take good care of it. Maybe you want to take it home with you every night after your shift. You need to guard it like it's the most precious thing."

*****

At Rock'n Hollywood Sushi, everyone sharpened their knives with a shared set of whetstones. The restaurant covered the cost, so we didn't have to buy our own. I later learned that traditionally, in Japan, you are expected to have your own set of whetstones. When used frequently, the stone's surface becomes uneven, which results in an unevenly sharpened knife. You need to take care of the whetstones to make sure they always have a flat, even surface. When you share a stone, it's hard to keep it at an optimal level because some people take good care of it, and some people don't.

"The whetstones come in many different grades. There is a medium grade, and there is a fine grade, which we use for finishing," Toshi explained. "This brown one is 1000 grade. It's medium, so it's rough. You want to start first with the brown stone."

I nodded.

"After the brown one, you want to switch to the white finishing stone, finer and harder stone," he continued. "You must first immerse it in water entirely to get it wet until the stone soaks up as much water as it can before you start sharpening your knife,"

"How come?" I asked

"That is because when the stones are not wet enough, you will break them when you move your knife on them," Toshi explained. "Wetting makes them softer, so it's easier to glide your knife."

"I see."

"It takes a good ten minutes, maybe fifteen for the stones to get ready," he said.

"You soak them in the water like this," Toshi placed the white finishing stones into a small bucket filled with water. "You see the bubbles coming out? Stones are soaking water now. When the bubbles stop, then they are ready."

"The sharpening technique is very simple," Toshi pulled out one of the non-bubbling stones. "First, you start with the backside of your *Yanagiba*. Lay your knife flat against the whetstone, and let it slide up and down like this." Toshi held his *Yanagiba* with his right hand, and placed his left fingers on top of the blade, moving both hands together to slide the knife.

"To sharpen, you can either apply the pressure when you move it forward, or when you move it downward, but not both ways," Toshi said.

"Which one do you do?" I asked.

"I tend to press when I go forward," Toshi replied.

"Make sure to keep a firm grip on the knife and avoid slipping your left fingers from the surface of the knife," he said. "Sometimes, when you put too much pressure, you slip your left fingers and can cut them."

I imagined my left fingers sliding on top of my knife and cut on the whetstone. It looked painful.

"Yes, that is not a pretty image," Toshi said.

"After you slide the flat side, then you flip the knife, slide the backside with the same amount of pressure. Make sure to keep the angle of the blade. It's about twelve-to-thirteen degrees. Also, make sure to slide the knife the same number of times as the flat side."

"What do you mean?" I didn't understand.

"For example, if you slide your knife ten times on the flat side, you slide it ten times on the other side," he explained.

"Oh, I see."

"Now, you try," Toshi said.

I slowly put my knife on top of the whetstone, flat side down, and moved it up and down. I couldn't figure out how much pressure I needed to apply. My hands moved at an awkward, uneven speed.

"Try doing it more smoothly," Toshi said. "I think you are pressing too hard."

I tried to relax, but I was haunted by the image of accidentally cutting myself with the blade. It was like trying to drive a stick shift for the first time. It was scary.

I flipped my knife and did the same to the other side. I angled the knife and lifted the backside like Toshi showed me, but each time I moved it, I couldn't keep the same angle.

"Try keeping the same angle," Toshi said.

"I know, but I cannot," I said.

"You just need to practice more," he assured me. "Oh, by the way, always sharpen your knife before you start your shift, during your break, or after your shift. Never during your shift. That is just a rule for the Sushi Chef."

"I understand," I told him, though, I really didn't understand why. Several years later, I figured out that to work in a kitchen was like going to battle. Just like a soldier should have his gun ready, a chef needs to have his knife ready for battle.

When Toshi left, Jun admitted, "I have been practicing it for three months, but still cannot sharpen my knife well." He showed me his *Yanagiba* with its curved tip. "No matter how many times I sharpen, it never gets as sharp as Toshi's knife."

I started to think maybe it was the knife that was bad, not Jun's technique. I really wanted to get a better knife, but I couldn't afford one.

"How much does a decent *Yanagiba* cost?" I asked Jun.

"About $300," Jun said. "There is one by Masamoto, one of the leading knife makers in Japan."

$300 was 100 days' worth of living expenses in my world. I had no idea how I could save enough money to buy a better knife. So, for now, I was stuck with my current $60 *Yanagiba*.

*****

After years of using and sharpening knives, slicing, and gutting fish, I came to understand that it's not the quality of the knife that matters, it's how you sharpen it. One of the most experienced Sushi Chefs I've ever worked with, Jin-san, used only two sets of ordinary chef's knives he bought at a restaurant supply store. They each cost around $15, but when he used them, he cut the fish faster and more beautifully than anyone I'd ever seen.

I had a fascinating encounter, one time, at a knife store in Tokyo. It taught me a valuable lesson about knife quality.

It was 2005, I was strolling in the Kappa-Bashi district in Asakusa, Tokyo. Kappa-Bashi is the restaurant supply mecca of Tokyo, with over 170 stores on an 800-meter-long street. You can find just about anything you need to run a restaurant in Kappa-Bashi. Japanese plates, Western-style plates, pots to serve noodles, soup dishes, pans of all sizes, shapes, and colors; chopsticks ranging from $1 to $30 a pair; traditional Red Lanterns, with calligraphy words written on them, like the ones displayed at *Yakitori* and Ramen shops; lacquerware, in both black and red, traditional and modern; store signs and uniforms, like the ones worn by Sushi Chefs in the U.S.; to-go containers and refrigerated showcases; even wax food displays, some that even looked better than the actual food. You name it, they'll have it. It's a restaurant supply wonderland.

I stumbled upon a knife store with a few hundred, knives on display. Japanese knives, Western knives, short blades, long blades, small, and big, most of which I'd never seen. Everything was laid out so beautifully in the display case. As I was browsing, I wondered why there were so many different types of knives. Then, behind me, I overheard a conversation. A customer, a middle-aged man, was looking at a long, shiny, beautiful chef's knife resembling a small *Katana* or Samurai sword. Beside him was the store owner, an older man in an apron, who gave him a wary look.

"Can I see this one and this one, and...this one, please?" the customer asked the store owner.

"Yes, sir," said the owner. He opened the display case, took out three knives, and placed them on the table.

The customer looked at them for a minute, and the atmosphere got tense. He held each knife one by one, holding each up in the air to examine the blade, the handle, and the weight. He continued looking at the knives, stopped, and finally asked, "So, which one do you think is the best knife?"

"Well, they are all great knives."

"Yes, I know they are all great. But what I'm asking is which I should buy? Which one do you recommend?"

"Let me see…" the owner said as he frowned. "Well, I can tell you this from my experience. Almost all professional chefs buy inexpensive knives because they use their knives every day. They sharpen them every day, too. They know that they will damage expensive knives, so that is why they buy cheap ones."

The customer held his breath, stood still, and listened to the owner.

"Almost all the amateurs and semi-pro chefs end up buying expensive knives if you ask me," the owner said.

The customer squinted but said nothing. The owner continued.

"I suppose amateurs want to own and collect knives instead of using them. I suppose I don't mind whether they use the knives or not, as long as they buy from me," the store owner said. "But, if you are going to use them, I want you to get a knife that fits you the best."

The store owner stopped, and silence followed. I left the store right after their conversation, so I have no idea which knife he wound up buying. I'm guessing he bought a more expensive, nicer-looking knife because clearly, he was not a professional chef. I sensed he was more attracted to the quality of the steel and its price. It reminded me of the day I got my first inexpensive *Yanagiba* at Rock'n Hollywood Sushi. Even after the store owner shared his opinion, I felt the customer thought, the higher the price of the knife, the better its quality was.

As I learned through my experience, as well as from other Sushi Chefs like Jin-san, the quality and the looks of a knife is secondary, if you intend to use it every day in the kitchen.

*****

57

"I cut my finger a thousand times, but now I cut my finger no more." I heard some Sushi Chefs say. Honestly, I don't remember how many times I cut my finger during my professional sushi career. Toshi never cut his fingers. During the year-and-a-half I worked with Toshi, I never saw him cut his finger. No once. I just couldn't understand why.

It's embarrassing to cut your finger at the Sushi Bar mainly because your fellow chefs know what happened. It's even worse when your customer notices. It hurts, but the pain really isn't the biggest issue. It's kind of like getting into a traffic accident, hitting the car in front of you. You know you just made a simple, stupid mistake, but you're fully aware of it, and so is everyone else. It's embarrassing. At the Sushi Bar, you have to excuse yourself and treat the wound with a Band-Aid. Luckily, we used something called Liquid Bandage at the Sushi Bar. It's basically a fast-drying glue that coats, disinfects, and seals your cut all at once, and it works its magic in just a few minutes. Most of the time, I didn't have to wear Band-Aids or a plastic grab, which is pretty obvious to the customers. There were also medical finger condoms I could wear, too, but they didn't look great, either. Either way, after you cut yourself, two things happen: One, your finger didn't look good, and two, it felt pretty awkward making rolls and *nigiri*.

*****

It was a busy Thursday evening. Toshi, Kai, and I were standing at the Sushi Bar. Table order tickets were piling up, and I was busy taking care of them, while Toshi and Kai took care of the customers at the Sushi Bar. All fourteen bar seats were full. I picked up one ticket and noticed it was printed fifteen minutes ago. In some restaurants, orders have to go out within fifteen minutes after they're placed in the POS system. Even though there wasn't a time limit at Rock'n Hollywood Sushi, fifteen minutes was not good. It meant that the customer had been waiting at least twenty minutes for their food.

The order had two California Rolls, one Spicy Tuna, one Rainbow, and two Salmon *Nigiri*. I calculated that it would take me about ten minutes to make everything. I started with the two California Rolls first, placing two sheets of *nori* side-by-side at the same time. This way, I could make the rolls much faster. After placing the Crab Mix, cucumber, and avocado, I rolled up two rolls, squeezed them with the *makisu,* and cut the first roll with my *Yanagiba.* I made hundreds of California Rolls by this point, so my body moved almost automatically. And that's was when it happened. I moved my knife to cut the California Roll in half when I realized that I cut my left thumb at the same time. Because I placed my left hand almost unconsciously over the California Roll, I must have misjudged and didn't realize my finger was right underneath the blade. I didn't feel anything, but I immediately knew what happened because I started to see blood pouring out from my thumb.

"Oh, shit," I said, but not shouting. "Don't panic, don't panic," I mumbled to myself.

Toshi looked over and saw a sea of blood spreading over the cutting board.

"Jesus, what happened?" Toshi shouted.

"I must have misplaced my finger when I tried to cut my roll," I said, reaching for the paper towels.

Two ladies were sitting in front of me and saw the whole thing through the glass *Neta* Case. "Oh my God, are you okay?" One of them asked me, concerned.

"I think so. I am sorry about that," I was embarrassed. "No, not really, I mean, I think it will be okay," I quickly responded, trying to stay calm.

"It always happens when you are thinking of something else," Kai said.

He was right. I don't remember what I was thinking about at that moment, but I'm sure it was something else.

There was no way I could continue making sushi. I excused myself to the back kitchen and grabbed the first-aid kit. When I opened the paper towel to look at my thumb, blood was still pouring out. The cut was about halfway through my fingernail, making it look like the top part was just hanging. The cut had been so sharp, but I felt very little pain. I threw away the old paper towel now smeared with blood, grabbed a new one, and wrapped my thumb again, applying pressure. I stood there for five minutes. I started to think maybe I couldn't go back to the Sushi Bar tonight. I felt terrible leaving Toshi and Kai during such a busy night.

A chef once showed me the quickest way to stop bleeding: sprinkle salt on the wound and let the blood crystallize. The salt soaks up the blood, quickly turning red, like a Hawaiian Shaved Ice. I was skeptical at first, but within seconds, the salt hardened, quickly sealing the wound. It worked just like magic. Plus, it didn't hurt much, either.

I looked down at my thumb; it was still bleeding. Maybe I could salt it if the bleeding continued. I was hoping it would stop soon. I kept applying pressure. Five minutes. Ten minutes. Blood was still flowing. I applied extra layers of bandage, wrapped it with medical tape, and put a plastic glove on my hand. I headed back to the Sushi Bar.

"How is it?" Toshi asked.

"It's deep, halfway through the thumb and still bleeding," I said. Kai wrinkled his nose. "I put some bandages and wrapped tightly with the tape. I will be okay for now."

"Okay," Toshi said.

The two ladies from the Sushi Bar were gone, and now a couple sat in front of me. They had no idea what just happened, and neither did any of the other customers at the Sushi Bar. I was back from my "penalty box," but the glove on my left hand was a reminder of my mistake. I wanted to take it off, but I couldn't, at least not tonight. I told myself never to cut my finger again and picked up the next ticket order.

Of course, the following day, I cut my left finger.

SUSHI

MY FIRST MEMORY OF SUSHI

Circa 1975.

I probably had my first taste of raw fish in my hometown of Yasugi, a tiny fishing village in Japan. The village was famous for *Unagi, Iwashi, Saba, Maguro, Kani, Karei,* and *Tachiuo* (Belt Fish) in winter and many shellfish: Clams and *Sazae* (Turbo Cornutus). But my first memory of sushi goes back to when I was nine years old in Tokyo.

I always thought my mother was an excellent cook and loved eating whatever she made. I never knew that she didn't know how to cook before she got married. She made a variety of dishes for us, and my sister and I didn't ever fuss during our meals. My first memory of sushi is as clear as ever, even after so many years.

*****

I suffered from a series of unexplained, severe headaches. The headaches attacked me almost every month, and every time a one struck, I had to call in sick and stay in bed. My head felt like it was splitting in half, and there was no permanent cure. I took aspirin to ease the pain temporarily, but it still lingered, with just a little numbness.

My mother tried all the pain medications, read all the home doctor books trying to find the cause and solution of my headaches. After a lot of trial and error, she finally found that Bufferin worked best. Since she still wanted a permanent cure for me, we started going to doctors. My mother took me to the University Medical Hospital in Shinjuku for an MRI. I didn't know it back then, but that hospital was one of only three hospitals in Japan that had an MRI machine at the time.

One morning, my mother told me to get dressed.

"Where are we going?"

"To the hospital in Shinjuku."

"How about school?" I asked her.

"You are not going today. It will take us the whole day."

"A whole day?"

"Yes, so get dressed now. Hurry."

I had no idea why we had to go to a hospital so far away. But it didn't matter where we were going, I was just glad I didn't have to go to school. For me, it was a small excursion, and I loved it.

We took a bus from our home to the Oizumi-Gakuen train station. We took the Seibu Line to Ikebukuro, a more metropolitan part of Tokyo. From there, we transferred to the Green train, the Yamanote Line, that took us to Shinjuku. The Ikebukuro station was a big hub— one subway and three different train lines, each operated by a separate company.

In the mornings, my father also transferred to the Ikebukuro station to the subway line to get to his office in Marunouchi (downtown Tokyo). I remember it being very crowded. If you didn't walk fast, people ran into you from every direction. They would look at you, silently yelling, "Hey, walk fast!" Luckily, we arrived after the morning rush, and the station wasn't nearly as hectic as I remembered.

The entire trip took us about an hour and a half. The hospital was a lot bigger than any hospital I'd seen before. Until that day, I was only used to visiting small local clinics. This hospital had a small convenience store, like a 7-Eleven. They sold coffee, canned drinks, and snacks. We found the general waiting area and went into a second waiting area on the opposite side of the room. We were the only ones waiting. I felt special because no-one else was there. My mom never told me what we were doing, so I wasn't nervous, only curious. Above all, I was happy because I didn't have to go to school. Everything was new and exciting.

A nurse opened the door and called my name a few minutes after we sat down. They gave me a paper-thin, light blue, cotton disposable hospital gown, the kind you tie in the back and asked me to change my clothes. Once I changed, the nurse told me to go into a different room, where I saw a big doughnut-shaped machine the size of a car with a metal bed attached to it. The nurse told me to lie down on the metal bed and stay still. The metal bed looked cold and didn't have any sheets. I had no idea what was about to happen, but I kept saying "Yes" to every instruction she gave me.

I laid down on the cold metal bed and waited for another instruction. The bed started to move slowly and slid me into the giant white doughnut. I heard a deep mechanical humming sound, like metal drumbeats resembling nothing I've heard before.

I suspected the machine was doing something, and although I didn't know what was happening, I somehow knew everything was going to be just fine, I was in good hands. If I had been three years old and the nurse told me it would be just as fun as the Peter Pan ride at Disneyland, I would have believed her.

I couldn't keep track of time while I was inside the machine. It felt as if I had been lying there for thirty minutes. I felt nothing, and only heard the strange mechanical noises, so I figured it was doing something only doctors could understand.

As the bed brought me out of the doughnut machine, the nurse told me it was over. I looked at her, confused because I felt no pain. I wanted to ask why there was no pain, no medication, no shots. They didn't even check my temperature or my heartbeat. I also wanted to know the result. I asked the nurse, and she said that we had to come back in two weeks to find out.

As soon as I changed back into my clothes, I rushed to my mother in relief. We left the hospital and took a bus to the Shinjuku Station, where my mother decided to have lunch—a Kaiten-Zushi restaurant: Nigiri Sushi on a conveyor belt.

What a great idea! I thought. Until that day, I never had nigiri. We made Sashimi and Hand Rolls at home for dinner, but never nigiri. Contrary to popular belief, not everyone in Japan is a nigiri expert. In fact, most Japanese (my guess is over 90%) don't even know how to make it at all. There are, however, other forms of sushi that the Japanese enjoy at home. Chirashi sushi is a form of sushi with vegetables and fish sprinkled over shari. It can be served either individually in a bowl or on a large plate and is usually shared among the family. Hand Roll is another popular dinner in Japan. Also known as Tamaki, Hand Roll sushi takes shari and fish and wraps them into a cone with seaweed.

One time I remember my mom buying a pre-sliced fish Sashimi pack at the supermarket. The Sashimi assortment had Maguro, Tai, Hirame, Ika, Tako, and Ama Ebi. She made shari, using the sushi vinegar she also bought at the store and prepared vegetables - cucumber, pickled daikon, and shiso leaves - and laid everything out on a large plate.

Salmon Sushi wasn't popular in Japan until the 90s, so I never had it until I came to the U.S. Sweet Shrimp is another one of my favorites, and I love natto maki, fermented soybeans, notoriously famous for their foul smell. Maguro was always my second favorite fish, and of course, Toro, the most expensive item. I also enjoyed the tsuma—a thin strip of daikon radish garnish. It's white, translucent, and beautiful, creating a nice contrast with the green shiso leaves in the package. Plus, when you dip them into soy sauce, it's very refreshing and will cleanse your palette after the raw fish.

*****

As we entered Genroku Sushi, a famous *Kaiten-Zushi* restaurant chain, all the chefs shouted, "Irasshaymase!" My mom and I took a seat at a counter in the back of the restaurant.

My mom took two teacups and poured green tea out of the hot water dispenser in front of us. Everything was self-serve, and it was one of the reasons why *Kaiten-Zushi* was affordable.

The counter seat-only restaurant was packed with salarymen. They picked up plates from the revolving conveyer belt and ate their sushi fast. In the middle of the conveyer belt, four Sushi Chefs were making all kinds of *nigiri* in great haste. It was exciting. The way chefs moved made me think of a choreographed dance. They didn't waste any time, and every move was calculated. It was beautiful.

The conveyer belt was full of plates, two pieces of *nigiri* on each one. I immediately saw my favorite item moving toward me, Red *Maguro Nigiri.* I picked up the plate, took one piece, flipped it, dipped it in soy sauce, and then put it in my mouth. The flavor of Tuna spread through my mouth, mixed with the aroma of *wasabi* and soy sauce, and instantly made me happy. I was feeling weak and sad about the constant headaches and the long trip to the hospital. But at that moment, I didn't have a headache, and I was eating Red *Maguro Nigiri* for lunch.

Each plate was a different color, and each color was a different price. The Red *Maguro Nigiri* was a blue, ¥100 plate. I knew I could eat a lot of them without hurting my mom's wallet. When I finished the first plate of *Maguro*, I watched to see if another plate was coming my way.

Then boom! I saw two plates on the conveyer belt, three seats down from me. I waited fifteen seconds for the two plates to move in front of me, and snatched them off the conveyor belt like a cat stealing food. Once I finished them, my eyes fell on a plate of cooked shrimp, *Ebi. What color plate is the Ebi on?* I wondered. It was blue!

Great, it's blue, and I can have two, but wait, let's just take one, for now, I thought. Once I gobbled up the *Ebi*, it was time for *Ikura* and *Uni*.

I knew *Ikura* and *Uni* would be more expensive than *Maguro*, and they don't come around very often. I patiently waited for an *Ikura* plate to come my way, while I sipped my cup of green tea, and ate *gari* to kill time. *Ikura* was on a green plate, and *Uni* was on a red plate, the most expensive of all.

The only time I had *Ikura* was on New Year's Day during *Osechi Ryori*—the traditional Japanese New Year's Meal. I was four years old and loved it the moment I put it in my mouth. *Ikura* has a rich, oily flavor that just spreads through your mouth. I had to have one. But the biggest finale was *Toro*, Tuna Belly, the king of *nigiri*. I liked *Chu-Toro*, a medium-fatty Tuna, the most. *O-Toro*, the fattiest Tuna, was overwhelming for me, and the most expensive *nigiri*, a rare item on a special gold plate. I didn't dare grab one.

*****

I was still relishing the dishes around me, trying to savor the taste and smell of my lunch. My mother asked me to stack up the finished plates to see how much sushi we ate. I saw a total of twenty plates in front of us: twelve for me, eight for my mom.

"Bill, please!" my mother shouted to one of the elderly waitresses, who came to collect the plates. The waitress counted the plates, added up the prices, and handed the bill to my mom. That was when I learned that stacking plates wasn't just for us to see, but to make it easier for the waitress to calculate the bill.

"¥2,500, please," the waitress said.

"Okay, time to go," my mom told me. We stood up from our chairs and walked back down the narrow aisle to the front entrance.

"Excuse us, excuse us," my mom kept saying.

My mom handed three ¥1,000 bills to the cashier, and we left the restaurant after receiving the change.

I was happy. The sushi had satisfied my appetite and nourished my body. It was simple, yet there was something special about *nigiri*. I didn't know exactly what it was, but I was too content at the moment to try and figure it out. All I knew was I wanted to go back there again. Soon.

A couple of weeks later, we went back to the hospital to get the reports. I found out that the big doughnut machine was checking my brain waves. I heard the doctor tell my mother that I had irregular brain waves, but it was nothing to worry about. Either way, none of it made any sense to me, and I didn't care. All I could think about was having sushi for lunch again. I didn't ask my mom if we were going back. I was afraid she wouldn't take me there if I did. Nonetheless, I had a strong feeling that we were going to the same *Kaiten-Zushi* restaurant again.

I was right! When my mother told me we were going back, I jumped with joy, dashed out of the hospital to the bus stop, and shouted, "Hurry, mom!"

The place was packed, just like the last time. Since it was my second visit, I knew exactly what to do. I planned out which sushi to start with, and the order of my plates on the bus. As soon as we sat down, I reached for the tall teacup and poured myself some green tea. I grabbed a pair of chopsticks, took some *gari* and *wasabi* from the container, and poured some soy sauce on my plate. I pretended I was a regular. I felt like I was part of the grown-up lunch crowd and ready to pick up my plates of *nigiri*. *Maguro*, shrimp, *Ikura*, *Tai* were all on the revolving conveyor belt, eagerly waiting for me to pick them up. I was about to pick up my first plate of *Maguro* when I heard a middle-aged businessman at the end of the table, talking to the Sushi Chef. The chef nodded, grabbed his knife, sliced a couple of thin pieces of fish, formed a *nigiri*, and plated it.

"Here you go, Mirugai," the chef said, smiling at the man as he handed him the plate.

"Thanks a bunch." I heard the man say. He was beaming with a satisfied smile on his face.

I saw him eat two pieces of giant clam from the plate.

Wait. What just happened? The salaryman ordered a nigiri, and the Sushi Chef custom made it for him? I thought we were only supposed to eat what was on the conveyor belt. Does that mean I can order something if I don't see it here? Do they have more fish inside the Sushi Bar, hidden from our eyes?

I was only nine years old and couldn't figure out what was going on.

"How did that man over there order a *Mirugai Nigiri*? Can we do the same?" I asked my mother.

"Sure, you can. Do you see the names of the fish on the wall? That's the menu. You can order any one of them," she told me

What menu? The large wooden tags on the wall with names of fish on them? I thought they were decorations? What the heck is *Engawa*? *Kohada*, and *Suzuki*? "I have no idea," I mumbled. I wanted to order from the menu, but I was intimidated. I just couldn't ask the Sushi Chef to make me a *nigiri*. I couldn't even ask him what *Kohada* was. I was afraid everyone in the restaurant would laugh at me. So I didn't. I picked up another plate of *Maguro* from the conveyor belt instead.

THE GALLOPING GOURMET

Circa 1980.

It's a Saturday afternoon. I came home after a half-day at school, and my lunch was waiting for me on the table. My mother was out, she worked at a café downtown part-time as a server. My dad had the day off and was watching TV in the living room. I started to eat my *Yakisoba* lunch when I heard laughter coming from the TV. I think it was an American TV show because the host was a Caucasian man wearing a tie and a burgundy velvet shirt with a glass of wine in his hand. The audience was filled with blondes, brunettes, and dark hair with all sorts of colors.

The host was talking to the audience while sipping wine at the same time in a kitchen. Wait, is this a cooking show? I'd seen a cooking show on TV before, but nothing like this. A typical cooking show featured an instructor who talked about ingredients, and an assistant, who just repeated what the instructor said, adding precise measurements like, *"Yes, that is 2 grams of salt, isn't that right, Chef Tanaka?" "Yes, that is correct."* It was informative but amazingly boring. But this cooking show... I had no idea what it was called, and this man... I had no idea who he was, were more entertaining than any other cooking shows I'd ever seen. He chopped onions and slammed meat on the cutting board. It was crude, but fun to watch. Even I could tell he wasn't like other professional chefs. He was clumsy and made jokes. He ridiculed himself when he made mistakes, but it made his audience laugh. It made me laugh. At one point, he jumped over the couch next to his kitchen and started talking to the audience. When he tasted his food, his expression was exquisite. His food must be so mouthwatering that I wanted to taste it. I wanted to cook the same dish as he did.

At the end of the show, he sat at the dining table and drank more wine while he sliced up the large piece of beef he just cooked. He picked a piece up with his folk and put it in his mouth. There was a close-up shot of a woman in the audience. Her face said, "Oh, my gosh, I want to taste that, too." The host stood up, ran into the audience, grabbed the hand of that same woman, and invited her to sit down at his table. At the end, the credits played with music while the two talked and enjoyed the meal — what a great show. I asked my dad what the show was called. He told me *Sekai no Ryori Show*, The World Cooking Show in Japanese. The name of the host was Graham Kerr (Gra-ham Kerr in Japanese). Since Graham was speaking in Japanese, I had no idea that he had a British accent or that the show was called the Galloping Gourmet, until some twenty years later.

Watching the Galloping Gourmet became my Saturday ritual for a while. My favorite part of the show was always the end. I tried to guess who Graham would pick out from the audience. I always thought he would choose a woman because I imagined he was a womanizer because of the way he dressed. But sometimes picked a man from the audience instead. Either way, whoever he chose, they never failed to show how fantastic the food tasted.

Without realizing it, I started to understand the magic of cooking and liked how happy it made others. I don't know if I secretly wanted to be like Graham Kerr, but he must have made a strong impression on me because when I started teaching Sushi Class in San Francisco years later, my wife suggested I wear a colored shirt and a bow-tie. When I asked her why, she said, "Well, you told me you were watching Galloping Gourmet, so I thought Graham Kerr had a big influence on you. You should wear a bow-tie and make it your style just like he did."

AMERICAN–STYLE SUSHI

Circa 1990.

The California Roll was invented 5,000 miles away from Japan, in Little Tokyo, Los Angeles. The story goes like this:

A chef at the Sushi Bar, Tokyo Kaikan, was asked to make something special, but he didn't have any unique fish he could use. Out of desperation, he quickly sliced avocado, added crab, and made a Crab and Avocado Roll. The customer liked it so much that he ordered it again. Soon after, other customers found out about this Special Roll and kept ordering it. Thus, a California Roll was born. Since some of the customers didn't like the taste of *nori*, the chef decided to make this roll inside-out, so the first thing you taste is the *shari* instead of the *nori*. I never understood why people didn't like the flavor of *nori*.

I recently came across an article indicating that sushi-eaters in Japan have developed certain stomach enzymes that help them digest seaweed through their systems. Westerners, like Americans, don't eat sea vegetables as the Japanese do and, therefore, don't have these same enzymes. It didn't make a lot of sense to me at the time, but it could explain why many of the customers I met at the Sushi Bar didn't like *nori* at all.

A few traditional Japanese Sushi Chefs may still consider the California Roll to be "disgraceful" or "not sushi at all." In my opinion, these versions are unquestionably sushi because they use *shari*, and the word "sushi" refers specifically to the seasoned rice. If the chef at Tokyo Kaikan thought using avocado in sushi was wrong, there wouldn't be a California Roll.

Something similar frequently happens in Japan, as well. Though some Japanese chefs won't admit it, Salmon Sushi is a good example of experimenting or creating your own version of sushi.

About thirty years ago, in Japan, no one used Salmon for sushi. But now, if you go to any *Kaiten-Zushi* restaurant in Japan, you will see many varieties of Salmon *Nigiri*. They come with toppings, such as thinly sliced onions, seared with *katsuobushi,* or dried *Bonito* shavings. According to many surveys, it's currently the most popular *Nigiri Neta*, especially among Japanese children. It just goes to show you that traditions can change, even in Japan. They even have Banana Sushi as well as Corn and Mayo Sushi.

*****

My first encounter with "real" American-style sushi was at the Crazy Fish restaurant in Los Angeles back in the 90s. At that time, I was still a Graphic Designer for a small ad agency in Beverly Hills, designing movie posters. I was twenty-five, just out of college, and happy to have a full-time job. There was a sense of freedom, I felt motivated, eager to do whatever it took to advance my career. I was making $25,000 a year, which was more than I ever made in my life, and it was a great feeling.

Those days, I enjoyed going out to eat with my friends, and Los Angeles offered plenty of dining opportunities for a variety of cuisines. I bought the *Zagat Guide* to look up notable restaurants. Before the *Zagat Guide*, I only knew of the most common places like The Cheesecake Factory and Red Lobster. The *Zagat Guide* led me to lots of wonderful discoveries. Chinois on Main - Wolfgang Puck's restaurant in Santa Monica, Fama on 4th Street - an Italian-California restaurant, Röckenwagner - California cuisine with European influence, and Joe's contemporary American fare in Venice. It was fun to find new restaurants, taste their food, experience the ambiance and service. Those days, I spent a good part of my salary dining out. I probably could have saved or invested that money instead, but I didn't, and I have no regrets. Those dining experiences were priceless and helped shape my life. They've allowed me to work at a restaurant, teach Sushi Classes, and offer private *Omakase* Sushi dinners.

*****

Every evening on my way home from work, I saw a long line of people waiting outside of a corner shopping mall. The mall consisted of a copy store, Federal Express, a dry cleaner, and a Bank of America. The line came out from the smallest store in the building with a little neon sign that said, Sushi Café.

A Sushi Café? I said to myself, wondering who would open a restaurant here. It was a residential area with mainly houses, apartments, and just a few businesses. I thought it was a rather unusual place to have a restaurant. Let alone, one with a long line of people waiting.

After watching the lines and that place for months, I decided to try it. I didn't want to go alone, so I asked my friend Tom to come with me. We decided to go on Wednesday evening, thinking the line would be shorter than on Friday night.

*****

We arrived at the Sushi Café at 7 PM, put our name on the waiting list, and waited outside. There were six names in front of us, and about fifteen people waiting outside. I peeked through the glass door saw a sign on the back wall, Crazy Fish.

"Hey Tom, this place is called Crazy Fish, not Sushi Café. Did you know that?" I asked.

"Yes, I am looking at the menu now," Tom said.

"Let me see the menu," and I took it from him.

The menu was a long white sheet like the one you'd see at a sandwich shop with a section for rolls and a section for *nigiri*. I understood the *nigiri* section with its familiar fish such as *Maguro* and *Hamachi*. But I couldn't understand all of the rolls on the menu and wondered what they were. "California Roll, Spicy Tuna Roll, and what the heck is a Spider Roll?" I mumbled.

"Do you know all these rolls? I like *Tekka*, Tuna Rolls, a traditional roll in Japan, but I guess these are not "traditional" at all?"

"I've had the California Roll and the Spicy Tuna Roll at other places.

A California Roll has crab and avocado. A Spicy Tuna is really good too. I don't know what Jewish Roll is," Tom chuckled.

"A Jewish Roll? What the hell is that?" I said to Tom, with a confused look.

"Look, all the people are eating rolls, like the orange one over there," I pointed out to the one table inside the restaurant.

"Yeah, those orange ones look good. I wonder what they are," Tom said.

"We should ask someone when we are inside," I said, watching the people eating.

After a thirty-minute wait, the waitress called our name, and we were seated at a small table for two, but the waitress quickly disappeared into the kitchen, coming back with a tray full of food, taking it to different tables. The small thirty-seat restaurant was running at full force. Sushi Chefs made sushi at high speeds, and waitresses were running back and forth with plates full of Sushi Rolls from the Sushi Bar. They took orders from customers and shouted across the restaurant. They cleared tables and escorted new customers inside. The scene was more like a Sunday brunch at a busy diner, like Denny's.

"Excuse...me," Tom grabbed one of the waitresses on her way to the back kitchen.

"Yes, what can I help you with?" she shouted.

"How do we order?" Tom asked.

"You circle the ones you want and write down how many you want, right here in the empty box. Once you are done, just hand it to any of us. That's it," the waitress explained.

"Wait," Tom grabbed her as she was about to leave our table.

"We don't know any of these rolls," Tom said.

"Which one?" the waitress said.

"Well... how about Spider Roll?" I asked.

"Tempura Soft Shell Crab."

"Let's see how about Caterpillar Roll?" Tom asked this time.

74

"*Unagi* inside and avocado on top with Sweet Eel Sauce," she said.

"Hmmm, how about..." Tom was about to ask her another question.

The waitress quickly interrupted him, "Look, I'm sorry; I don't have all night to answer your questions, so you can ask your neighbor to see if they can answer your question, okay?" The waitress rushed into the kitchen.

"Gee, that was nice of her," Tom said to me as she left.

"Well, look at what they are eating. It has Tempura Shrimp in it. It must be... this one, Shrimp Tempura Roll," I said to Tom. "Let's get this one and a Spider Roll."

"How about Jewish Roll? It sounds interesting. What's in Jewish Roll?" Tom asked the man at the next table.

"It has Cream Cheese with Salmon. It's delicious," he replied.

"Cream cheese?" I said. "That sounds too weird."

"C'mon, Kaz. It sounds good, actually. Let's order one and see what happens?"

We circled the rolls we wanted, wrote down "1" for each roll, and handed the order sheet to a waitress. Our order was in. Now, we could relax.

Ten minutes later, the waitress brought our first roll: Caterpillar Roll, Fresh Water Eel, *Unagi*, inside, and thinly-sliced avocado wrapping around the outside to make it look like a caterpillar. Sweet *Unagi* Sauce was drizzled all over the roll and plate.

"OMG, is that a Caterpillar Roll?" a young Beverly Hills 90201-type blonde girl asked Tom.

"Ummm, yes, I think so," Tom said.

"It's my favorite. It's soooo good. It's like dessert for me because the BBQ Eel Sauce is so sweet," she told us in excitement.

"OMG, Tom. Our first roll is supposed to be a dessert piece. What should we do?" I asked, imitating the girl while keeping my voice low.

"Well, why not?" Tom said.

Until then, I had never had *Unagi* with avocado. The way I used to eat it was called *Una-Jyu*, grilled *Unagi* over rice, or *Kabayaki*, plain grilled *Unagi*, with a side of rice. I couldn't imagine how it would taste with avocado. When I put the first piece in my mouth, I immediately said, "Wow! Tom, this is good. This is better than good!"

The buttery flavor of avocado matched well with the smoky flavor of *Unagi*. I'd never guessed it would be this good.

All of the sushi at Crazy Fish was nothing like I'd ever seen or tasted. The Spider Roll had Tempura Soft Shell Crab inside, and legs were sticking out of each end, like spider legs, with a bright orange flying fish egg, called *Tobiko*. The Jewish Roll had Salmon, avocado, cucumber, and Philadelphia Cream Cheese, and was named after the Lox Trim Bagel Sandwich served at a Jewish deli.

Despite my expectations, I loved all the rolls we ordered and was pleasantly surprised. It was not like the sushi I knew. Crazy Fish introduced me to a whole new world of American-made sushi.

After that first visit, Crazy Fish made me crazy for their sushi. I ate there frequently, sometimes more than once a week, and told all my friends about it. They, too, all tried it out, and everyone said it was excellent and worth the wait.

I saw American-style sushi as just another form, or creative variation of sushi, like *Chirashi*. Even as I began to relish and enjoy the American-style Sushi Rolls at places like Crazy Fish, I never abandoned traditional Japanese-style sushi, like *nigiri*.

*****

I moved to Los Angeles and lived in my friend Brian's apartment near the LAX after spending three years at college in Iowa. Brian worked at a financial firm downtown, and one of his colleagues, Takeshi, was Japanese. One day, one of Takeshi's friends called to let him know that some of his friends, who worked for Japan Airlines (JAL), were going to be in town for a few days.

"Can you take care of them while they stay in town? They will stay at Hotel Nikko in downtown L.A., and they will be off for a couple of days.

They are my friends, so please show them around, okay?" Takeshi's friend asked on the phone.

Takeshi agreed and invited us to meet the JAL flight attendants too. We drove them out to Manhattan Beach, watched beach volleyball, and took them to a Mexican Restaurant. We drank Margaritas and ate taquitos, chimichangas, and enchiladas. The flight attendants came back to visit several times, sometimes three times a year. Each time, we took them to new places, restaurants, and areas around L.A.

When I met the flight attendants for the fifth time, I went alone, as both Takeshi and Brian had gone back to Tokyo. I decided to take them to Crazy Fish because I wanted them to try American-style sushi, too.

"So, this place is very interesting, they have American-style sushi. I thought maybe you'll like it," I told Momoko, one of the flight attendants.

"That sounds good. All the places you took us before were good, so I trust your judgment," Momoko said.

It was Thursday night, and the place was moderately crowded—a typical thirty-minute wait.

"Have you ever had California Roll?" I asked Momoko.

"California...What?"

"It's American sushi with crab, avocado, and the *shari* is on the outside, not seaweed like a traditional roll. It's terrific. I don't know if you and your friends will like it, but I thought it would be a good experience. I like them a lot," I told her.

Since there were no tables available, the waitress told us to sit at the Sushi Bar. When we sat down, we looked at the menu, and I started to explain all the rolls, like Caterpillar, Spider, and Spicy Tuna.

"I think we are going to leave it up to you, Kaz. Would you order whatever you think is good?" Momoko asked.

"Okay," I replied. I ordered the rolls that I was used to—Caterpillar, Shrimp Tempura, Spider, and Jewish Roll. "These have become my standard rolls," I told them after I placed the order.

As we waited for our food to arrive, we started to chat. One of the young Japanese Sushi Chefs heard us speaking in Japanese and started talking to two of the attractive girls in our group of four. The young Sushi Chef began asking questions.

"Hello. I didn't realize you were Japanese. Sorry to interrupt, but how are you?" the chef started while rushing and speaking in an excited tone.

"Umm, hello," Momoko said, hesitantly. She sensed his awkwardness.

"Where are you all from? What are you doing here? You're obviously from Japan, right? Are you on vacation?" His excitement continued.

"We are just visiting for a couple of days. We are here for work, and we'll fly back to Japan the day after tomorrow. Our friend, Kaz, here, told us about this place, and he said the American sushi is good here, so we thought we'd try it," Momoko said, without mentioning that they were *flight attendants* for Japan Airlines.

"Oh, yes, that's good. You know how busy it is here? You see, it's a crazy place to work. It's not somewhere you work too long," he said. I wondered why he was sharing this information. It didn't seem like an appropriate topic of conversation.

Next to him stood another Japanese chef, who was smiling and looked a little embarrassed.

"I'm sorry about my co-worker. I think what he is saying is that we rarely get Japanese customers here, let alone attractive young women from Japan. So he is, well, slightly excited, if you know what I mean," he explained.

"Oh, yes, slightly...," I tried to hide my sarcasm.

"Anyway, what are you all doing tomorrow? How about we all go to the beach or something? I mean, it's not what you think, you know?" the chef continued. It was obvious that he was hitting on my friends because he wasn't making any sense.

"I'm sorry, we have plans to meet other friends tomorrow, so perhaps next time," Momoko politely declined his offer.

The chef continued talking even after our food came, saying that he had no time to meet girls. It was funny watching the women being hit on by a Sushi Chef at an American Sushi Café. Of course, at that point, I never thought I would do the same thing, hit on an attractive girl sitting in front of me at the Sushi Bar.

*****

A few years later, I came across a restaurant in West L.A. that had a bright yellow sign and black letters stating California Roll Factory. I didn't know why, but something just didn't feel right about that place. But, the California Roll Factory was only a few doors down from my favorite Japanese pub, or *izakaya*, Terried *Sake* House.

Terried *Sake* House was a hole in the wall that served authentic, at-home classic *izakaya* fares, like *Yakitori*, *Agedashi* Tofu, and Tofu Steak. They had two types of Tofu Steak, No.1 with Egg, and No.2 with Egg and *Katsuobushi* (*Bonito* flakes). They also offered grilled fish a la carte, and *Teishoku* dinners (set meal) with rice and Miso Soup. Their sushi and *Sashimi* weren't the best, but it was pretty decent. The best part of Terried *Sake* House was the price. They were so affordable, the food was good, and they were always packed, especially on weekends.

Every time I visited Terried *Sake* House, I couldn't help but see the bright yellow sign three doors down, as if it was beckoning me to come in. Finally, one evening, I decided to visit the California Roll Factory to see what I was missing. I walked in alone and sat at the bar. The chef who greeted me looked familiar, but I couldn't figure out where I met him before.

After a few moments, I realized he was the chef at Crazy fish. Not the one flirting with my JAL friends at the Sushi Bar, but the one who stood next to him.

"I remember you from Crazy Fish," I said to him. "Remember your co-worker hitting on my friends?"

"Oh, yes. I remember that night," he said, looking embarrassed. "I remember you, too. That was the night that my co-worker went crazy," he laughed.

"Crazy indeed." I agreed.

"I am sorry about that," he apologized.

"No, no need to apologize. It was not you and wasn't your fault. There was really nothing you could do. Besides, the girls did not mind him at all," I said.

"He acts like that all the time. In fact, every time he sees an attractive Asian woman at the Sushi Bar, he always tries to ask her out, but never succeeds."

"That's a shame. He seemed like a nice guy. Anyway, I would like to order something. It looks like you have lots of rolls," I diverted the topic quickly, as he was ready to take my order, too.

"Yes, I quit Crazy Fish and opened this place a few months ago. Many of the rolls are the same ones from Crazy Fish, and I keep adding new ones with unique names."

"I see. I'll take whatever you recommend," I said.

"Ok. No problem. I will make you some sushi," the chef said.

His name was Kaz, just like mine. He created several different rolls for me that were similar to Crazy Fish and were all good. But something was different. Something was missing, I thought. But I wasn't sure what it was. The inside of the restaurant looked a lot like Crazy Fish. There were handwritten menus on the wall and casual tables like a café. The fish and the *shari* were both good, but different.

The other Kaz made a couple of rolls that I knew, Caterpillar and Rainbow. He also handed me a few slices of *Hamachi Sashimi*.

"This one is on the house," he said.

"Oh, thank you so much," I responded, as I enjoyed the rolls.

As I looked around the restaurant, I noticed there was only one couple seated in the back. There was a Latino chef at the Sushi Bar and another one in the back kitchen. There was a TV on the wall, and the L.A. Dodgers were playing against Pittsburg Pirates.

"Every night, it's nerve-pinching," Kaz said, noticing me looking around the empty restaurant.

"I worry how busy we are going to get. I think what if... what if no customers show up for the evening? What would I do with all the fish, you know? Will I have enough money to keep the restaurant open next month? How about the month after that?" Kaz said.

"I see...." I nodded my head and wondered why he was sharing all of this with me.

"Also, I need to teach the kitchen staff how to cook Japanese food. Most of them are from Mexico, and they don't know anything about Japanese food. Let alone how it should taste. I was telling them how to make Miso Soup, and they have no idea it had *dashi* broth. They thought adding Miso paste to hot water would make Miso Soup," Kaz complained.

"That must be tough," I replied. I thought I understood what he was talking about, but I didn't.

I didn't truly understand how he felt because I didn't own and run my own business as he did. I'd never trained an employee or taught them how to cook Japanese food. I never taught anyone how to cut fish or make Sushi Rolls. I didn't know anything about borrowing money from a bank or about keeping a cash flow. I didn't have employees, payroll, or business rent to pay. I didn't have to worry about health inspections, licenses, or food safety and foodborne illness. I also didn't have to think about lawsuits from customers or employees.

I listened to Kaz tell me how challenging it is to run a small business and to be a Sushi Chef. I only started to realize what he was saying when I started my own sushi business fifteen years later. I never dreamed that a little over a decade after that conversation, I would become a Sushi Chef.

*****

Another Sushi restaurant I visited and still remember vividly was the famous Sushi Nozawa—the highest Zagat-rated restaurant in L.A. for its food. Out of the perfect thirty points, Sushi Nozawa consistently received twenty-eight points every year and became not just a Sushi restaurant, but a restaurant phenomenon in Los Angeles.

While some said it was great, others complained the service was horrible. Nonetheless, Sushi Nozawa was still one of the most influential Sushi restaurants in L.A. Chef Nozawa was famous for his *Omakase-*

style, also known as, "trust me."

It meant, *don't ask any questions, just take what Nozawa-san offers, and you'll be just fine. If not, face the consequences.*

I heard a rumor that once a girl requested a California Roll and Nozawa-san asked her to leave the restaurant. A lot of similar stories surfaced, which gave Nozawa-san the nickname "The Sushi Nazi."

Nevertheless, the *Zagat Guide* was my bible, and I just had to try it.

When my sister's boyfriend, Taro, came in from Japan on a business trip, I finally got my chance. He mentioned sushi for dinner, so I thought it was the perfect opportunity to try out Nozawa Sushi since it was close to where he was staying. I picked him up at the Universal City Hilton, and we drove five minutes to Sushi Nozawa on Ventura Boulevard. It was set in an ordinary-looking, small corner shopping mall.

By 6 PM, there was already a long line of people waiting. Sushi Nozawa didn't take reservations. We put our name on the list and waited nearly an hour and a half before we were seated at the Sushi Bar. Just like the Zagat Guide said, the inside of the restaurant was nothing fancy—basic wooden tables and chairs, little decoration or art, a couple of neon signs, but there was one sign that said, "Trust Me." While looking around, I also noticed an Arizona license plate, that also said, "Trust Me."

Oh, I see. Omakase equals 'Trust Me' in English, I said to myself. I only told Taro that Sushi Nozawa was supposed to be the best sushi place in Los Angeles. I didn't mention anything about the chef's reputation, his nickname, or his alleged rudeness.

Shortly after we were seated, Chef Nozawa noticed us talking in Japanese. In a soft voice, he asked, "We only have *Omakase*, is that okay?"

"Yes, that's fine with us," I replied.

I sighed in relief and knew I had made the right choice. Nozawa-san, despite the rumors, was not rude to us at all.

*****

At the Sushi Bar, we saw Nozawa-san and two assistants. There was also one elderly waitress who appeared to be his wife. We ordered a bottle of Sapporo and started drinking before our sushi was served. Nozawa-san was the only person making *Nigiri* Sushi, serving all the thirty or so customers in the restaurant, so we knew it would be awhile. We didn't mind, though, we know good food takes time.

Maybe that's why Nozawa-san had so many complaints. In Japan, it's common for people to spend two, sometimes three hours at a restaurant, especially when the food is good. Perhaps some of the non-Japanese customers at Sushi Nozawa were unfamiliar with this custom, or maybe they couldn't wait for their food to arrive, so they complained, giving Nozawa-san a bad name for what was his legitimate service.

The first *nigiri* was *Maguro*, which was a surprise to both of us. Taro looked at me with wide eyes and whispered, "*Maguro?*" I looked at him, nodding, but said nothing, fearing Nozawa-san would hear us. Typically, the first *Omakase* piece should be a Whitefish or something light, followed by a fish with a stronger, fattier flavor. As such, *Maguro* is not usually introduced until the middle of an *Omakase* experience.

The world-famous Sushi Chef, Jiro Ono, supposedly introduced this idea. According to Jiro, when you serve fish with strong flavor at the beginning of *Omakase.* He said it will overwhelm the taste buds, and should only be served toward the middle or the end of the course. I was never a sushi connoisseur, but even I was caught off guard. When I put the piece of *Maguro Nigiri* into my mouth, I was shocked again to taste warm *shari*. None of the sushi I ever had before included warm *shari*. It's said that the best temperature for *shari* is body temperature.

Nozawa-san's *nigiri* was different. "A warm *Shari*? What was going on?" Taro asked. The aroma of vinegar filled my mouth, and the sweetness of the rice created a wonderful harmony with the savory taste of Tuna and dash of *wasabi*. It was nothing like the *Maguro* I had had at Genroku Zushi in Shinjuku after my hospital visit. I don't even remember what I had after that *Uni, Ama Ebi*, Whitefish, and other sushi. We had at least ten different types of fish, until we told Mr. Nozawa, "Thank you, that's it for us."

"Thank you," he replied with a slight nod.

Aside from the first *nigiri* being *Maguro*, the sushi was excellent, and the service was good. There was nothing unusual, rude, or shall I say "Nazi-like" about Nozawa-san. We took whatever he offered because after all, that's what *Omakase* means, trust the chef, leave everything to him, and you'll be in good hands.

I suppose the term "Sushi Nazi" was just a label from the media or by someone who wanted to sensationalize the different culture, the custom. Back then, *Omakase* was a very unfamiliar term, even to most sushi-goers in Los Angeles.

Even to this day, performing *Omakase* requires experience. It's both a custom and a culture. Someone once said that sitting at a Sushi Bar and ordering *Omakase* is like getting an invisible membership to a private club. No one will explain the rules, so you have to figure them out for yourself. It's very complex. I mean, how are you supposed to order something when there is no menu and no price?

Our bill was around $100 per person with one drink each, very reasonable for Japanese standards, in 1997, at a restaurant given the highest Zagat-rating for food. If we were to dine at a high-end sushi restaurant in Tokyo, it would cost us at least $200-$300 each.

*****

I didn't realize how many rock 'n' roll sushi-styled restaurants I visited in L.A. during these years, long before I first started working at the rock 'n' roll sushi restaurant in West Hollywood. One of them was Tokyo Delve's in North Hollywood, known for wild disco dancing, beer, and *sake* drinking, and partying, but not for sushi.

One of my friends lived near Studio City, close to Universal Studios in Hollywood. Every Los Angeleno knows that Universal Studios is not in Hollywood, but in Studio City, and Studio City is NOT Hollywood. It's over the hills, also known as "the Valley" to the locals. There are cities there like Burbank, Van Nuys, Northridge, Reseda, and Canoga Park. The Valley is also part of the so-called *Greater Los Angeles*, which includes Ventura, San Bernardino, Riverside, Orange, and Los Angeles Counties.

Those who live in L.A. County tend to make fun of Valley residents because it gets hot and smoggy there. Also, suburban families live in the Valley, so it doesn't fit the stereotypical image of L.A. County. The Valley isn't a *happening place*, and it's *not cool*. Valley residents come to the city of Los Angeles to dine and play, but Los Angelenos don't go to the Valley.

*****

A friend once told me about a sushi place close to where he lived with his girlfriend. They invited me to join them for dinner.

"It's a fun place. We've been there before, and we should go," my friend told me.

"Why not?" I replied as I always loved to try new places.

"Tokyo Delve's is seriously a rocking place," he exaggerated. "It's crazy there. They have dancing, couples' time during the evening, and all the customers and Sushi Chefs start dancing on the tables. They even play disco music; it's really, really fun. They also spin the Wheel of Fortune, and whoever wins gets a free drink or sushi."

I was in my late twenties, and it sounded like a fun experience, so I decided to give it a try. It was just a social dinner, and my expectations for the sushi were really low. Besides, I had never been to a rock 'n' roll sushi restaurant before. I was certainly curious.

The restaurant was located in North Hollywood, also called NoHo, where the city was promoted as the "NoHo Artist District." Each time someone tried to imitate SoHo, which is in New York City, I felt like saying, "It's not New York City, and stop trying to be like New York City." We were in front of a building that didn't look like a sushi restaurant, but rather, it looked like a small night club, where a local rock band would play. It did, however, have a neon sign out front which said, "Tokyo Delve's Sushi Bar."

We got there early, around 6 PM on a Thursday night. My friend told me we'd have to go early or there'd be a long wait. Even then, the only seats available were at the Sushi Bar. Inside, the restaurant was dark. It felt like a strange blend of 50's dinner café memorabilia, disco lighting, and an American Japanese restaurant interior. The music was so loud that it was flooding my eardrums. They played Sly and the Family Stone, AC/DC, and The Who. I couldn't hear what my friend was saying. Most of the crowd was young, in their twenties and early thirties at most.

The menu looked similar to the one at Crazy Fish, so I knew what to order—Caterpillar, Spider, Shrimp Tempura, and Spicy Tuna Rolls all sounded good. But when the food came, it was bad. The rolls were sloppy—uneven cuts of fish, different thicknesses, and in all different sizes. Some of the rolls weren't perfectly round, but others were broken, and their fillings popped out from every edge. It looked like an inexperienced Sushi Chef made them all.

Oh boy, I'm going to eat this? I thought to myself. Well, I guess I had no choice. I didn't come here for the sushi, I came for the experience. I reminded myself.

I slowly reached out for one of the scary-looking rolls and picked it up with my chopsticks. I dipped the roll in the soy sauce, not once, but twice, to give it an extra coating of flavor. Hesitantly, I put the roll in my mouth. It tasted exactly how I expected it to taste like, sloppy. Again, I reminded myself, I'm here for the experience, not for the food.

Suddenly, I remembered a time when my Jewish co-worker, Shelly, took me to Benihana in Beverly Hills. A Mexican chef, Jose, cooked our food - fried rice, Chicken Teriyaki, Japanese steak, and stir-fry vegetables. While he was cooking, he performed tricks with his metal spatulas. He flipped shrimp tails in the air that landed in his chef coat pocket. He sliced white onions, made a small "mountain," lit up the top, and called it a "volcano." None of this ever happened in a teppanyaki restaurant in Japan.

Shelly asked me, "Well, how did you like it?"

"Well, none of it is authentic, and it's an American Japanese-style restaurant, but not really Japanese. I suppose we are here for the experience, not the food." I told her.

*****

"I wonder when they'll start dancing," I asked.

"I think they do it twice an evening," my friend replied.

A few minutes later, a man in a cheap looking black tuxedo came out and started shouting into a microphone.

"How's everyone doing? Are you ready to party?"

It reminded me of the opening of a heavyweight world championship boxing match in Las Vegas, "Are you ready to ruuuumble!!!"

The loud disco music started, and all the staff and Sushi Chefs began to dance. As they danced, some of the customers started to dance too. A few were even dancing on the tables. Since we couldn't just sit there, watch, and eat while everyone else was up dancing and singing, we quickly stood up and joined the rest of the crowd.

I have to admit it was fun, thanks to a couple of bottles of Sapporo. I doubt I could ever dance like that sober. Other customers started to scream, so I screamed, too. Everyone was dancing to *Stayin' Alive*, imitating John Travolta's moves. Now, everyone in the restaurant was standing. Disco lights were flashing, and the lights were dancing, too. For a couple of minutes, I forgot we were in a sushi restaurant.

When the music ended, we sat back down, told each other how much fun it was, and started to eat more sushi and drink more beer. The sushi still tasted like there was something wrong with it, but after a large bottle of Sapporo and dancing on a table, I didn't care. All I wanted to do was drink, eat, and have more fun. After the first dance, they played the Wheel of Fortune. One lucky customer got to throw a dart for a chance to win a great prize, like a free drink, a free appetizer, or free sushi.

By the time we left the restaurant, I didn't know how many bottles of Sapporo and cheap warm *sake* I had. I didn't realize how full I was until I started to feel sick. We were just about to get in the car when I really got sick.

"Wait, wait," I shouted, waving my hands in the air. "I think I am going to throw up."

I ran to the back of the restaurant and threw up everything I consumed over the past two hours. As I threw up, all of the something-tastes-strange sushi and warm *sake*, I told myself, *Bad idea. I will never come back here again. Ever!*

Well, what do you know? After a couple of years, I went back to the beloved Tokyo Delve's for more dancing, sushi, drinking, and fun with my friend, Tom. We were both single, looking for a fun night out, and Tom suggested we go there.

"I've been there only once, but it was a really bad experience for me. However, I have to admit it's a good place to party. The food is awful, so I say we go there and just drink some Sapporo, order one or two rolls, and appetizers," I told him.

Then, I had a better idea. "In fact, how about this? Let's not order sushi. Let's order Tempura or something cooked from the kitchen. Maybe the cooked food is not so bad,"

"Whatever, dude. Let's just go there and have fun," Tom said.

"All right, I'll see you there at seven, then."

During my second visit, I remembered not to go overboard and drink too much, just to make sure I was *Stayin' Alive.*

MAKANAI & FISH

MAKANAI

"You can use anything you want in the walk-in," Saito-san said to me one afternoon during my prep shift. "Except fish, of course."

"Really?" My jaws dropped. "For *makanai*? Everything?"

"Yes. It will be a great practice, so make whatever you want to eat."

Recipe ideas started pouring in my head. I closed my eyes to imagine what we had in the walk-in. Carrots, cabbage, onions, potatoes, tomatoes, lettuce, garlic, ginger, beef, whole chicken, butter, milk, green onions, oranges, broccoli, *kabocha* pumpkin, Japanese yam, Japanese cucumber, parsley, herbs, and so much more.

Great! I can start with Curry Rice, I thought to myself. *I'm getting tired of eating Tempura and Udon noodles for dinner.*

I ran to the back kitchen and saw Toshi prepping fish.

"Did you hear what Saito-san just said? He said I could use whatever we have in the walk-in," I exclaimed.

"Yes, I heard," Toshi said, without changing his facial expression.

"How come you are not excited? Aren't you tired of eating Tempura every day?" I asked him.

"I just don't like cooking that much." Toshi mumbled. "I prefer eating."

*****

Makanai means "employee meal" in Japanese. It's customary for the chefs to take turns cooking the daily employee meal at a Japanese restaurant. Chefs look at making *makanai* as training, an opportunity to learn and improve on their cooking skills. One of the basic rules is to use whatever is available. You also don't use the expensive ingredients, and the dish must be delicious enough to satisfy the sophisticated taste of your co-workers and the other professional chefs.

At Rock'n Hollywood Sushi, there was no *makanai* tradition. No one cooked for others. No one took turns. Everyone cooked whatever they wanted, or they asked the kitchen chef to prepare something for them. At first, I ate what was on the menu: Tempura, Teriyaki Chicken, Teriyaki Beef, Udon Noodles, *Yakisoba* Noodles, and Stir-Fried Vegetables. They satisfied my hunger and that was it.

After a while, though, I got bored. For one, everything was cooked by a Mexican chef who never had Japanese food until he started working there. He only knew the American versions of Japanese food, so it was just different from what I was used to eating in Japan. Naturally, I got tired of everything. I needed something new. Something delicious. Something exciting. Something, not Japanese. Something not sushi. And definitely something not on the menu.

During my two and a half-hour break between lunch and dinner, I laid on the couch upstairs and started to think about what I want to make. I thought about my favorite restaurant in L.A., Alejo's. It was in the corner of a strip mall, right in between a doughnut shop and a 7-Eleven on Lincoln and Washington Boulevards in Venice Beach.

There was always a long line of people waiting. Inside there was one long "communal" table in the middle, enough to seat about sixteen people, or eighteen if they sat tight. There was nothing fancy about the décor, except for some large framed pictures of pasta with tomato sauce. Because they didn't have a liquor license, they couldn't sell any alcohol, but they did allow customers to bring their own for no corkage fee. So, a lot of people brought their favorite wine, some even bought it from the 7-Eleven next door. "Of all the 7-Elevens in Los Angeles, this one has the best selection of wines," I heard one customer say. There was no way for me to check the validity of that opinion, but it sounded about right.

More than their tasty Pasta and Chicken Parmigiana, Alejo's was famous for one thing: the basket full of bread with garlic oil that was served the moment you were seated. The garlic oil was so addictive that, once you dipped your bread in, you couldn't stop eating, like buttered popcorn at the movies. Everyone joked, saying you may as well call in sick the day after going to Alejo's because you'd stink of garlic.

Linguini Pescatore was my favorite dish at Alejo's. The linguini was perfectly cooked *al dente* every time I ordered it. The fresh clams, squid, shrimp, and octopus also added fantastic *umami* to their original tomato sauce. I never missed emptying the plate. Ever.

I thought I could try to recreate Alejo's Linguini Pescatore for *makanai*. That would be great, but a significant challenge. My mind then shifted to the time I spent in Thailand, where I had nothing but great food.

*****

In 1997, I was in a food court at a shopping mall in Bangkok. It was lunchtime, and the place was packed with people. I didn't know how to read Thai, but I could look at the pictures and guess. This was my second trip to Thailand. I loved it there, especially the cuisine. I love their street food, Satay Chicken, Yellow Noodles, Rice Noodles, Yellow Curry, Green Curry, Red Curry with Sticky Rice, Panang Beef Curry, Pad Thai, Papaya, Tom Kha Kai, Tom Yum Kung, and Phat Phrik Khing.

I wondered if they had the Crab Curry I tried in Patong Beach, south of Bangkok. I looked at all the pictures, but I couldn't tell. Then, I saw something familiar. I pointed to the image of a Papaya Salad to the woman at the register. She said something in Thai, but I just looked back to the picture and said, "Som Tum." She repeated the same thing, nodded, and took out a small stainless bowl. She grabbed some ingredients, poured sauces into the bowl, and started to mix everything up. When she handed me the salad, I thanked her in Thai and seated myself at a small table. I took my first bite; it was refreshing and tasty. I loved the mix of sweet, sour, and the freshness of young green papaya. It went well with the rice I ordered. I then took another bite and another.

Within a minute, I started to feel the hot Thai chili peppers, Prik Nu, aka "Mouth Shit Chili." They say it's one of the hottest chili peppers in the world. "Oh shit, I did not realize she put so many of them," I said to myself. Tears started to pour out of my eyes, as I stuck out my tongue, drank lots of water, and ate a lot of rice to cool my tongue off.

I then knew what the woman at the register was trying to ask me. She was asking if I was okay with "Mouth Shit Chili." But now it was too late, and I was a mess. There was family eating right next to my table, and they were all laughing. Yes, laughing, not smiling. They were probably thinking, "Look at that Japanese tourist. He must have eaten Prik Nu, and that is why he is sweating and crying like that."

When I told the story to my friend Tony living in Bangkok, he said that the Thai people use Prik Nu to test boys.

"What do you mean test?" I asked Tony.

"If a boy can eat Prik Nu without sweating, he is a grown-up."

I suppose as far as the Thais were concerned, I wasn't a grown-up yet.

*****

Thai food it is, I decided.

I went to the Santa Monica library to search for Thai Cookbooks. I found about ten or so and picked one up to browse. I always wondered why American cookbooks have very few pictures. I grew up reading Japanese cookbooks, every recipe included a picture, so a recipe without a picture looked more like an academic paper to me. It wasn't as fun as the ones with pictures. Oh well. I chose the two books with the most pictures to take home and study.

When I read Japanese recipes, I can imagine how to make them by looking at the ingredients. However, reading a Thai cookbook was different. I couldn't get a good picture in my head by just reading because I'd never heard of most of the dishes or the ingredients. I couldn't imagine how they would look or how they would taste. Furthermore, I'd never heard of *galanga, kafir* lime leaves, Thai basil, fish sauce, cane sugar, lemongrass, sweet soy sauce, or Thai eggplant.

What the hell is coconut sugar? Can't I just use regular sugar instead? I asked myself. *Where can I find all of these ingredients?* I was confused and didn't know exactly what to do. It was too early to give up. After about an hour of brainstorming, I remembered a place my friend Eiji had told me about: Thailand Plaza, a restaurant famous for a Thai Elvis impersonator. Maybe Eiji knew where I could find the ingredients.

"Hi, Eiji. I am looking to get some fresh ingredients to cook Thai food. You told me about the Thailand Plaza Restaurant. I thought maybe you know a place?"

"Yes, go to Thailand Plaza," Eiji responded.

"Isn't that a restaurant?" I asked.

"Yes, but on the first floor, there is a Thai Grocery Store. They sell all kinds of stuff," Eiji said.

I was more than thrilled. Now I could cook Thai food!

It was still 12:30 PM., a couple of hours before I started my shift. *If I leave now, I can get there and still be on time for my shift*, I thought. I jumped into my car and rushed to Hollywood.

Thailand Plaza was in an area of East Hollywood known as Thai Town. Located on the east end of Hollywood Boulevard, past the Chinese Theater, at the end of the Walk of Fame, Thai Town encompassed the six-blocks between Normandie and Western Avenues. East Hollywood isn't exactly a place where you want to hang out after dark. It's a part of town where your car could get broken into. You could be robbed at gunpoint if you walk around alone at night. And it's definitely not an area where you want to use the ATM. You get the idea.

Thailand Plaza reminded me of a restaurant in Bangkok and if you've been there, I am sure you know what I am talking about. There were hundreds of blinking Christmas lights surrounding a stage filled with speakers, microphones, electronic keyboards, and drums for a live band. On Fridays and Saturdays, the famous Thai Elvis impersonator performed two live shows each night, singing all of the Elvis hits, like *Love me Tender* and *Blue Hawaii*.

In front of the store was a big, tall, faded, reddish-purple neon sign, resembling a Thai Temple. By the entrance was an *Apsonsi*, a mythical half-human, half-lion angel. The first floor was Silom Supermarket, my destination.

Upon entering, I smelled something familiar. It was kind of like landing at the Tokyo Airport. That feeling of *home*. I felt like I was at a street market in Bangkok with its fresh, exotic herbs, spices, sauces, dried seafood, meats, and vegetables. The white, half-lit fluorescent lights, narrow shelves packed full of groceries, and the altar with a picture of the Thai King all made me feel like I was in a foreign land. Foreign yet familiar. There was something about that store that made me feel at "home."

Thai Green Curry was tonight's *makanai* menu. I created a list of ingredients to buy from the recipe in the cookbook, so I started searching for everything I needed in the store. I thought I still had about an hour to shop, but now I only had a half an hour. Fish sauce was the first item I looked for. I navigated through the narrow aisles and found a sauce section. There were at least five different types of fish sauce. I saw the Squid Brand, but it had a picture of shrimp on its logo, and another one with a fisherman on the label. *Is this fish sauce or shrimp sauce?* I leaned in to get a closer look. *It says fish sauce...how confusing,* I thought. I picked the Squid Brand mainly because it was the second cheapest option. I figured the cheapest wasn't the best quality, but the second cheapest would be a little better.

Next up was curry paste. *Where would that be?* There was no one at the register, so I circled around the store until I found the curry paste section. There were three different brands to choose from, and they were color -coded: Red, yellow, and green labels. No English and something was written in Thai. *Oh no, not again,* I winced. Since I was running out of time, I just grabbed the first one I saw. I dashed over to the produce section for a piece of *galanga* and picked up what I thought to be lime leaves out of about ten different lime leaf look-a-likes. *I hope I got everything I need*, I thought.

From Thailand Plaza, I drove directly to Rock'n Hollywood Sushi, arriving just in time for my shift.

"*Ohayo Gozaimasu,*" I said to Toshi.

"*Ohayo Gozaimasu,*" Toshi said.

"I bought some Thai ingredients at Thailand Plaza today," I told him. I was excited. "I am going to make Thai Green Curry for *makanai* today."

"Thai Curry? Really?" When he saw me with a bag full of groceries,

Toshi looked excited, "That will be great!"

After spending two hours setting up the Sushi Bar and prepping, it was time for my break. I took out all the ingredients I bought earlier at Silom Supermarket and started making the curry, carefully reading the recipe I copied from the book.

I was confident that I remembered what Thai Green Curry tasted like. But to make one was another story. I had no idea what was in it. I learned that coconut milk, fish sauce, and good chicken stock were the key. I wanted my first curry to taste just like the one I had in Bangkok.

After mixing the broth, vegetables, chicken, and curry paste together in a pot, it started to look and smell like the Thai Curry I remembered. I was thrilled. I put my spoon to take a taste. Toshi was also anxious and stood by my side, "Well, how is it?" he asked.

I squinted my eyes and said, "Umm, something is not right. Something is missing, and I don't know what it is."

"Let me try," Toshi grabbed a spoon and dipped it into the curry sauce. "I think it tastes good.

"No, no, no. I think it needs... more coconut milk," I said.

After adding more coconut milk, I added some more fish sauce to try and give it a good base and *umami*. I added some soy sauce, more chicken broth, sugar and salt, and a little bit of lime juice. I tried it for ten minutes, but nothing seemed to satisfy me. Toshi kept saying the curry tasted great, but it wasn't good enough for me. I read the recipe one more time to see if I missed something.

"Nothing is missing. I have everything in the recipe," I sighed.

"I give up. It's done," I surrendered.

I was disappointed with my own curry, so the next day, I went to a Thai restaurant and ordered their Green Curry. It had a more complex flavor than mine did. It was thick and had a richness of coconut milk, broth from the fish sauce, vegetables, and meats, all nicely blended with the fresh scent of Thai herbs.

What was I was doing wrong? Was it the curry paste I used? The book said that each household in Thailand made their own curry paste fresh, by mashing their own blend of herbs and spices in a stone grinder. I wasn't into making my own curry paste. It sounded interesting, but too time-consuming. I knew I could use the ready-made curry paste and still make a good curry.

A few days later, I decided to give it another try. It tasted better than the first time, but still not like the one at a restaurant. Something was different, like a Miso Soup at a Japanese restaurant in Kansas City. I knew it was just a matter of "a pinch of salt," or more like, "a pinch of fish sauce."

I made Thai Curry over and over until it tasted closer to the one I ate at the restaurant. Still, it wasn't the same, but I finally realized it was as good as it got.

After the curry, I made Papaya Salad, buying fresh young papaya from the Silom Supermarket, along with fish sauce, lime juice, cilantro, and dried shrimp. I used a Japanese mandoline to shred green papaya, then seasoned it with sweet vinegar and fish sauce for an hour or two, added peanuts, lots of lime juice, minced cilantro, and dried shrimp to add more *umami*. I learned fish sauce is like *dashi* stock in Japanese cuisine and works as a base for almost all Thai dishes. It's also the source of *umami* and glutamate. No wonder Thai people love *Ajinomoto*, a chemically engineered monosodium glutamate.

In no time, making *makanai* became my second job, or more like a hobby, playtime during my breaks. I had all of the ingredients and professional appliances at my disposal (for free!) and got to experiment, cook, and eat. I couldn't wait for my lunch break every day, so I could make a new Thai dish from the cookbook. Thai Ginger Chicken was my favorite dish at this small hole-in-the-wall Thai Restaurant in Hollywood. Just like the curry, it wound up tasting completely different when I made it, but I was glad I tried. I found a recipe for Thai *Chawanmushi*, which resembles a Japanese steamed egg custard dish. The Thai version has red curry paste, cilantro, and lots of seafood, like shrimp and clams. I wrapped all the ingredients in aluminum foil and steamed them for a good fifteen minutes. When I opened it, the curry and egg aroma was so exquisite I knew it would be delightful. Sure enough, we all loved it.

Although my *makanai* practice wasn't as traditional as using only what's available in the kitchen, I was still glad I used the opportunity to expand my horizon as a chef. I'm grateful that Saito-san gave me the permission and the freedom to cook whatever I wanted. I disagreed with most of the things he said but allowing me to cook *makanai* was the best idea he ever had.

A few unexpected things came about from this experience. First, Saito-san added one of my *makanai* recipes to the restaurant menu. Second, the Thai Curry cooking experience helped me to cook Vegetarian Curry at Greens Restaurant in San Francisco.

One thing always leads to another, but you're never going to know how what you're doing right now will serve you in the future. You just need to trust that it will.

MAGURO

It was 60°F, a windy evening in November. A "frigid" day for Los Angelenos. I thought it wasn't going to be too busy because of the weather. It was too cold to go out. It was too cold to eat sushi. It was a perfect evening to stay at home and watch The Sopranos, Law & Order, or Buffy the Vampire Slayer on TV.

After three months of basic training, I could now finish all of the Sushi Bar prep by myself—setting up, placing the fish, cutting the vegetables, and making *shari shari kiri*). However, cutting the fish was way beyond my abilities. I was barely making rolls. No *Sashimi.* No *nigiri.*

I entered the walk-in to grab some cucumbers and noticed a long, rectangular container full of fish and ice. It must have been a delivery from the fish company. There was a large cut of Yellowfin Tuna in the container. I remembered Toshi placing an order the night before. He always said, "*Maguro shibuichi.*" I knew it meant Tuna, but I couldn't understand *shibuichi.*

"What is *shibuichi?*" I asked Toshi, who was busy cutting *Hamachi* in the back kitchen. "You say that every time you order Tuna. Is that a type of Tuna?"

"No, it's not a type. It means a quarter cut," Toshi replied. "Just read one-quarter in Japanese. The number four first, shi, then the number one, ichi."

"Oh, yes, that makes sense," I nodded.

Toshi cut the *Hamachi* into three blocks, skinned it, wrapped it in plastic, and then placed it in the walk-in. He then came out with the Tuna *shibuichi* in his hands. He was about to cut the Tuna into *saku* blocks.

"Can I watch?" I asked, like a child asking his parents for permission.

"Sure."

The first thing Toshi did was remove the bloodline, *chi-ai*, the thin dark line on the side of a Tuna. Toshi moved his *Deba* knife in slow motion.

"Can you eat it?" I asked Toshi. He was holding the long, thin piece of dark burgundy Tuna bloodline he just detached.

"Well, I suppose you can," Toshi replied. "It won't kill you. I heard some fishermen in Japan eat it. They grill it with some soy sauce. I never heard of anyone eating it raw."

"How does it taste?" I asked.

"Be my guest," Toshi handed me the piece.

I cut off a small piece and put it in my mouth.

"Hmmm, it's not bad," I said. "It's intense and a bit bitter with iron?"

Toshi squinted his eyes.

"Well, I don't find it tasty," Toshi said. "I think the color doesn't look appetizing. You know it's too dark. We never serve it to the customers."

Toshi cut and removed more bloodline from the Tuna, which looked like it weighed about half a pound.

"Wow, that's a lot," I said.

"We are not done yet. We need to take off the skin, which is another pound," Toshi explained. "This is why sushi is expensive. We have to throw away a lot before we can serve it."

Toshi cut the Tuna into three blocks, about ten inches apiece; two were the same length, which left one short tailpiece. From one block of Tuna, Toshi cut five or six pieces of *saku* blocks. Each *saku* was about four fingers wide, or about 2.5 inches, and 6 inches long. Less than 1 inch thick.

"The tail part is for Spicy Tuna. I am only going to cut one of the large blocks into *saku* and leave the second block in the refrigerator," Toshi explained.

"How about the skin?"

"We keep the skin on. It prevents discoloring," Toshi said.

The skin was thick, like leather, and hard, like plastic. Toshi grabbed white sheets of parchment-like paper and started wrapping the Tuna block.

"This is a special paper we get from the Japanese food distributor," Toshi explained. "We call it a magic paper because it keeps the Tuna nice and red."

"Really? How does it work?" I asked.

"I don't know. All I know is it works. When we wrap Tuna in this paper, the color stays nice and red longer. But, it's expensive, so we can only get it from time to time," Toshi said. "I think we should use it all the time, but Saito-san says no."

After wrapping the Tuna in the magic paper, Toshi also wrapped it in plastic.

"Here you go. You can put this in the walk-in," Toshi handed me the plastic-wrapped block of Tuna.

Next, Toshi put another large Tuna block on the cutting board and reached for his *Yanagiba*. From the side, the Tuna block had a triangular shape. Toshi placed his knife about two inches from the top and cut the top part off. "The top is called Ten-Pa and is the softest and most delicious part," Toshi explained. The top piece was slightly darker than the rest of the Tuna. "This part has no grains because it's right against the bones. It is very soft, so it makes great *Sashimi*. You want to save this part for a special customer if possible," Toshi explained enthusiastically.

"What do you mean by a special customer?" I asked.

"A regular at the Sushi Bar who loves *Sashimi* or *nigiri*, who doesn't eat American-style rolls like Caterpillar. You know what I mean, right?" I understood what he meant.

"If you see the Ten-Pa inside of the Sushi Case, make sure to ask me first before you use it."

"Got it," I said. "Is there any other part of Tuna that is 'special'?"

"Well, yes, but we don't get those parts," Toshi shook his head. "The best part is the head."

"The head?" I exclaimed.

"Yes, *No-Ten*, the head meat, by the spine. That is absolutely the best part, but you can only get four-to-five servings from one large Bluefin Tuna. Also, the cheek meat is just exceptional, better than *Toro*."

I really wanted to taste both parts, but I knew it was a desperate wish; all of the Tuna came without a head because the heads weigh too much. It would be too expensive to airship Tuna with a head from the Tokyo Fish Market.

"There are other parts like the top of the *Toro's* belly, and the part by the anus is also good. But I never had those parts, either, so I don't know how they taste."

"You see this part close to the skin? Do you see white strings?" Toshi showed me, getting back to the Tuna blocks. He moved his fingers along the bottom of the block, close to the skin. "It has too many tendons. They are very tough to chew, so we need to separate them."

"How would I do that?" I asked.

"Here, use this," Toshi handed me a spoon. "You can go to the Sushi Bar and scrape this part using a spoon. Once you scrape it, we will mix it with the spicy sauce," he told me.

"Why a spoon? Can't we just chop with a knife?" I asked.

"No, that's not a good idea because when you chop Tuna with a knife, it loses nice Tuna flavor," Toshi said. "Tuna tastes good when chunky and thick. When you make Tuna *Sashimi*, you want to cut it slightly thicker than, say, *Hamachi* or Salmon."

"Really? How come Tuna needs to be chunky and thick?" I asked, surprised.

"I don't really know why," Toshi said. "I just know you never want to cut Tuna paper-thin because it tastes horrible."

I took the tail part of the Tuna to the Sushi Bar and placed it on the cutting board. I moved my spoon to the left and to the right, but it hardly collected any Tuna meat, so I applied more pressure. It didn't make a difference. I scraped and moved my spoon furiously for about ten minutes until my right arm was too tired to move. Something was wrong, but I couldn't figure out what to do. My arm was sore, so I stopped, shook my it in the air, and looked back at the big Tuna tailpiece. *I already moved my arm left and right, so why not try a different direction, maybe forward and back?* When I moved my spoon forward, I scraped more Tuna meat with less force. When I moved it backward, it scraped almost none. *Oh, I get it. I can scrape along the grain with less force. I need to scrape the same way as the tendons are running,* I thought to myself.

From then, it was just a matter of time. I moved my spoon forward for another ten minutes until all I could see was the Tuna skin and very little meat.

I got a good three-to-four pounds of scraped Tuna, enough to make about thirty rolls, I guessed.

"I am finished scraping," I told Toshi.

"Good. I can show you how to mix Spicy Tuna," he replied. He walked to the Sushi Bar and picked up a small ladle from the square stainless container.

"This is our House-Made Chili Oil. You put two to three ladles full of this, then, add some mayo, shichimi," Toshi explained.

"How much?" I asked.

"This much." He showed me the large stainless bowl. "We don't have a written recipe, so you just have to remember it by doing and tasting it," Toshi said. "For the first two weeks, make sure to bring it to me to taste whenever you mix Spicy Tuna."

"Yes," I replied. "So, I heard someone saying that Spicy Tuna is not good because it's old Tuna?" I asked Toshi.

"Not, really," Toshi said. "Sure, you can cover the fishy smell using Spicy Hot Sauce, but you can still taste the fresh fish even after you mix it. I mean, sometimes, we may use Tuna from yesterday to make Spicy Tuna, but they are not bad Tuna. Sometimes, color is not great for *nigiri* or *Sashimi*, and they taste fine, good enough for Spicy Tuna. We will never use smelly Tuna to make Spicy Tuna."

*****

It was a busy Saturday night around 10 PM. We were almost down to the last quarter pound of Spicy Tuna Mix, and we had two *saku* left in the Sushi Case. Toshi looked inside of the *Neta* Case and squinted his eyes.

"Hey, Jun-chan, do we have more *Maguro*?"

"I think this is all we have left. I know there is nothing in the walk-in," Jun replied.

"That could be a problem, "Toshi said. "That would be very embarrassing to be out of Tuna."

I sensed Toshi meant that we would be eighty-sixed, *Yama*, out of Tuna soon, but I couldn't understand why it was such a big deal. Why is it embarrassing? Couldn't we just say, "Sorry, folks, we are out of Tuna!" and be done with it?

"How come it is embarrassing to be out of Tuna?" I asked Toshi.

"That is because Tuna is the main *neta* for *edomae*-style sushi," Toshi explained. "The best *Akami* and *Toro* are the signature pieces at a Sushi Bar, like the main dish for a French meal. *Maguro* is the highlight of *Omakase*. It's the main course, you know?"

"So, not having Tuna is like not serving the main dish?" I asked.

"Absolutely," he replied.

I understood what Toshi was saying, but I just couldn't relate to how he felt, especially the embarrassment part. At that moment, I didn't want to know, and I didn't really care either. I guess I didn't understand the pride of a Sushi Chef like Toshi did. I didn't consider myself a master artisan (*shokunin*) or a high-end Sushi Chef (*itamae*). I was just a Sushi Chef in Los Angeles, making American-style sushi. So why bother? It was one thing to respect the tradition, but another to follow it. Do the customers even care? Do we bother to explain the history of sushi or the pride of *itamae*? Do we ever mention that our Spicy Tuna is made from fresh Tuna, and not from smelly old Tuna? No, we didn't. We never told them how much Tuna we threw away before we served them. Did anyone ask? Did anyone care? I didn't have any of the answers, and a large part of me said that none of it mattered anyhow. But there was a small part of me that screamed, *maybe it did*. It might not matter to the customers, but maybe, it was more important for it to matter to me, to us, and to anyone who knew about sushi traditions.

In some ways, we were carrying not all, but some, of the sushi traditions with us. Like how we cooked our rice, how we held our knives, how we handled the fish, how we filleted the fish, how we served our customers, how we cleaned the Sushi Bar. There was no denying that without our cultural heritage, we wouldn't be here making sushi. Even though we weren't making traditional sushi, all of our customers assumed we were traditional because we were, in fact, Japanese Sushi Chefs. Such a contradiction. All of our customers assumed everything was authentic because they never doubted or asked. In a sense, I guess we took advantage of it all because everyone just made assumptions based on how we looked.

But now, Toshi was explaining a very traditional Sushi Chefs' philosophy, and I now I was confused. Are we following the traditions? And if we are, why? Is there a reason we should? Is there someone who is telling us we should? Is it a must? What if we decided not to follow the traditions? These are the questions I still think about every time I make sushi.

There isn't a right answer, and there isn't a wrong answer, either. It's simply a choice. What's important is the how and the why because it affects everything I do as a chef. Consequently, it affects the taste of the sushi I make, and that affects my customers.

FUGU

"Have you eaten *Fugu*?" A young male customer at the Sushi Bar asked me.

"Oh, yes, of course," I replied hesitantly, thinking, *not again*. It was another question about *Fugu*. I knew he was going to tell me how lethal the fish was.

"Well, how was it?" He was curious, like asking me how old I was when I lost my virginity.

I knew it was going to be hard to deal with this. For one, the man was drunk, and drinking lowers one's I.Q. You care less about the seriousness of a conversation when you're drinking. This man wanted drama, so I knew my answer wouldn't satisfy his appetite for sensationalism, like a headline for *The National Enquirer*.

What should I tell him? I thought. Should I let him know that no one in Japan died from eating *Fugu* in 2012 or 2013? That more people died from eating raw oysters in the U.S. than *Fugu* in Japan? That 3,000 people die from foodborne illnesses each year in the United States? I knew what he was looking for, "over a million Japanese die each year from eating *Fugu*, yet they continue to eat it and serve it in restaurants." He probably watched the famous *Fugu* Episode on *The Simpsons*, where Homer Simpson eats *Fugu*, not knowing how lethal it is and thinks he only has a few days to live. I knew that, in this man's mind, *Fugu*, like in the Simpson's episode, was prepared by an inexperienced chef, looking at a cookbook showing off how to fillet the poisonous fish.

I feel like the *Fugu* myth in the U.S. is very similar to the one about sharks. Many people believe that every shark in the ocean is going to attack and eat any human being in sight. Thanks to movies like *Jaws* and documentaries like *Shark Week* on Discovery channel, the Great White Shark is portrayed as a dangerous, man-eating fish. The fact remains that most sharks are harmless to humans. Out of more than 470 species of sharks, only four have been involved in a significant number of fatal, unprovoked attacks on humans. According to the International Shark Attack File (ISAF), the average number of fatalities worldwide, each year from unprovoked shark attacks, is 4.3 (2001 - 2006). That's one person per year out of more than six billion people in the world (as of 2001). The deaths associated with *Fugu* is also one per year, and in *Fugu's* case, that's only one out of the one hundred and twenty-six million people in Japan.

I could go on and on, but I saw that his mind was already made up. No matter what I said, no matter how many facts I gave him, he wasn't going to believe me. He was already convinced: *Fugu is a very lethal fish, and you're going to die if you eat it.* I once read a book that explained how human brains are incredibly inflexible when it comes to changing a formed opinion or belief. Once our minds believe something, it's hard to change the mindset because our brains are developed to adapt to the complex social world we created.

Nevertheless, I decided to tell this young man a truth, hoping to educate him, and maybe he'd find it entertaining.

"You see that there is nothing dangerous about eating *Fugu* in Japan," I started to explain. "In Japan, they remove the poisonous part before they serve the fish, and a certified chef does it, so they are very safe. There are many *Fugu* restaurants in Japan. For Japanese, going to a *Fugu* restaurant is as casual as going to any other restaurant. No one thinks it's dangerous."

"How about the numbness or tingling sensation that comes from eating *Fugu*?" he asked.

"So, that is from eating the poisonous part. Some stupid people fillet *Fugu* by themselves or an uncertified chef and eat the parts like the liver, which has the most poison. Until twenty or thirty years ago, a chef did not have to have a certification to filet and serve *Fugu*. Many chefs learned at their job," I answered.

"Really?" He asked.

"Many chefs cheated and served the 'dangerous part' of the *Fugu* because some daring customers who requested it," I said. "Some of them died, which made a newspaper headline. But again, that was a long time ago."

"At a restaurant, it is now illegal to serve those poisonous parts, so at *Fugu* restaurants in Japan, there are no tingling sensations," I continued. He still looked suspicious.

"Can *you* fillet *Fugu*?" he asked.

"No, I am not certified. It's a government certification to fillet *Fugu*," I said.

"How can you get it?" he asked.

"First, you must be a licensed chef for at least five years in Japan before applying for *Fugu* certification. The certification process involves a few years of rigorous training and testing. Because of this, it is very safe to eat *Fugu*," I said.

"Do you serve it here?" he asked.

"No. Again, I am not certified, and no one here is certified," I said. *Fugu* is not a popular sushi item in Japan. Most sushi restaurants and Sushi Chefs in Japan never serve *Fugu*."

"Why is that?" he asked.

"I never asked so if I had to guess, I think one of the reasons could be the possibility of cross-contamination," I explained. "Also, there are *Fugu* restaurants in Japan. Because of the poison, *Fugu* is not a traditional sushi fish. I suppose there are plenty of other 'non-poisonous' fish out there you can use for sushi, so why risk serving *Fugu*?"

"That makes sense," he said. "How do they taste?"

"They taste close to *Hirame* or *Tai*, Whitefish *Sashimi*. Very lean," I said. "They serve it with *ponzu*. I personally like *Fugu Karaage*, fried is the best. I think *Fugu Sashimi* is rather bland. I don't like it that much. I don't understand why some people make it such a fuss."

"Really? I want to taste it," he said. "Is there a restaurant that serves *Fugu* in L.A.?"

I knew it. He wanted to eat it so that he could "live to tell" others. It was his way of showing off how daring he was to eat this lethal fish. How

American he was, I thought, but then, I suppose some Japanese men have similar traits.

"I don't know any restaurant in L.A., though, I heard there are some in New York City that serve *Fugu*, or you can go to Japan. Wintertime is the *Fugu* season," I said.

"New York, huh?" the man said.

"Yup, New York, or Japan."

Now, I thought it was time to ask, "Have you seen the *Fugu* episode on *The Simpson's*?"

"Oh, yes, I have. That was a funny episode, man!"

Yep, that's what I thought.

SASHIMI

How hard can it be? After all, isn't it just slicing fish? I was watching Toshi prepare a plate of Sashimi.

For weeks, I watched Toshi slice *Maguro, Hamachi,* and *Sake.* It didn't look that difficult. All he did was move his $600 *Yanagiba* and cut the fish about two centimeters thick, three, or five pieces at a time. Then, he plated the *Sashimi* with the *daikon tsuma* decoration, one leaf of *shiso,* and a small mound of *wasabi.* It was beautiful - white *daikon,* green *shiso,* red Tuna, orange Salmon, and white, light red-pink *Hamachi.* All of the *Sashimi* slices were exactly the same width.

"*Sashimi* is the most difficult to master," Toshi mumbled, recognizing my intent gaze.

"Really? How come? Why it's so difficult?" I asked as I shook my head.

Toshi was quiet for a second, "Because it is. Fish is soft, and to slice it without damaging the flesh, it takes practice. You must master the knife," he explained. He sounded just like Mr. Miyagi from *The Karate Kid* movie, I thought.

"Too much force fractures the delicate texture of the fish, you will." Now, he sounded like Yoda from *Star Wars.*

"Really?" I continued to watch. "I had no idea."

"Of course you didn't," Toshi said. "How could you know? You've only started a few months ago."

"You also need to move the knife so that you have a straight edge on each slice of fish. No wavy surface. When done right, *Sashimi* is the most beautiful thing on a plate."

I was quiet for a while. In awe, I looked at Toshi's *Sashimi* plate one more time, when he continued: "Oh, one more thing, you think all my *Sashimi* slices are the same thickness, but look carefully, they are not."

He was right, and once more, I was wrong. Nothing was easy. I was starting to finally grasp the concept and feel the true sense of the Japanese proverb: *The simplest thing can be the most difficult thing to master.*

*****

It was two in the morning when I arrived home after my shift at the Sushi Bar. My East Hollywood/L.A. City College neighborhood was quiet, but I was wide awake. I played some Jazz on my stereo to try and calm myself down, I needed to get rid of some of the energy from the restaurant. I still couldn't stop thinking about what Toshi told me about *Sashimi.* I had a hard time understanding what he meant.

I reached for the *Sushi Technique Encyclopedia* and opened it to a section on "*Sashimi.*" Some slicing techniques and pictures showed how to make *Maguro Sashimi.*

The instructions explained how to hold the *Yanagiba*, and the diagram showed the importance of knife skills or, more precisely, knife movement. The arrow in the diagram showed the knife moving straight down and back all at the same time. I tried to imitate how Toshi moved his knife by moving my arm with the same movement. I didn't know if I was doing it right. It felt awkward. Isn't this whole thing backward? Shouldn't I be learning how to make *Sashimi* first, not how to make rolls?

My mind started to wander, looking for answers. The book dedicated more than ten pages just to plating *Sashimi*. The section did have a lot of beautiful pictures, and it explained how to make garnishes using *daikon*, carrot, and cucumber. But I was too tired to go through it all. Before I even finished reading the first two pages, I fell asleep.

*****

The following day, it was back to Sashimi training. Toshi was just about to explain plating Sashimi.

"When plating, you have to think about the front and the back," Toshi said, holding a small plate of *Sashimi.*

"The front?" I asked.

"Yes, the front," he said. "In Japanese cuisine, the plated food always has the front and the backside. In other words, when you plate, you have to think about the front and the back."

"I see," I nodded, pretending to understand what he said.

"Before you start slicing fish, you always grab your plate first, and place it on top of *Neta* Case in front of you," Toshi said. "The plate is your canvas. You should visualize how the final plate look like with *Maguro Sashimi.*"

Toshi grabbed a handful of *daikon tsuma* soaked in water from a side container. He squeezed the *tsuma* to drain some of the water and placed it in the middle of the plate. The *tsuma* made a triangular shape.

"When placing *tsuma*, you make it look like a mountain. A Western cuisine chef like a French one would plate it flat. But for Japanese cuisine, we plate the food more three-dimensionally," Toshi said. "That is why there is a front side and a backside."

"Now, I am going to explain how to cut *Sashimi*," he told me.

"First, when you slice fish, you need to pull your knife like this," Toshi held his knife in the air and moved his right arm backward, just like the diagram from the sushi book.

"When you pull your knife, slice the fish with one stroke. Never force your knife down. If you use the force to cut the fish, you will damage the fragile meat and the cell of the fish," Toshi said, in a firm tone. "Also, never go back and forth like a saw. If you do that, the surface will be uneven."

"Why is uneven not good?" I asked.

"Because it does not look good. A nicely sliced *Sashimi* should have a straight edge when plated. When the edges are wobbly, it is not considered beautiful. Also, it is hard to plate them," Toshi said. "It affects the taste, too."

"How come?

"You want to have a flat cut surface to maximize the contact with your taste buds on your tongue," Toshi said.

Toshi made the knife-pulling motion several times. I watched him and imitated his movement using my steel *Yanagiba*.

"No, not like that," Toshi said. "Move your knife in a slightly circular motion like this," Toshi corrected my movements. "Move your whole arm, not just your wrist."

"Now, try with this block of tofu." Toshi brought me a block of tofu from the walk-in.

"Think of it as a *saku* and move your knife like slicing *Sashimi*," Toshi told me.

"Cut this tofu into five slices, just like *Maguro Sashimi*," Toshi instructed.

I slowly moved my knife backward, like Toshi showed me, slicing the tofu into equal lengths. The knife sliced easily, and I made small slices of Tofu *Sashimi*. It was easier than I imagined. But I knew I wasn't moving my knife the way Toshi told me to.

"That's not bad," he smiled. "You need to move your knife more in a circular motion like I said."

"I know what you told me before," I said. "I need more practice."

"Yes, I know that, too. *Sashimi*, as I said, is very difficult. It will take you a few years just to do it right. To do it perfectly, it would take more," Toshi said.

"I still feel I cannot make a perfect *Sashimi* even after working for seven years," Kai chimed in. "So, don't feel bad. I think you are learning a lot faster than any of us."

"Now you know how to move your knife, all you need is practice," Toshi said.

"Yes, but how?" I asked Toshi.

"Little by little. You will start by slicing a small piece for *nigiri* first, then gradually move on to slice the whole plate of *Sashimi*," Toshi said.

"How did you learn how to cut *Sashimi* first?" I asked him.

"Before I became a Sushi Chef here in Los Angeles, I worked at Fish Wholesaler in Tokyo, filleting whole fish. That's how I learned how to slice fish," Toshi answered.

"May I try cutting this *Maguro*?" I asked.

"No, not *Maguro*. How about Salmon? It's cheaper than *Maguro*," Toshi explained. He then grabbed a block of Salmon and placed it on the cutting board in front of me.

"Now, try slicing it," Toshi told me.

I stood facing the cutting board and placed my knife above the Salmon block. I moved my knife just like Toshi showed me, or at least how I thought he showed me. My knife made a small incision, but halfway through, the flesh started to fracture.

"Oh no, what is happening?" I asked in a panic. My Salmon slice is all torn apart.

"Look, you are using too much downward force. What you need to do is to slide your knife. Let your knife 'run.' Let your knife do the work," Toshi said.

"Run...?" I asked.

"Yes, run. Let it run. No force. Use less force when you have difficulty slicing," he explained. "Now, let's try one more time."

"Okay..," I agreed hesitantly. What Toshi told me sounded counterintuitive.

Once more, I placed my knife above the block of Salmon, but this time I reminded myself to use less force. As I was about to put my knife on the Salmon, Toshi stopped me and said, "Wait. Use my *Yanagiba* knife instead."

"Really? Is it OK?" I was shocked, as I recalled a famous proverb: *A Yanagiba to a Sushi Chef is a rifle to a soldier. It's a tool only he can use. It's not something you lend to others.*

"It's all right. You can slice better with this one," Toshi smiled.

"Thank you," I said, placing my knife on the cutting board.

Toshi's *Yanagiba* was heavier and longer than my $60 stainless-steel knife. It felt good in my hands. When I held the wooden grip, the blade felt almost like an extension of my index finger.

I placed it on the Salmon and moved it slowly backward, without forcing downward.

"Gee, this knife slices a lot better than mine," I said in excitement. When I looked down at the slice, it looked a lot better than the first one, but it still didn't look like anything sliced by Toshi or Kai.

"Not bad, not bad," Toshi smiled. "As I said, keep practicing, and you will be better soon. Maybe in a few weeks, you can try filleting small fish like *Saba*. *Saba* is pretty cheap and is easy to fillet."

After two more slices, I handed Toshi his knife back and switched back to mine. Suddenly, my knife felt miserable and cheap. I wanted a more expensive knife with better steel.

"Speaking of Salmon," Toshi interrupted my thoughts. "Did you know a male Salmon tastes different than the female Salmon?"

"No, I did not know," I replied.

"Usually, the female Salmon tastes better," he said.

"How come?" I asked.

"Well, Salmon has to go up the river to where they were born. The females have to lay their eggs, and they store the energy in the form of fat," Toshi explained. "So, the female Salmon tastes the best just before they lay their eggs. Not after, because they would consume all the fat, they become lean."

"Really? That is so interesting," I felt mesmerized with the new fact. Maybe I could share it with one of the customers when I was finally allowed to stand at the Sushi Bar.

*****

The following day, I was watching Toshi make *Kihada Maguro shibuichi*, Yellowfin Tuna quarter-cut, into small *saku* blocks. The Tuna was about eighty-centimeters long. He moved his *Deba* knife in many different directions, separated its skin, cut it into three large blocks, removed the tail, and finally, cut twenty- centimeter long rectangular blocks. I tried to remember what he did, but it was too complicated.

"How is this Tuna?" I asked Toshi.

"Well, this one is so-so," he replied. "If the Tuna looks like *Yokan*, then that is a good sign."

"*Yokan*, like jellied red-bean paste?" I asked.

"Yes, *Yokan*."

The Tuna had a beautiful red color. It was translucent and dark, but not muddy, and its shiny texture and looked nice and fresh. I'd noticed that as Tuna gets older, its color gets darker.

"Can you tell the taste by its color?" I asked.

"Yes and no. The color is just one indication. The darker the Tuna, the tastier it is in general. Pink Tuna has very little Tuna flavor unless, of course, it is *Toro*."

"Do we ever get *Toro*?"

"Sometimes," Toshi said. "Most *Toro* comes from Bluefin Tuna. Bluefin is too expensive for us."

"How expensive are they?"

"Let's see. Yellowfin is about $14 per pound, and *Toro* is about $40 per pound right now," Toshi said.

"$40 per pound?"

"Yup, $40," Toshi said. "We once had Bluefin Tuna *Toro* caught in Boston for $100 per pound."

"$100 per pound?!" I exclaimed.

"That was the best *Toro* I ever had in my life," Toshi said. "Boston Tuna is the best. I wish we could have it one more time."

"How do you know how to cut them?" I asked.

"There is a way," Toshi answered. "You can look at the picture in the sushi book I lent you."

"Okay," I said.

Toshi finished disassembling the Tuna and carefully wrapped each *saku* in a white paper towel, and again with plastic wrap.

"How come you wrap the Tuna with the paper towel first?" I asked.

"To prevent discoloring," Toshi replied. "Without the paper towel, Tuna gets dark faster. It doesn't change the flavor, but it just doesn't look good. We need to wrap it tightly, so the oxygen doesn't get inside."

"Really?" I said, feeling enlightened by the answer.

Toshi taught me a lot more about Tuna - When slicing Tuna for *Sashimi*, cut it thicker than the other fish because Tuna tastes better when it's cut thick, about one and a half to two centimeters each. Never cut the Tuna paper-thin because it loses flavor. When you're making *nigiri*, again, cut the Tuna thicker than other the fish, but thinner than you cut it for *Sashimi*.

"When cutting *Toro*, you need to cut it a lot thinner." Toshi went on.

"Thin? Why is that?" I asked.

"Because of the fat content," he said. "If you cut *Toro* two centimeters thick, the flavor is overwhelming. It will be too much fat. So, when we get *Toro*, make sure you cut it thin."

*****

Toshi was making *Hamachi*, Yellowtail *Nigiri*. *Hamachi* was one of the most popular sushi *neta* on the Rock'n Hollywood menu. We used farm-raised *Hamachi* that was air-shipped in from Japan.

It arrived in a tightly vacuum-packed plastic bag, a whole fish without a head. It was called *Doresu* in Japan among Sushi Chefs.

"Why is this *Hamachi* called *Doresu*?" I asked Toshi. "It sounds like 'A Dress.'"

"I know, it sounds strange," Toshi said. "I heard that it is from the word 'headless' in English, not a dress."

"Headless?" I asked.

"Yes, headless. Remove 'head' from the word headless. It will leave you with 'dless,' thus *Doresu* in Japanese," Toshi said.

"Strange," I said. "There's no double D in it," I mumbled.

Toshi and Kai used lots of words related only to Sushi Chefs, industry terms that I was unfamiliar with. I heard them use the same words over and over again during my first few months at the restaurant, and I finally memorized all of them. *Doresu* was one of those words. *Shibuichi*, a quarter cut of Tuna, was another. I often heard Toshi use that one when

117

he placed a fish order on the phone. *Yama*, which means mountain in Japanese, means "no longer available," same as "eighty-sixed" in the U.S. *Oaiso* means "check." *Shari* is Sushi Rice. *Shari Kiri* is to mix the Sushi Rice, but in Japanese, it means to "slice" the Sushi Rice. Then, there are other sushi terms like *Murasaki* meaning "purple" refers to soy sauce, *Agari* is the green tea. But since no customers or waitresses knew these terms, we never used them at the sushi bar.

I also found that Toshi didn't say, "Make *Sashimi*." Instead, he said, "Pull *Sashimi*." In Japanese, it is "*Sashimi o Hiku*."

"The reason is you pull your knife backward when slicing for *Sashimi*," Toshi explained.

"How come *Hamachi* always gets darker just two days after we open the package?"

"I don't know. I guess that's because it's farm-raised?" Toshi said.

Toshi took the *Hamachi* from the package and filleted them in half one-by-one. He separated the belly from the back. The belly was reserved for special customers and was served as *Hamachi Toro* at a higher price. The half fillet was now cut into four smaller pieces and placed inside of the *Neta* Case.

Toshi removed the collar, wrapped it in plastic, and handed it to the kitchen chef. They served it as Grilled *Hamachi Kama* Collar with *Daikon Oroshi*, Grated Radish, and *Ponzu* Sauce.

"I like *Hamachi*," I said to Toshi.

"Really? I used to like it, too. But that was before I became a Sushi Chef. Now, I cannot eat it anymore," Toshi said.

"You cannot eat it? Why?"

"It's too oily. It's very typical of a farm-raised fish. They feed the fish with food that would make them grow faster and fat," Toshi said. "They don't get enough exercise, which is good because they get fatter that way. That's why a lot of people like them."

"That doesn't sound appetizing," I said.

"Also, I heard they give antibiotics," Toshi cast a doubtful look at the piece on the table.

"As I said, I used to be able to eat it, and now, I just don't like the taste of farm-raised *Hamachi* anymore. It tastes funny and weird. Just too oily, unpleasant, unnatural."

It may have been unpleasant for Toshi, but I didn't agree. I still enjoyed *Hamachi Nigiri* and *Sashimi*.

After the *Hamachi* conversation, a few months passed by, and I'd forgotten all about it. One day I tasted it again, and my opinion quickly changed. I didn't like it, something tasted different. In fact, it was awful. It was too oily, just like Toshi had Kai told me it would. It was overwhelmingly fatty, and the oily flavor was unpleasant to my palette.

"Toshi-san, you were right about *Hamachi*," I told him.

"I cannot eat *Hamachi* anymore," my voice raised unexpectedly. "Like you said, it tastes too oily."

"See, what did I tell you," Toshi said, smilingly. "No more *Hamachi* for you, Kaz. I think you are becoming a sushi chef."

Over the course of my sushi career, I've met many Japanese sushi chefs who share the same feelings I have about farm-raised *Hamachi.* No one ate *Hamachi* once they became a chef. I also met a lot of people who told me they *love Hamachi*, but none of them were chefs. Whenever someone told me it was their favorite fish, I had to hold back my opinion, reminding myself that everyone's taste is different.

*****

When I started my training, all I wanted to do was learn was how to cut fish, especially a large one like *Maguro*. Every day, I saw Toshi filleting *Maguro*, *Hamachi,* and Salmon. I thought it looked cool. I didn't understand the techniques. It seemed simple but complicated, like learning how to play the guitar. It had a depth to it that I just didn't understand. Every day, I prepped at the Sushi Bar while Toshi cut the fish in the back, so I only saw bits and pieces of his technique. I watched him a couple of minutes at a time, whenever I had a chance to walk to the back kitchen. It was like watching five minutes of a half-hour TV drama every day. I had no idea how the whole story went.

It had been over a year since I started working with Toshi. Every day I anxiously waited for him to teach me how to fillet fish. As a tradition, it wasn't polite to ask because that would be begging. So, I waited patiently, watching Toshi cut the fish every day.

One day, Saito-san walked into the back kitchen during the prep hours. He saw Toshi cutting the fish and me standing there, watching.

"Toshi, how come Kaz is watching you?" Saito-san asked. He was not angry but seemed surprised. "Haven't you taught him how to cut fish?"

"No, not yet," Toshi answered.

"Why not?" Saito-san said to Toshi. "You've taught him pretty much everything else, right?"

"Yes, pretty much," Toshi answered.

"Well, let's teach him now," Saito-san said. "Is there a reason we cannot?"

Toshi hesitated for a moment then said, "Ok, I will teach him."

"Good," Saito-san said.

Great! I screamed in my mind but chose to stay silent.

If I were at a sushi restaurant in Japan, I'd probably have to wait another three, four, or maybe even five years before I was allowed to touch the fish. They say you need to spend your first three years cooking rice. So even though it took over a year, I was excited and grateful for the opportunity.

*****

"Let's talk about the anatomy of fish," Toshi said, as I looked at a beautiful Red Snapper on the cutting board.

"First things, first. I will show you how to handle fish," Toshi said. "You always place its head facing left, as we both are right-handed."

"Why left side?" I asked.

"When you cut the head off, it's easier to angle your knife with the head on your left," Toshi explained. "You place the knife at a 45-degree angle by the head."

"When picking up the fish, never grab it like this." Toshi grabbed the tail of Snapper and lifted it up in the air. "When you grab it by the tail, you will damage its meat, causing *mikuzure*, breaking of the meat."

"*Mikuzure*?" I said.

"Yes. When there is *mikuzure* in the fish, we cannot use it for *Sashimi* or sushi," Toshi said. "So, you must handle the fish gently and carefully without causing any damage to it. The muscle of the fish is connected to its tail and the fin. So when you grab its tail and move the whole thing around, you'll damage its flesh."

"I never knew that," I replied.

"You may have seen people holding fish by its tail, swinging upside down in the air. Trust me, that's the worst thing you can do," Toshi said. "If you want to hold the fish by its tail, cut the tail fin halfway over the skin to disconnect the tendons from the tail." Toshi moved his *Deba* over the fin and made a small incision.

"You see, now I can grab by its tail because I detached the tendons," he picked up the Snapper, and placed it back on the cutting board, slowly.

"Always handle the fish gently. The flesh of fish is softer than the land animal. Never throw it on the cutting board. Never drop it either. Always pick it up with both of your hands, like handling a small baby," Toshi explained.

"Do you know why fish is softer than the land animal?" I asked.

"Because there is less gravity in water. Less gravity means less binding force to connect tissues and muscles, which makes fish flesh softer," he told me. I liked how Toshi explained it. It sounded very scientific and made sense to me.

Toshi explained many things— how to hold a knife, where to place it, and at what angle, which direction to cut, how far to push the knife, etc. I was overwhelmed. I couldn't remember most of the things he talked about. On my first day of fish cutting training, I was only allowed to watch, just like when I first started my sushi training a year ago.

The next day, Toshi told me to cut *Hamachi* because it was the easiest. Jun already knew how, and I felt like I wanted to master cutting

Hamachi today.

The vacuum-packed half-filleted *Hamachi* was already gutted and cleaned. It didn't have a head or gills. All I had to do was to remove the chest bones first, then move my knife into the middle to cut it into two pieces, and finally, cut the belly part. When I finished, I would have three long pieces of *Hamachi saku*. I did not have a *Deba* knife yet, so I borrowed one from Toshi.

"You should get *Deba* knife if you want to fillet fish," he told me.

"I am going to Little Tokyo tomorrow to buy one," I said.

Cutting *Hamachi* went pretty smooth. The most difficult part was removing the chest bones because it was hard to figure out the angle of the knife. I had to place the blade almost flat against the bones and slide the knife underneath the bones. After removing the chest bones, it was just a matter of letting my knife "run."

The following day, Toshi told me to fillet the Salmon. Our Salmon came whole. Before we cured it in salt and vinegar, we had to fillet it. Salmon was a lot more difficult because its flesh was the softest of all the fish we carried.

"Remember how to cut its back, just above the bones?" Toshi asked, pointing at the back of the Salmon. "Be careful. It's very soft. Softer than any other fish."

When I placed my knife on the Salmon, it didn't go in through the skin. I pushed harder, and by the time I cut through the skin, I already fractured its flesh. The cut wasn't clean, and I couldn't place the tip of my knife between the backbones. Toshi saw me struggling.

"Wait, wait," Toshi grabbed my hand. "Your knife is not hitting the right spot."

"It's right here, right in the middle, and you place your knife just slightly above the centerline," he guided me.

When Toshi cut the Salmon, it was like magic. His knife went through the back of Salmon smoothly, cutting it in half. I tried to remember how he did it and placed my knife on the Salmon again. This time, the knife went through the skin, and I was able to cut all the way from its head to its tail. But, I still didn't cut through, so I let my knife run one more time.

After the third time, I was able to detach the top half of the Salmon. The surface didn't look as clean-cut as the one Toshi did.

"How can you tell where to place your knife? I couldn't figure out where?" I asked, still astounded.

"Oh, you just feel it. You just know it. It only takes practice. I'm sure you'll get it after a couple of practices," Toshi smiled.

By this time, I started to understand why sushi apprentices in Japan spend years practicing small chores and prep work. The idea is to get used to a knife so that it feels like an extension of your arm. That's also the reason each chef owns and uses his own knives.

*****

"Looking for fresh fish is just like looking for fresh tomato," Toshi said. "We look for color, shine, firmness, and smell."

It was a slow evening, so Toshi decided to give me a lesson in *mekiki*, the ability to tell the quality and taste of fish by just looking at it.

"When it comes to the color, white fish like Snapper, Flounder, and Halibut should be a clear translucent color," Toshi explained, pointing to the Snapper fillet in the *Neta* Case.

"The cloudiness is a sign of older Whitefish," Toshi said.

"When *Maguro* is old, you will start to see a rainbow, like dark rings on the flesh," Toshi picked up a *Maguro saku* and showed me its side. "You can see it right here."

"Shininess is another sign of freshness," Toshi continued. "It's a sign of how much water the flesh is retaining. The more water, the shinier the reflection is. As the fish gets older, it loses water from its flesh and becomes dull."

"That makes sense," I agreed.

Since I grew up watching whole fish, I already knew a few things to look for.

"The very first thing you want to look for is the eyes, right?" I asked Toshi.

"No," he replied. "It's the gills. Gills will get dark and muddy."

"Really, not the eyes?" I asked him again.

"Eyes are the second to look," Toshi said. "Fresh fish gills are bright red. The fish gills catch lots of bacteria because lots of water goes through them. Because of that, it is one of the first places that start to deteriorate."

"I did not know that," I told him. "By the way, I love fish eyes. I only eat the eyes from fresh fish, old fish eyes don't taste good," I added.

"I grew up in Tokyo, so we did not eat fish eyes."

"Well, that's too bad," I said.

"I started eating fish eyes after I started working here," Toshi offered.

"Fresh fish has eyes that are crystal clear as if you can see the bottom of the ocean through the water," I said.

"There should be no blood in the eyes," Toshi explained. "You know that the older the fish gets, the cloudier their eyes turn."

"Yes, I do, and I have seen those," I answered.

"The last part you want to look at is its stomach," Toshi continued. "A firm stomach is a sign of fresh fish because it means its intestines are in good condition. As they deteriorate, the stomach loses its water. Thus, firmness is lost too."

"That is why they gut the fish first?" I asked.

"Yes, that is correct," he said. "Also, lots of enzymes in the stomach, which break down the flesh."

"Do you know what a fresh fish smells like?" Toshi asked me.

"Umm, well, like fish?" I asked.

"No. They smell like ocean and grass," he said amusingly.

"Grass?" I raised my eyebrows.

"Yes, like grass," Toshi said. "The fish smell comes from a bacteria and parasites gone bad on the skin of the fish."

"Bacteria, huh?" I nodded thoughtfully. "You know when I was in college in Iowa, I was trying to explain to my friends from Nebraska and Wisconsin what *Sashimi* would taste like," I told him. "They never understood what I was trying to tell them. They all said I was crazy saying a fresh fish does not smell like the fish they know."

"I know what you mean," Toshi agreed. "That's hard to explain what *Sashimi* tastes like to someone who never had fresh seafood, let alone a raw fish in his life."

"I know, I know. Well, I tried to tell them that *Sashimi* does not taste like anything they tasted before. In fact, it tastes nothing like the fish they know."

After a little pause, I continued, "But now, I understand why. The fishy smell was bacteria. When my friends said the fish smells like fish, they were talking about the bacteria on the fish."

SEX, DRUGS, AND ROCK 'N' ROLL

EMMA, BABY GIRL, AND SHAUNA

Everyone loved Emma—a petite Asian waitress, full of energy, upbeat, friendly, talkative, and just fun to be around. Emma did a better job than any of the other waitresses. She listened to the managers and followed the rules. Emma was honest and never cheated. She never tried any tricks when ordering, even when she placed an order verbally. She always remembered to put it in the system later. I loved working with Emma, and so did all of the other Sushi Chefs.

It was only natural that she made more in tips than anyone else. All of the waitresses shared their tips with the Sushi Chefs, kitchen chefs, and busboys. At the end of Emma's shift, she always came to the Sushi Bar and handed over a portion of her tips as a "tip-out" and said, "thanks!" I felt she was sincere, and the other chefs agreed. I learned that Emma wanted to be an actress, and had tried a few auditions. Sadly, she never got the "break" she was looking for, but I never thought she was really the "actress" type anyhow. She was too nice to be in the Hollywood Movie Industry.

I met a few movie studio executives from back when I was a graphic designer. My impressions about almost all of them weren't so positive. They weren't exactly mean, but they weren't exactly nice either. They were very demanding and didn't give us graphic designers a chance to negotiate. Their actions always seemed to say, "Well, if you can't do it, we will find someone else who can." An honest and nice girl like Emma didn't have a place in Hollywood.

Emma lived with her boyfriend in an apartment just three blocks from the restaurant. Her boyfriend came in frequently to take advantage of her employee discount. He loved to throw parties, and occasionally brought his friends in and ordered *Sake* Bombs for everyone. He, too, was an aspiring actor, looking for his break in Hollywood.

"Emma is always smiling, and she is always positive. I wonder if sometimes, she goes home and cries by herself," Kai said, out of the blue.

"Gee, why would you say something like that," Toshi shook his head.

"Oh, I just wondered," Kai said.

As I heard them talking, I watched Emma talking to a customer with a huge smile, and I wondered if Kai was right. Was that just part of her act? Was she smiling to hide her pain?

*****

Unlike Emma, not everyone liked working with Lillian, also known as "The Baby Girl." She was a tall, blonde, California bombshell who called everyone "Baby" and ended every sentence with "Baby." The Latino busboys all loved her because she was nice to look at, but she didn't get along with all of the waitresses. Lillian only worked on Wednesday and Thursday nights. She spent her weekends going out with her friends and hitting all of the Hollywood nightclubs and bars. We assumed she was looking for her future husband. Every Wednesday, she told us all about what she did over the weekend, where she went, and who she met. Listening to her talk was like listening to a daytime Soap Opera on TV.

Toshi once told me that Lillian lived with her wealthy parents at the top of Hollywood Hills.

"I've been to her house once," he said.

"Really? What was it like," I asked.

"Well, it's huge, like five or six bedrooms. Her dad likes cars, and he had Porches and Mercedes in the garage. I think there were five garages," Toshi explained. "They have a huge backyard with palm and orange trees and, of course, a swimming pool where you can invite all your friends and have a poolside party, you know? What shocked me was her room."

"Her room?" That sounded interesting. "What about it?"

"Yeah, she showed me her room, and you know what? It's all pink, like Barbie-pink. Everything from her bed to her pillow covers, the sheets, room slippers, and the walls. Everything is so freaking pink, and it's so scary. I would never want to date a girl like that. No way," Toshi shook his head.

I looked over at Lillian, talking to her customer, and imagined her being in the pink bedroom. The image scared me too. But the scariest part for me was it all made perfect sense and I couldn't understand why.

*****

Apparently, Lillian didn't have to work at all, thanks to her wealthy parents. So, she had never held a steady job before Rock'n Hollywood Sushi. The rumor was she just stayed home doing close to nothing, hung out with her friends, and smoked pot. Her parents finally forced her to get a job. I'm not sure who hired her here. When I met her, she had already been working there for more than six years. This made her the longest working waitress at the restaurant.

Baby Girl was friendly to everyone, though, she never came and visited us on her days off. She never brought her boyfriends or her friends to Rock'n Hollywood Sushi.

"Why would I come here on weekends? I spend two days a week here, and that's enough. Besides, this isn't a place I want to hang around," she told me one day. "I don't want to be around other waitresses here. I mean, they are nice and all, but they're not my friends. It's not like I dislike them or anything. I just party with my friends at different places."

I knew she was lying; she didn't like most of the waitresses. Lillian complained about, well, just about everyone except for Emma. I tried to imagine what Lillian's friends would be like. But the image of five or six Lillian-like blonde girls, drinking, talking, and partying was too scary for me to handle. It would be something like Barbies on acid. Yikes. I quickly erased the image from my mind.

"Where do you go?" I asked.

"Like, Bar Marmont at Chateau Marmont, Sky Room, The Standards Hotel, and places like that," she replied.

"So, you go to those "happening" places, huh?"

"I like going to those places because, there, you find a different crowd, not like the people who come here. There, no one starts to scream after doing a shot of *Sake*. Sure, people party, but they behave and don't get out of control," Lillian explained.

Lillian also loved to complain. She always complained. Mostly about the young Hollywood wannabes who acted out and behaved obnoxiously. They drank too much Sapporo and did too many *Sake* Bombs. She hated them, they lacked respect. Most of those types of customers came on the weekends, which is probably why she chose to only work during the week. I did agree, in some part, with what she said. Those testosterone-infused-*Sake*-Bomb-drinking young males weren't exactly my kind of crowds either. But then, we all chose to work here, which, made us part of the scene also. How ironic.

I was going to ask her about her boyfriend but stopped myself because I wasn't really interested in who she was dating. She already said that other waitresses weren't her friends, so she wasn't my friend or even someone that I wanted to be friends with. We just happened to work at the same restaurant, two days a week, and that was enough. We were just too different.

*****

Occasionally, Lillian would take a Wednesday night off and had to swap her shift with another waitress. This meant she'd wind up working on a weekend. Any of the other waitresses would love this opportunity to work on the weekends because of the higher tips, but not Lillian. She cared more about going out with her friends than making more tips on weekend shifts.

When Lillian wasn't complaining, she was actually fun to work with. She rarely made mistakes with her orders and was usually cheerful and friendly. Unfortunately, she had terrible taste in music, or should I say, her taste was different from mine and most of the restaurant staff. She only played two CDs, one with disco music like *Got to be Real*, by Cheryl

Lynn, and the other was Bob Marley. Now, thanks to Lillian, I can no longer listen to *No Woman No Cry* or any other Bob Marley songs.

*****

"Hi Toshi, Kai, and Kaz," Emma greeted us when she walked through the door. "This is Shauna." It was just like a scene from a movie—everything was in slow motion. Shauna looked at me; I looked at her. She smiled. I smiled back. Unfortunately, it was probably one of those geeky smiles. I was never very good at looking at girls. I always felt awkward, like I shouldn't be staring. Needless to say, I didn't date a lot in high school or in college.

Shauna was a petite, with long brown hair all the way down her back. Her ponytail looked like an actual pony's tail. She wore bright red lipstick, and her whole look reminded me of one of the girls in the Robert Palmer music video, *Addicted to Love*. I imagined she would look great in a red leather jacket. I liked that image.

Shauna had a great smile. Not like Lillian's, it was more of a quiet smile. Her dark eyes were mysterious and sad all at the same time as if she had a million secrets reserved within her. There was something different about her, and I wanted to find out more.

"She will start working here. Tonight is her first training shift, and I will be her trainer," Emma smiled at Shauna.

"Nice to meet you," Shauna said, in a lower tone.

"Nice to meet you, too," everyone said.

I looked at her and smiled again. She looked at me and did the same.

Emma told us that Shauna and her boyfriend drove from Boston to L.A., after a brief stop in San Francisco.

"What were you doing in San Francisco?" I asked right away.

"We were planning to move there, but we couldn't find a place to live because the rent was too high. Besides, we couldn't find any work either. So, we decided to come here and stay with my boyfriend's brother. Well, you know that's Emma's boyfriend," she smiled. "When I told Emma I

131

was looking for a job, she talked to Big Earl, and I got the job. So, here I am now."

"Are you staying at Emma and her boyfriend's apartment?" I asked.

"Yes."

"Is it big enough for four of you?"

"No, it's only one bedroom. We're only staying there until we find our own place," Shauna told me.

"I see," I nodded.

I was surprised that I could carry on a conversation with her. I'm usually nervous in a situation like this. I'd ask a question or two, and that was it: no more words, awkward silence. But with Shauna, things seemed to be different, easier.

I asked her where she went to college, what she studied, and when she decided to drive from Maryland to California. She listened to my questions and answered every one using carefully chosen words. "I studied Psychology in college. We left Maryland a couple of years after I graduated in an old Mazda RX-7 my boyfriend got from his father."

Since she went to San Francisco first, I figured she must like The Grateful Dead. I imagined that she's very liberal, like the students at U.C. Berkeley, engaging in heated political discussions about environmental issues and organic food. I couldn't help but project an image of how I wanted to see her.

When she wasn't busy, she sat at the end of the Sushi Bar and read books. Every time she worked, she was reading a different book. I was never a bookworm growing up. My father always told me to read as many books as I could, which made me hate reading. But I always admired people who liked to read.

My father made me read Japanese literature and books by famous authors, nothing I was ever interested in. My high school Japanese teacher made me read the *Tale of Genji*, a classic novel consisting of over ten books. Books always made me sleepy, and I usually lost interest before I hit page ten. And if there were more than five characters in the story, I had trouble following it, figuring out who was who.

So, watching Shauna read through one or two books a week was inspiring. I wish I could read like that. I wanted to read the same books as she did so we could talk about them. But I couldn't do that while everyone else was working around me. I had to find a situation where only she and I worked alone. I never dreamed it would happen, but one day, it did.

*****

On one Wednesday afternoon, Saito-san walked into the restaurant and asked Toshi. "What do you think about opening for lunch at 12 PM?"

"I don't think anyone would come. No businessmen are working around here. No one comes out here to do lunch. It's dead during the day. Sunset Strip is where you go out at night."

Toshi was right. He didn't tell Saito-san at the time, but the previous owner, Shige, tried to do the same and failed miserably. In fact, it was one of the few mistakes Shige ever made, but for some reason, Toshi didn't say anything. I knew he was right, lunch wasn't a good idea, but he knew that Saito-san would not listen. Later on, I asked Toshi why he didn't say anything, and he said, "Well, do you think telling the story would have changed his mind? I don't think so."

"So, can we do it?" Saito-san asked Toshi.

"Sure, if you want, we can. But, again, I just don't think it's a good idea," Toshi said without looking up.

So, Rock'n Hollywood Sushi opened for lunch. This meant that Jun and I had to start at 11 AM instead of 3 PM. But it also meant that twice a week, I could spend three hours alone with Shauna. I was thrilled, to say the least. The night before my first lunch shift, I wished that tomorrow would come sooner.

The waitresses had very little to do during the lunch shift. After setting up the tables, which took about fifteen minutes, there was nothing left to do except wait for customers.

My lunch shift started at 11 AM. The first thing I did was wash and cook the rice in the back kitchen. Then, I went out to the front, turned on the fridge, laid out the fish, cut the cucumbers, make the *daikon tsuma* garnish, scrape the Tuna, and mix the Snow Crab. I then took out the frozen fish to thaw, filled the *gari,* and made the hot sauce for the Spicy Tuna. I did all of this while taking care of an occasional customer or takeaway order. I was there four hours before the other chefs came in, and usually, there was more prep work than I could finish in those four hours.

One day, Shauna and I were alone in the restaurant. She sat at the Sushi Bar by the entrance, and I was standing behind the Sushi Bar prepping vegetables. As usual, she just sat there, reading. I asked her what she was reading, and she told me it was *Harry Potter.*

"Har...what?"

"*Harry Potter,*" she repeated.

"What is it about?" I asked. I had no idea what *Harry Potter* was.

She showed me the book and explained the story. I pretended to be interested, but, in reality, I wasn't. I was only interested in getting to know Shauna.

"It takes place in England, about a boy and a magic school. It's a fantasy. It's a worldwide best-seller," Shauna said.

At first, I was only attracted to her physically, but as I got to know her, I started to be attracted to her personality too.

"Every time I see you here, you are reading. Do you read a lot?" I asked Shauna, as I was peeling the skin off an English cucumber with my *Yanagiba.*

"Yes, I do, about one or two books a week. Sometimes, three, when I'm not working."

"What books do you like to read?" I asked.

"Umm, I like novels. I like stories, complex stories with many characters. I don't like horror stories, and I definitely never read Harlequin Romance Novels," Shauna said, with a tiny smile.

For some reason, the word "Harlequin" made me think of San Francisco.

"Why did you want to go to San Francisco?"

"I had a friend who moved there, and she said The City was so beautiful, and I should live there too. They call it The City, like people call here L.A. I heard people there hate when others call it "Frisco." When my boyfriend and I got there, we planned to find an apartment and find a job. But the apartments were so expensive, $2,000 for a small apartment, we couldn't afford it. So, we just stayed at my friend's apartment and visited touristy places like Fisherman's Wharf, Chinatown, North Beach, and the Mission district."

"Chinatown, huh? Did you ever go to House of Nanking?

"Yes, yes, yes. I did. I loved it," Shauna raised her voice.

"Really? Me, too. I liked it there, too. Did you order their famous eggplant dish?"

"Of course I did!"

When I saw her eyes widen, I found myself excited, too, knowing that we both had visited the same restaurant, enjoyed the same food.

That excitement lingered with me for the rest of the day. I even wrote it into my diary that night just to preserve the memory.

It was a trivial, small thing, and maybe she didn't care at all, but in my mind, having something in common with Shauna gave me hope. I thought perhaps I had a shot at winning her over. *Would she choose me over her boyfriend?* I wondered. *If she did, what would happen to her? Where would she live? With me? Would she keep working here? What about Emma and her boyfriend?* I tried to straighten out my thoughts— *why would she?*

*****

During my three-hour lunch break between 4 and 7 PM, I always cooked *makanai* for Shauna, and we sat together at the Sushi Bar to enjoy it. I knew I couldn't impress her with my conversation skills, so I figured I could at least wow her with my cooking skills. Offering her something to eat allowed me to sit down and share a meal with her. There's a saying in Japan: *The depth of a relationship is measured by how many meals you've shared with a person.* I always thought that was true. I also remembered what Graham Kerr did on Galloping Gourmet.

I wasn't sure if she would eat what I cooked, so I tried to figure out what she liked. I asked her questions like where she likes to go to eat and what kinds of food she cooked at home. I tried not to be too obvious. I already knew she liked the Chinese food at the House of Nanking in San Francisco. She also once told me that she liked Thai food, so I started cooking her Thai *makanai*. To me, sitting in an empty restaurant with Shauna eating Thai food felt like being on a date.

In fact, it was better than being on a date because I didn't have to pretend to be nice or cool. I was just me. I didn't know if she'd like my food, and if she didn't, it was okay. We all come from different backgrounds, eat different things, and like different foods. So it's perfectly okay if someone doesn't like what I like. It is not a matter of right or wrong. It's not even a matter of tasty or not tasty. It's all a matter of what we're used to eating, and more precisely, what we used to eat when growing up.

We frequently looked out the window at the beautiful blue daylight and evening orange L.A. skies while we ate. Homemade Tom Kha Kai, or Thai Coconut Chicken Soup with *galanga*, or Thai ginger, made with coconut milk, palm sugar, bamboo shoots, mushrooms, plenty of lime juice, chicken stock, and Nam Pla, fish sauce. Quite often, we exchanged just a few words. I'm not sure if she enjoyed the silence, but I loved eating *makanai* with her. I enjoyed her presence.

She was quiet, too—or at least with me—perhaps because I didn't talk a whole lot, except for a few questions here and there. When she was with the other waitresses, they talked, and so did she. I always wished I could be more like the girls just so I could find out more about her. Most of all, I wanted her to like me. So I cooked, every chance I had. I made a variety of dishes, Chinese, Italian, Japanese, just so I could figure out what she liked.

Eating *makanai* with Shauna became my favorite time of day. I couldn't wait for her lunch shift. She only had two lunch shifts with me: Friday and Saturday. I wished there were more, so I could spend more time with her alone without her boyfriend or anyone else interrupting.

I always made enough for the Sushi Chefs and sometimes another waitress, but it was mainly for Shauna. I didn't want anyone to know that it was all for her. I didn't want anyone to find out that I was secretly attracted to her. If they did, then Shauna's boyfriend could find out too, and that would mean big trouble for her.

Emma always told me that my food was delicious, and Toshi, Kai, Jun and Juan, too, but I only cared what Shauna thought. I anxiously waited for her comments and smiled when she tried my food.

*****

Sometimes the waitresses ordered takeaway sushi at the end of their shift. When Shauna put an order in, I'd always add extra sushi, *Sashimi*, or *nigiri* for her. She loved the Double Shrimp Roll, so I'd sometimes add that too. I just kept trying to get to know her better.

After a month of lunch shifts, Shauna started to get some evening shifts too, filling in for Emma and the other waitresses. Occasionally, Shauna worked a double shift on Fridays, taking Emma's shift. I loved it when she worked a double because it meant I could spend all day with her at the restaurant.

The party crowd came in on Fridays, and we all got busy. Every time I had a chance to look away from my cutting board, I'd look over at Shauna, and she'd looked back at me and smile. That one, simple gesture made me so happy. I knew she had a boyfriend, but I didn't care. It may not have been romantic, but she was clearly interested in me.

When Toshi and Kai started to talk about Shauna one day, I finally told them that I liked her, even though she lived with her boyfriend. They knew I was flirting with her, so whenever she ordered takeaway sushi, they'd let me make it for her.

Kai made fun of me a few times. Once, he saw me picking up Shauna's order. "So, you are going to put some love in that order," he teased.

"Yup," I mumbled, blushing.

*****

I had been making Thai Curry at least once a week for *makanai* for the past two months. I felt pretty good about my Thai Curry, so I decided to venture onto something more elaborate. My mind wandered back to when I initially started making *makanai* at the restaurant. I remember thinking about trying to recreate the Linguini Pescatore from my favorite Italian restaurant, Alejo's in Marina Del Rey. I thought this would be a great chance to give it a try. I ordered Manila Clams, fresh Monterey Squid, and White Shrimp from the fish company to use in the pasta dish the next day.

Since the sauce had to simmer for several hours, I started it at the beginning of my shift in hopes that it would be ready by the time I went on break. In between my shifts, I tasted the tomato sauce; it was excellent and reminded me of cooking with my Italian friend, Barry. His grandmother taught him how to make authentic tomato sauce from scratch.

"Don't burn the sauce, keep watching, and make sure to stir," Barry used the same words his grandmother said to him as we cooked. It reminded me of a scene from the movie *Goodfellas*, which Ray Liotta's character is saying, "Don't burn the sauce."

Obviously, I couldn't stand in front of my sauce while I prepped, so I asked Pedro in the back kitchen to look after my sauce and stir it consistently. After two hours of simmering over low heat, the sauce was thick and rich with *umami* flavor. All I had to do was add fresh seafood and Parmesan cheese. I made that Linguini Pescatore many times after that, and it was always good. But no matter what I did, I just couldn't make it the way they do at Allejo's.

"What do you think about this pasta? I made the sauce from scratch," I asked Shauna.

"This is excellent. I love it, especially the seafood," she replied with a smile. I couldn't help but feel my heart skip a beat.

A MOVIE DATE

For the past three months, I'd been working hard to win Shauna's heart. Making her tasty *makanai*, taking an interest in her books, engaging in small talk with her. Every time she came to the Sushi Bar to pick up an order, I tried to talk to her and get her attention. Some days I was successful, and some days I was not. I had Sundays off, but I'd just sit at home thinking about Shauna, so I'd get in my car and visit during her lunch shift, pretending like I had some business to do. At first, I thought she might be suspicious, but by the time I started driving, I didn't care. I knew that seeing Shauna, even for only ten minutes on my day off, would make me feel better. I knew she liked me, but I wasn't sure how much she liked me. Did she like me as a co-worker, as a friend, or maybe more than a friend? Did she like me enough to go on a date? I desperately wanted the answers, but how? She was still dating and living with her boyfriend, so it wasn't like she'd just dump him and start dating me. But I still hoped that she liked me more than a co-worker.

One Friday, I made Thai Ginger Chicken and Tom Ka Kai Soup for our *makanai*. I sat next to Shauna in my regular seat at the Sushi Bar. It was a hot, bright summer day in L.A. There was a copy of *L.A. Weekly* on the table, so I was browsing through the movie section. We started talking about movies, and I saw a big ad for *Crouching Tiger, Hidden Dragon*, which was starting to catch people's attention.

"I heard it's a good movie. I want to go see this one," I said to Shauna.

"Me, too!" she agreed.

I couldn't believe what she just said. I didn't mean to ask her if she wanted to go see the film, but now I knew she wanted to. My heart started to beat faster, I wanted to ask if she'd see it with me.

"Let's go see it together," I said.

"Yes, that would be great," Shauna replied.

I was shocked. The words came out so naturally, it didn't even feel like I asked her out on a date. Maybe I didn't? I went back and forth in my head for a few seconds and decided that I really did ask her out. *And she said yes?!* I thought I might be dreaming.

I immediately looked back at the paper for showtimes, because if we didn't make a plan now, maybe we never would. "They are showing it at the theater on La Cienega at 12 PM. How about tomorrow? You switched shifts with Emma, right?"

"Yes, we can go tomorrow. That would be fun!" she smiled.

I smiled back and finished my Tom Kha Kai. I could hardly wait until tomorrow. That night, the rest of my shift felt longer than usual. Shauna was done at 6 PM, and I saw her clock out by the cashier. She gave me a quick glance and then left without saying goodbye. But she smiled at me, ever so slightly and briefly so no one would notice. We had a secret. A secret date that no one else knew about. Not Toshi. Not Lillian. Not Emma. Not Big Earl. And definitely not Shauna's boyfriend.

The next morning, I woke up around 10 AM, got ready, and made sure my car was clean. At first, I wanted to pick her up at her apartment, but then I realized it would probably be a bad idea since she lived with her boyfriend. Instead, I called and asked her to meet me at the theater at 11 AM.

I got there about ten minutes early and waited. While I was waiting, I started to worry. What if she didn't show up? What if she called and told me she couldn't make it? What if she changed her mind?

But at precisely at 11 AM, Shauna was walking toward me, waving her hand in the air. She was wearing a pair of Levi's and an orange t-shirt. I was only used to seeing her in black pants and a black shirt at the restaurant. It was strange but refreshing. Seeing her in a bright color made me happy.

"How are you doing?" I asked her.

"Oh, I'm doing great," she said. "How was last night after I left?"

"It was busy, a typical Friday night. I got off around midnight, went home, and slept—as usual," I shrugged, trying to sound cool.

"Do you go to sleep right after you come home? Because I can't. I need to relax for a while, like an hour or two before I can go to sleep.

Normally, I am too wound up from work. I have to release some of the energy," she smiled.

"After work, I am exhausted and have no problem falling asleep. Toshi and Kai both tell me that they stay up all night long and go to sleep around 6 AM. They play video games and watch movies and Japanese dramas. I can never stay up all night," I smiled back.

We both exchanged smiles. Then, there was a moment of silence, not awkward, but a pleasant one.

I walked up to the box office, bought two tickets, and handed one to her. She opened her purse and tried to take out some money.

"That's okay. It's my treat," I said and smiled at her.

"Do you want some popcorn?" I asked. I wanted this to feel like a real date, even though neither one of us had said it was.

"No thanks," Shauna said, laughing.

"What's so funny? Was popcorn funny?" I asked.

"No, nothing," she said. "I just didn't think you'd ask me that question."

Since I was the one who asked her out, I wanted to make sure I took good care of her. Also, I had a rising feeling like boiling water in my head. I don't know why I felt such a strong need to protect her.

But protecting her from what? I guess my thoughts had answers, too. She wasn't in any danger. As far as I knew, her boyfriend wasn't a bad person or abusive. Sure, sometimes the customers at Rock'n Hollywood Sushi tried to hit on her, but there weren't any stalkers. It was just me, trying to win her over, showing her I was worthy. I was, both unconsciously and consciously, suggesting that she ditch her boyfriend and start dating me.

None of that mattered right now because I was the one with her, right here and now.

We chose seats side by side, near the back of the theatre.

"I am so glad that we could come and watch this movie today. I have wanted to see an Ang Lee movie ever since I heard about him," Shauna said in a quiet voice.

I knew very little about Ang Lee or the movie we were about to see. It was supposed to be a Kung Fu action movie, but it turned out to have a romantic side too. I wanted to hold Shauna's hand every time a romantic scene came up. But every time I thought about it, I stopped and reminded myself that she had a boyfriend.

On the other hand, if this were a date, it would be okay to reach for her hand, and maybe she'd hold my hand back. But then again, what if she didn't? That would be awkward. We worked together. And we worked together tonight. But she was right here next to me, so close yet so far away. For an hour, I struggled, trying to suppress my desire. I just wanted to put my hand on top of hers, look her in the eyes, and whisper, "I like you, Shauna. I like you a lot." But I couldn't. I fought with myself for the rest of the movie. I could hardly keep up with the story.

When the movie was over, the lights came on. We looked at each other again and said, "Wow, that was a good movie."

"I don't have to start work until 4 PM today. So, let's get some lunch. Only if you want to?" I waited for Shauna's reply.

"That sounds good. Where do you want to go?"

"There is a Café inside of that flower shop, right next door. I think they have sandwiches, soups, and salads."

*****

I heard the Café was originally just a flower shop, and the owner decided to turn the whole shop into a Café so the customers could enjoy flowers and food together. When we walked in, I saw a bouquet of roses - red, yellow, orange, pink, and white - and thought about buying one for Shauna.

Then, I remembered the Mexican Flower Lady, who visited Rock'n Hollywood Sushi every night. She liked to meet all of the couples in the restaurant and sell them a single-stemmed rose for $8. These roses were different from the Mexican Flower Lady's, but there is just something about red roses. I looked at the flowers, wondering if I should buy them for Shauna. *Would it make me look cheap?* I took a deep breath and turned my attention to the other side. I decided not to buy them. Besides, what would Shauna do with all those roses? She couldn't possibly take them home. I didn't like the silence, so we began to talk about the movie.

"I did not like the people laughing at the wire effect, people flying during a Kung-Fu fight. Sure, it looked rather cheesy, but that's the style in a Chinese movie. They just don't understand it," she said, playing with the spoon on the table.

I nodded in agreement. Every time we shared our thoughts and agreed on something, I felt closer to her. Of course, the closer I felt, the more I wanted her in my life. During lunch, I hoped we would talk more about our personal lives, but we didn't. I couldn't gather the courage to ask her if she liked me.

After lunch, we went our separate ways. We both had to work in a couple of hours. After we said goodbye, she started walking towards her apartment. She looked back at me, smiled, and waved her hand in the air. I wanted to walk with her so we could spend more time together, but I knew I couldn't. If I walked her home, her boyfriend might see us, and that would not be good.

Everything was normal at work that night like nothing happened during the day. We didn't tell anyone about our date. But every time I looked at her, she looked back and smiled. Just like usual.

Even though she was smiling, there was something different about the way she looked at me. Something told me that she didn't consider our daily excursion a date like I did.

The next two months were awkward. She didn't look at me like she had before. We talked less. We sat together and ate *makanai* less. It seemed like we lost our momentum. My feelings were still strong, but hers were definitely gone. I had no idea what had happened. *Did I do something wrong? Was it something I said? Was it something I didn't say?*

And then, it was Christmas.

CHRISTMAS

Shige, the previous owner, used to throw a Christmas party for all the employees every year. He always invited his friends and some regular customers too. Shige was Saito-san's partner, and a friend, as well as the Sushi Chef who came up with the idea of opening the very first rock 'n' roll sushi bar on Sunset Strip, long before most people even heard of a California Roll.

According to Toshi, Rock'n Hollywood Sushi became a phenomenon and the "to go" place for the Sunset Strip Crowd from movie stars, rock 'n' rollers, aspiring actors and actresses, weekend party people, wannabees, to drug dealers. He told me all about the wild things that happened during those parties. Mostly involving sex, drugs, and rock 'n' roll. Everything changed, though, when Saito-san took over.

For the Christmas party, he decided to close the restaurant at 10 PM Saito-san wouldn't let us make sushi. He kept telling us, "Fish is expensive." So, Pedro made most of the food. Lots of Tempura, Chicken Teriyaki appetizers, and boiled Edamame.

"Rolls are okay. Use cheap fish like Salmon and Albacore and make Inside-Out rolls, not *nigiri*. You can make tempura rolls," Saito-san said.

"I was at the first Christmas Party five years ago," Juan said. "I got wasted and passed out on the stairs until the next morning."

"You did? And then?"

"Since the second year, I learned that I could make money, lots of money by setting up a bar, and serving beer and *sake* while collecting tips from other employees."

"That's better than passing out."

"Last year, I made over $200 in tips."

"Really?" I thought about doing the same as Juan, but then it would've been just like another night at the Sushi Bar. I wouldn't be able to enjoy the party and have fun. I wouldn't be able to talk to Shauna.

"Good Luck!" I said to Juan and went on to greet other friends.

*****

Everyone was there: all the waitresses and their friends, busboys, kitchen chefs, valet guys, the doorman, some regulars, and, of course, Shauna's boyfriend. Most people were drunk, and so were we. I hung out with the other Japanese Sushi Chefs drinking beer, while Shauna was with her boyfriend, his brother, Emma, and the other waitresses upstairs. They were shouting, laughing, singing, and having more fun than us Sushi Chefs downstairs.

Toshi knew how I felt about Shauna.

"Why don't you go upstairs and hang out with her?"

"I cannot. Her boyfriend is there," I said. "I wish I could, though."

"Let's all go upstairs together, and then it will be okay," Toshi said.

Toshi, Kai, Jun, and I all went up. We saw Emma's boyfriend dancing and singing loudly with Shauna's boyfriend. We sat across from them, in the corner of the room on a big couch. I stared at Shauna's boyfriend for a while and drank beer. Toshi, Kai, and Jun did the same. We didn't talk much.

"Kaz, why don't you go up and talk to her?" Toshi suggested.

"Yeah, you should," Kai agreed.

I had another sip of Sapporo, stood up, walked over, and sat next to Shauna. She was laughing at a joke and saw me sit right next to her, but she didn't say a word to me. I sat quietly for a minute or two.

"How are you doing?" I asked.

"Oh, I am doing great. Are you having a good time?" She asked, without looking at my direction.

"Yup, I am having a good time."

"Okay, that's good," Shauna said. Then she stood up and moved to another corner of the room with her friends. It was pretty abrupt and intentional. I felt like a giant wall was breaking over my head. I felt like a puppy whose owner had thrown him into a bush. I didn't know what to do. In fact, the only thing I knew not to do was to follow her. It was a clear sign. I shouldn't pursue her anymore.

And that was it. I looked at her for a long time, waiting to strike up a conversation. But she never looked back. She never smiled at me.

"You know you are asking too much, don't you? She is with her boyfriend, and they live together. It's too risky right now, and you're asking a lot. Something it's impossible," Toshi said, dragging me downstairs.

As I walked away, I turned around to see Shauna and her boyfriend hugging and dancing to the music. I wanted to join them. I wanted to hold her. I wanted to have a good time. But I wasn't. All of my hopes were gone, and there wasn't a reason to stay.

So I decided to go home alone. I crossed in front of Juan and wished him goodbye.

"I already made more tips than last year," he beamed. I nodded and smiled back. He looked happy, holding cash in one hand and a beer in the other. Big Earl was by the door, looking at me thoughtfully. "Goodnight," he said, as I got into my car.

The next morning when I woke up, I was tired. I didn't want to wake up, so instead, I laid back down like a piece of dead fish on a cutting board. I didn't want to go to work. I didn't want to see Shauna. I didn't know how to react or what to say to her. I wondered if she would even look at me.

But I got up anyway. I got myself ready and headed to work at Rock'n Hollywood Sushi, just like any other day. And did it because I knew Shauna would be there.

Just like me, she was in bad shape from drinking too much the night before. But, I knew that wasn't the reason she did not say hello. There weren't any customers during the lunch shift, so she decided to go upstairs and take a nap.

"Call me when a customer walks in," she said to me.

"Okay," I replied casually.

During my lunch break, I went upstairs and took a nap on the couch in the opposite corner of the room. I wanted to lie next to her, I still had feelings for her, but I could tell that she didn't feel the same way about me. When she saw me lie down across the room, she turned away. There was something awkward in the air. Big Earl walked in half an hour later, and Shauna walked back downstairs, told him how bad she was feeling, and asked if she could go home.

"Not a problem," Big Earl said.

Shauna grabbed her bag and left the restaurant without saying goodbye.

Nothing was the same after the Christmas party. Shauna didn't look at me the way she used to. She still talked to me, but only in a monotone, work-related, functional, non-chitchat kind of way. She carried on "normal" conversations with the other waitresses like Emma and Lillian, though. I still made *makanai* but stopped asking for her opinions. I just served the food. We didn't sit side-by-side at the Sushi Bar anymore either, she sat on one side, and I sat on the other, and we never made eye contact while we ate. After our movie date, I was going to ask her out again, but it didn't feel right anymore, so I just gave up.

One evening, Big Earl asked me about my date with Shauna.

"So, I heard Shauna and you went out on a date?"

"Well, sort of... yeah, something like that," I replied.

"Something like that, huh?"

"I don't know. I like her, but I just don't know. She has a boyfriend, and now things are not working out."

After I said the words out loud, I realized that I might be delusional. Things were never the way I thought they were. It wasn't a date. I hoped it was a date, but maybe she didn't think it was. We weren't dating. We weren't a couple. At the Christmas Party, she probably realized that I had feelings for her that she didn't have.

It didn't matter, either way, at least that's what I told myself.

Three months after our movie date, Shauna told me she was going back to Maryland. And that was that. It was too late. I didn't make up my mind fast enough to keep her. I didn't try hard enough. I was too afraid.

I gave up because I was scared. I worried about how others would look at me if I tried to steal her from her boyfriend.

All of those feelings are long gone now, and I don't want to see her again. But, even to this day, I regret letting my emotions and my fear get in my way. I didn't act when I should have, like when I decided to become a Sushi Chef. As the years' pass, I can't help but think, *what if I made a different choice back then?* Things might be different now.

A WHITE SUSHI CHEF

Tom was the only Caucasian Sushi Chef at Rock'n Hollywood Sushi. He only worked there part-time to make ends meet. His 'real job' was working as a dancer. To him, being a Sushi Chef was just another job, but for the rest of us, it was a career.

I knew how tough it was to make a living as a dancer. My friend, Bruce, was a dance major in college and told me the only steady job he could find was on Broadway in Manhattan, at shows in Las Vegas, or in Strip Clubs in Los Angeles.

"If you are lucky, you might get a job as a background dancer for concert tours or music videos, but you have to go to a hundred auditions," Bruce said. He also told me the pay wasn't great, even if you danced in the background for a major artist like Madonna.

"They never pay you enough. Madonna started out poor, and she didn't get paid well. She wants all of us to go through the same thing she did, paying us just enough to make a living, but not too much, so we stay hungry," Bruce explained. There was a lack of enthusiasm in his voice.

Therefore, I knew Tom had to work at Rock'n Hollywood Sushi because he wasn't making enough money as a dancer. But that didn't give him a right to do things half-way. I never liked his attitude. He only seemed to care about the tips.

Tom learned his sushi-making skills at Miyagi's, a large restaurant that used to be a legendary nightclub, the Roxbury.

Tom only knew the basics. I could tell he learned from an untrained chef, because of the way he handled his knife. When he cut fish, he pushed his knife instead of pulling it backward. He didn't know how to sharpen it correctly using the whetstones. He moved his knife on top of the stone, without angling it correctly.

I despised him because he didn't seem to care about the craft. I knew he just wanted to make some extra cash until his dancing career took off. He always talked about how much money he made producing a dance show at a nearby club on Sunset Strip. Every time he said that I couldn't help but think, *Well then, what the hell are you doing here?*

"Oh, the sushi at Miyagi's is really terrible. But, the girls are pretty," Tom told us. "On weekends, the place is packed and full of gorgeous-looking girls dancing and ordering at the Sushi Bar."

"Oh, really? Sushi is bad there, huh? That is exactly what I thought," Kai said, grinning.

"Yeah, it's really bad," Tom replied.

"So, it's a good place to go hang out, if you are looking for girls, right?" Kai continued. "Do they get better-looking girls there than we do here?"

"Oh, yes. The girls there are much better looking than here," Tom said.

"Shit, they get better girls than we do, huh?" Kai said. Toshi and I found it funny to listen to Kai speak English. When he talked in Japanese, he was fine. But the moment he started speaking in English, he sounded like a kid on the street or gang member from South Central L.A. He would use sentences heavily-laced with words like "shit," "fuck," and "you know what I'm saying."

I think he spoke that way because there was something inside of him he struggled to deal with. Maybe he was jealous of Tom, working at a place where the girls were prettier?

We were all single Japanese Sushi Chefs in our thirties, working ten hours a day, five days a week. We'd welcome any opportunity to meet our future wife. Therefore, prettier girls at another restaurant did sound appealing, but then again, I knew it wouldn't make for a better workplace. Kai knew this, too. In the end, it isn't really about the girls. It's about the integrity, devotion, and relationships you have with your coworkers that makes the difference. How you're treated determines your happiness. Pay comes at the end of that list.

I didn't become a Sushi Chef so I could date pretty girls and get laid more often. And I definitely didn't want to have a girlfriend who worked as a stripper at the Body Shop next door. Besides, we all cared about the craft, and we pushed each other to improve our skills. Tom didn't, and that's what made us angry.

*****

According to Tom, Miyagi's could easily hold three hundred customers. They had multiple floors, a disco ball, and flashing lights on every floor. Each level also had at least one Sushi Bar, and some were shaped in a circle instead of the traditional straight Sushi Bar style. Each station could hold at least one Sushi Chef, and customers would come and order their sushi just like they'd order a Martini at the bar. Miyagi's was definitely a dance club first, with the Sushi Bars as an afterthought. It was entirely different than Rock'n Hollywood Sushi. We were a restaurant that played rock 'n' roll music, not a dance club.

At Miyagi's, all of the prep was done in a kitchen on the first floor. Then, each chef had to bring all of the prepped ingredients up to the various Sushi Bars. They also didn't have an elevator, so if someone ran out of something, they'd have to run back down to the kitchen to get it. I thought about what a nightmare it would be if you were stationed on the fifth floor and had to run all the way down to the first floor to get more fish, rice, vegetables, or anything else, and then run back up five flights of stairs to your station.

"Oh, we just let the younger chefs go up and down to get what we need," Tom said.

That doesn't sound nice, it seems like punishment. I thought quietly to myself.

"How many Sushi Chefs work at Miyagi's?" I asked.

"I don't know exactly, but probably something like twenty Sushi Chefs on the weekend," Tom said.

"How do they keep an eye on every Sushi Chef on every floor?" I asked.

"They can't. There are only three managers at Miyagi's, four on the weekend. They just cannot keep track of what everyone's doing. We just make sushi the way we want to make it."

"Are there any Japanese chefs at Miyagi's?" Toshi asked.

"No. No Japanese Sushi Chefs. All American Chefs," Tom replied.

Based on what he told us, I could understand why Tom worked the way he did at Rock'n Hollywood Sushi. I also imagined that Tom received very little, if any, formal sushi training, let alone any Japanese work ethics. They probably showed him the sushi techniques just a few times, and after that, he was on his own. Many of the methods are simple to explain, but very difficult to master. It takes just ten seconds to show him how to make *nigiri*, but it will take a lifetime to master the technique. Even from my not-so-trained eyes, I could tell that Tom wasn't experienced at all.

Tom appeared to be a Sushi Chef to most of his customers, those who knew very little about sushi. He was an excellent salesman, but most of the time, he was bluffing. No one was knowledgeable enough to tell that he was making things up. He didn't even know how to pronounce the names of the fish in Japanese. I hated when Tom made things up, and I felt bad for his customers. I wanted to shout, *Hey, that's not right! Don't listen to this guy! He doesn't even know what irasshaimase means! That's not how you make nigiri! He doesn't know how to keep his cutting board clean! He's not a real Sushi Chef! He's just a dancer, pretending to be a Sushi Chef!*

Tom also complained a lot, just like Lillian, when he worked. Not only did he complain to us, but he also complained to our manager and our owner. Unity, hard work, discipline, loyalty, and *kaizen* (never-ending improvement) are the Japanese work ethics we all learned growing up. I didn't see any of these traits in Tom, who grew up in a different culture. In the U.S., he was in the majority, and we were the minority. But, at the Sushi Bar, we were the majority, carrying on the Japanese traditions. I wanted Tom to understand it, or at least show some respect. I think his lack of respect made us angry too.

We were also taught that complaining is a sign of weakness; hence, we hardly ever complained to our manager or our owner. Our job was to follow orders first, not to object, not to question. It may sound like being in the military, but working in a kitchen under a Sushi Master is exactly like that. The Master spent several decades figuring out the secrets, and now, he's ready to share them with you. If you just do whatever he tells you to do, at least in the beginning, your training time can be cut down by years. It's a great shortcut, but you need to have discipline and patience. Hence, "Your master knows more than you do. Do what you're told first, and then, if you must, question later."

Judging by the way he worked, Tom lacked the understanding of this concept, and all of the basic disciplines needed to be a Sushi Chef. He often came in late to work, showed up unshaven, in desperate need of a haircut, fatigued, hung-over, and in a dirty uniform. Tom used his apron to wipe off his cutting board and kept everything messy with fish and vegetable pieces scattered all over his workstation. His tools were poorly taken care of, and he carried his dull knife in scruffy a sports bag. He smoked more often than anyone else during his shift, and the list goes on and on.

To make *nigiri*, Tom formed a ball of rice on a cutting board and then placed the sliced fish directly on top to make it look like he made the *nigiri* with his hand. The rest of us know that the proper way to make *nigiri*, is to slice the fish, grab it with one hand, then grab some rice with the other hand and place it on the fish, squeezing several times, moving your hands rhythmically, flipping the fish and the rice together to form a perfect bite-sized piece. When done correctly, it's as beautiful as a skilled magician, shuffling a deck of cards. Forming *nigiri* requires a certain gentle pressure, not too firm, but firm enough so that the piece of *neta* sticks to the *shari*. And when you put the *nigiri* in your mouth, the rice breaks immediately, spreading all over the inside of your mouth, releasing the sweet and salty, vinegary flavor of the *shari*. Tom didn't know any of this. And he didn't bother to learn.

*****

On his day off, at least once, sometimes twice, a week, Tom visited Rock'n Hollywood Sushi to eat and drink because he knew he could get the employee discount. Tom also knew how to get "free drinks" and "free food" from the other waitresses and the manager.

Of course, almost all of the employees used the discounts and free orders, but none of us took advantage of the freebies like Tom did. It

153

was apparent that Tom came to eat just to save some money.

"Shit, man. Tom is here again," Kai squinted his eyes. "I don't want to make sushi for him."

Tom often sat at the bar, talking to Big Earl. He would order only one California Roll, then get a free glass of beer, a free order of Chicken Teriyaki, a free bowl of Miso Soup, and a free House Salad.

We didn't want to make the free orders that the managers put in for Tom. Usually, we just ignored them, even if the ticket was printed.

"Why is everyone treating him differently, or better, giving him freebies? What the fuck?" Kai started to talk shit in both Japanese and English.

"Are they feeling sorry for Tom? Why? He is not a good Sushi Chef. He doesn't clean up. He is slow. He makes mistakes with the orders all the time," Kai continued, complaining.

I, too, had difficulty understanding why Big Earl and the other waitresses gave him so many freebies. Maybe they thought it was charity or goodwill, but, in reality, it was merely pity and sorrow, not encouragement. I couldn't see Tom ever becoming a successful dancer. *There's nothing that makes him sparkle*, I thought.

Maybe they thought they were helping Tom, but it really didn't. If you want someone to succeed in life, as the saying goes, "teach then him how to fish, so that he learns to eat for the rest of his life, do not fish for him, so that he can live for only one day."

"Hey, Toshi, can you make one California and one Spicy Tuna Roll for me," Big Earl asked.

"Okay, who is it for? Is it for you or someone else?" Toshi asked Big Earl.

"It's for Tom," he said.

"Well, I need to see the ticket. Can I punch it in? When we get a ticket, we'll make it for you," Toshi said, looking directly at Big Earl.

Toshi knew what he was up to. He was trying to get free sushi for Tom again, and the only way to do it was to order without using the POS system. Of course, Toshi wasn't going to make free sushi for Tom. So, Big

Earl had no choice but to order it through the POS.

"All right, no problem. I'll punch it in right now," Big Earl said to Toshi.

The printer spat out Big Earl's order. Toshi made it and handed the plate to Big Earl.

*****

Even though none of us regarded Tom as a "real" Sushi Chef, his customers always gave him the highest reviews. One thing he did well was bullshit his way through things. Whenever he talked about sushi or the Special Rolls he made, served with "House-Made Sauce," most of it was improvising. He just used whatever he could find behind the Sushi Bar, like *gari*-marinated juice, *ponzu* sauce, mayo, and chili powder. Nothing that we would have used. Tom's Special Sauce never tasted good to us; but, his customers always exclaimed, "So good!"

Tom also copied other chef's recipes, serving them like his own. Once, he made Kai's Special Roll and served it to a customer. Kai was livid. When Tom talked to his customers, he bragged. *Like he knows the difference between fresh and old fish, or what kind of fish is available for sushi.* He had no idea where our *Hamachi* came from, or even if it was wild or farm-raised.

We wondered why Saito-san hired him. Toshi said he had objected at first, but Saito-san said it was good to have diversity. Having a Caucasian Sushi Chef at the Sushi Bar was a plus, it gave a good impression, and would bring in more novice customers.

Tom did excel in communication skills, he was friendly and talkative to the customers at the Sushi Bar. He explained the fish, how they tasted, and what the difference was between Albacore Tuna and Yellowtail. He talked about the sauces, explaining the process as he made the rolls, although most of what he said was made up. When customers asked him where he received sushi training, he said he learned from many master Sushi Chefs.

Tom gave his customers what they wanted: Special Inside-Out Rolls with Special Sauce. Although I was making California, Spicy Tuna, and Rainbow Rolls, I wanted to make *nigiri* instead. I didn't think of California Rolls as "real" sushi. *Nigiri* was the only real sushi in my mind, and I believed it was the best way to eat fish. *How can you taste the fish in a roll? The only thing you can taste in the Inside-Out roll is shari, isn't it?* This was why I hesitated to offer any Special Rolls to my customers. But for Tom, and most of the customers at Rock'n Hollywood Sushi, the Inside-Out Roll was "real" sushi. This was a concept I had trouble grasping at the beginning of my career. I was too narrow-minded and had a one-sided perspective. I thought my customers wanted what I wanted. I assumed they had the same taste buds as I did, which just wasn't true.

While Tom's style of splashing sauces all over the plate after deep frying the rolls was nothing traditional or original, he did capture his customer's attention and their taste buds. "Oh my God, this is so good," a customer would exclaim, while I was thinking, *These people know nothing about sushi,* as I stood by watching them.

I later realized that I wasn't only disrespecting Tom and his customers; I was also disrespecting all of the Sushi Chefs outside of Japan, making Inside-Out rolls, my Japanese co-workers, and ultimately, myself.

*****

One day Saito-san asked us to come up with a Special Roll. Tom quickly came up with a Forest Fire Roll: Albacore Tuna and Cucumber inside, Spicy Tuna on top, with some *ponzu* and scallions sprinkled on the outside. It was colorful; the red Tuna and green scallions were beautiful. When Tom showed us *his* Forest Fire Roll, we could tell it wasn't an original.

"He must have stolen it from someone else," Kai said, behind Tom's back.

Regardless, Saito-san decided to put the roll on the Special menu, and it became an instant success. It didn't matter whether Tom had invented the Forest Fire Roll or not. All that mattered was that it was a big hit, and made money for the restaurant. It made everyone happy: customers, waitresses, Sushi Chefs, and Saito-san.

Maybe it was the Hollywood way—as long as you can create a hit, how you go about creating it doesn't matter. I don't agree with that; never did, and never will.

CELEBRITIES

What do Leonard DiCaprio, Heath Ledger, Anthony Hopkins, James Woods, Denzel Washington, Helen Hunt, Paula Cole, Antonio Banderas, Gene Simmons, and Axl Rose all have in common? At a restaurant, they all appreciate being treated like a regular person. At least that is what I came to understand.

*****

Friday afternoon at 4 PM. It had been a month since Saito-san decided that we should open for lunch. Rock'n Hollywood Sushi was at the end of the Sunset Strip, not exactly the busiest business lunch area. Most of the so-called "power-lunch" spots, like *Le Petit Four*, were located on the far west side of Sunset Boulevard. So, lunch was slow; we would see only two or three customers in those four hours. Even though it was good training for me, as for the tips, not so much.

Shauna and I were working the lunch shift that day. Jun walked in to take over the prep work at the Sushi Bar.

"I pretty much finished everything, except maybe mixing some extra crab," I told him.

It was my break time. I went to the back kitchen to finish making Thai Noodle Soup, Bah Mi, Yellow Noodle with Chicken Broth Soup, Crabmeat, and Cilantro. I learned to do both Sushi Bar prep and *makanai* prep during my shift to shorten my cooking time during my break.

That day, I made two bowls, one for me and one for Shauna. We sat at the one end of the Sushi Bar, close to the front door, where Shauna always sat to read books.

"Here you go. Thai Noodle Soup with Crabmeat. It's called Bha Mi. I ate it when I went to Thailand and fell in love with it," I told her.

Shauna sipped the soup, slowly. "This soup is quite delicious. I love it," she smiled. I smiled back and realized how great I felt when she told me she liked my food.

At that moment, the front door slammed open, hitting the wall. Two tall African American men in jeans and T-shirts walked through. They sat at the opposite end of the Sushi Bar and grabbed a menu. One man had a huge blue fork-like plastic comb stuck in his semi-Afro shaped hair and wore a dark pair of sunglasses. Both of the men gazed into the menu like high school students trying to find the answer to an exam. The man with the plastic comb noticed us eating the noodles, looked back into the menu, then looked up again, with a confused look on his face and said,

"Hey, what is it that you are eating?"

"It's Bha Mi," I told the man.

"Bhaa, what?" he shouted.

"Thai Noodle soup with crab," I shouted back.

"Where is that on the menu?"

"It's not on the menu," I said.

"Why not on the menu?"

He stood up from the chair, looked over the Sushi Bar, pointed to Shauna's bowl, and shouted, "I want that. I want to order two, one for me, and one for my man, Eddy."

"I'm sorry, but it's an employee meal. I cooked it, and as I said, it's not on the menu. So, it's not available to order. Besides, there is none left," I said.

He stood at the opposite side of the Sushi Bar dumbfounded.

Then he sat down.

"They don't have that noodle on the menu, so they can't make it anymore," his friend said.

"No, no, I don't think they have French Fries, either. It's a sushi restaurant; they have raw fish, you know?" Now they were whispering.

"In fact, we do have French Fries," I whispered to Shauna.

"Yes, I know," she smiled at me.

The two men talked back and forth. It took them five minutes to order a California Roll and a Shrimp Tempura Roll. I noticed there was something strange about the way they talked. Nothing made sense, they were making irrelevant jokes, laughing for no reason, and their voices sounded weird. Suddenly, I realized they were high on pot.

Once their food arrived, they spent a good twenty minutes eating the two rolls and drinking a glass of beer. After that, they walked out, and we never saw them again.

"Do you know who that was?" Shauna asked me. She looked amused.

"No, I don't know who it was," I said.

"It was Bobby Brown, the singer, you know?"

"Oh, yeah? Wait, that was him, Bobby Brown?" I said. "I had no idea."

I tried to remember what he looked like in his music videos.

"Oh, yes, you're right. It was Bobby Brown, ha!"

"You said *NO* to Bobby Brown. That was too funny," Shauna smiled at me.

A few months later, a tall black woman walked in and sat right in the center of Sushi Bar during my lunch shift around 2 PM. No one else was in the restaurant at that point. When I looked up, I immediately recognized her. It was Whitney Houston. She looked directly at me and ordered six pieces of the Shrimp Tempura appetizer.

I don't recommend ordering Shrimp Tempura, is what I wanted to tell her, but I couldn't

"*Seis Camarones,*" I shouted to Pedro in the kitchen and smiled at Ms. Houston. I had a bad feeling, the Shrimp Tempura Pedro made never came out right. I had no idea what made his Tempura so not Tempura. Tempura is supposed to be nice and crunchy outside and fluffy and moist inside. But alas, it was just a big blob of fried butter-coated shrimp, resembling nothing like the ones you get in Japan.

Tempura Shrimp was the only thing Whitney Houston ordered.

"Would you like anything else? *Nigiri* or *Sashimi*?" I asked. I feared she would have nothing else to eat.

"No, thanks," she said firmly. "Oh, just a cup of green tea."

When Pedro brought out her six large Tempura Shrimp with dipping sauce, Whitney picked one up, looked at it carefully, and said, "These are not Shrimp Tempura. Real Shrimp Tempura never looks like this. These are too fat and too thick." I knew it. I was pretty sure she had "real" Shrimp Tempura in Japan.

"I'm sorry, should I send it back, or have the kitchen chef make another one?" I asked.

"No, that's okay," she said, with a disappointed look on her face. She ate three pieces of Shrimp Tempura, paid the bill, and dashed out of the restaurant in less than five minutes without saying a word.

A few months later, I heard about Whitney Houston and Bobby Brown's divorce. I figured they must have been in town to discuss the details. I didn't know what Bobby Brown was going through, but whatever it was, I assumed it must have been a difficult time for him by the way he behaved at the restaurant. But then, only they knew what happened between the two.

*****

One of the regulars at Rock'n Hollywood Sushi was a Mexican singer, Luis Miguel. I saw him at least four times sitting at the Sushi Bar. Every time he visited, all the Latino guys were extremely excited, like kids going to Disneyland. They asked for his autograph and took pictures with him. The way they reacted was charming and comical all at the same time. They would rush back and forth, forgetting that they were still on the clock. Even our general manager was excited about getting his autograph. Waiters would forget to bring out orders, and everyone just flocked around Luis. They probably thought, *Forget work, I'm busy! This is important, do you know who this is? It's Luis Miguel! He's a superstar, bigger than Michael Jackson! Leave us alone!*

I knew of Luis Miguel. I heard his songs and saw him on TV and in magazines, but I had no idea how famous he was in Latin America. When I asked about Luis, Javier said he was the biggest star in Mexico and all of the South American countries, next to Julio Iglesias. He was more

161

famous than the Beatles.

Toshi, Kai, Jun, and I had no interest in Luis Miguel's music. Therefore, to us, Japanese Sushi Chefs, he was just another customer sitting at the Sushi Bar. He was kind and bought us all drinks. He just sat there, talking to people who admired him and never made a scene. I thought he liked seeing other people happy to see him. Luis seemed to enjoy the attention. He was very friendly and had a charismatic aura, infecting everyone around him, but, at the same time, he was relaxed and never made a fuss about being famous. He never demanded anything extra and ordered his drinks, rolls, *nigiri*, and *Sashimi*, just like any other customers. It wasn't his intention to cause a commotion.

Juan was so excited that he left the Sushi Bar, sat next to him, took pictures, and talked to Luis for at least ten minutes. He also had some CDs with him and handed them out to the busboys. They immediately put a CD into the player and blasted the music through the restaurant. All of the Latino guys went crazy, singing and dancing together. All of the non-Latino customers seemed puzzled. *Why is everyone jumping and running around, taking pictures with this guy? What is this music they are playing?*

"Who is that guy?" one of the male customers at the Sushi Bar asked me.

"Luis Miguel," I replied calmly.

"Luis, who?" he said.

"Luis Miguel, the Mexican Singer. He is very famous, God-like in Latin countries. He is as big as Michael Jackson," I explained, but the guy didn't seem to care. It was all right with me, and perfectly all right to Mr. Luis Miguel. He paid attention to only those who cared about him.

*****

I could call it the most exciting encounter I ever had with a celebrity. It happened later on when I was working part-time as a manager at Miyako Sushi. Around 6 PM, I picked up the phone for a reservation request. "Six people for Phillips," the man said, in a low voice. I responded, "Yes, confirming a table for six at 7 PM. Thank you. We'll see you soon." I hung up the phone and didn't give it another thought.

At 7 PM, a tall man walked through the front door. I was talking to the Head Chef, Mako, when another tall man walked in behind him with a group of people. I didn't see his face clearly right away.

"Phillips for six," he said. "We have a reservation at 7 PM." As I looked up, I found myself face to face with Mick Jagger.

Mick!!! I almost shouted his name. I'm sure my mouth was wide open, but I held my breath.

The tall man standing right in front of me was Mr. Rolling Stones, Mr. Mick Jagger himself. I had been listening to The Stones since I was fifteen. When I was first introduced to rock 'n' roll, I listened to Deep Purple, and Emerson, Lake, and Palmer, but then, I discovered The Rolling Stones. I bought almost every Stones' vinyl records and bootlegs I could find and listened to them over and over during my high school years in Japan. I remembered all of the lyrics. I didn't know what everything meant, so I had to look things up in the English dictionary. Lyrics like, *"Pleased to meet you, hope you guess my name"* from *Sympathy for the Devil.* I learned what *Brown Sugar* meant when Mick sang, *"how come you taste so good?"* I had no idea what *Honky Tonk Woman* was about until I understood words like "gin-soaked bar-room queen," and "take me upstairs for a ride." Simply, brilliant.

I clearly didn't know what to say, or how to behave, because I was frozen, with my mouth hanging open. I don't know what happened. All at once, all of the teenage memories and Stones' lyrics poured into my head, like a broken faucet splashing water. I took a deep breath, trying to calm down and act normal. I had a job to do. For a minute, I forgot I was the manager.

"This way, please," I said and escorted Mick and his friends to a table in the center of the restaurant.

I handed out the menus.

"Could I get you something to drink?" I asked.

"A bottle of water," Mick said.

It was a complete surprise. I expected him to order Sapporo or *sake*.

"How about you, sir?" I asked another man from the group.

"Green tea and Evian for me, too," the gentleman said. No one ordered any alcohol.

Mick's friends looked like they were in the music industry, too. I left the table and placed the drink order. I couldn't hear what they were saying, but I assumed it was business. After the waitress brought their drinks and took their food order, I went outside the restaurant to call Toshi.

"Where are you? You are not going to believe this. Guess who is at Miyako, right now?" I said.

"Who?" Toshi said.

"It's Mick. Mick Jagger."

"No way!" Toshi exclaimed.

"Yes, way. It's Mick. It's really Mick." I probably said the word "Mick" more during this phone call than any other time in my life. "I'm not kidding. He is sitting at a table and just placed an order. You should come down. Where are you?"

"...I cannot," Toshi said, after a brief silence. "I am at a Lakers game at the Forum. It would take me over an hour to get there, and by the time I get there, Mick will be gone."

I was a little surprised to hear Toshi's response, as I had thought he would do anything to see Mick Jagger.

"He ordered some food, and they don't look like they are in a hurry. If you leave right now, you might make it." I shouted. Even though I was outside, it was likely that Mick and his friends could hear my voice.

"No, I won't. It's tempting, but I am going to pass this time," he said.

I was speechless again; oh well, his loss.

"Ok, no worries," I quickly replied and hung up.

*****

Toshi always kept a digital camera at the Sushi Bar, in case someone famous walked into the restaurant. He took photos with his high school rock 'n' roll heroes, Gene Simmons, Axl Rose, and Paul McCartney. I didn't have a camera, and this was long before cell phones had cameras.

"Do you have a camera here?" I asked the Sushi Chefs. Mako and Akio.

"No, we don't," Akio replied.

"Would you mind if I go to the gas station across the street to buy a disposable camera? It will only take me two minutes." I asked.

Seeing how excited I was, Mako gave me a permission.

"Thank you, thank you, thank you!" I shouted and rushed out of the restaurant.

I ran across the street and into the gas station, hoping they carried disposable cameras. I looked around and found one hanging by the cashier. I was so relieved, now I could take a picture and prove that Mick Jagger was here. I grabbed one, happily paid $15, and then rushed back to Miyako Sushi. The whole trip took precisely three minutes.

When I got back, Mick and his friends were still there. I must have called three or four of my friends to tell them, but no one was willing to come and see for themselves. Everyone said they were too busy or too far away, which sounded like a typical Los Angelenos' response. I couldn't understand why there were passing up this golden opportunity. But then again, *who cares?* I thought. Mick Jagger was in my restaurant, sitting less than ten feet away from me, eating sushi.

I did everything I could to get close to Mick every chance I had. I started by bringing the food to his table, I poured water and green tea, checked to make sure everything was okay their order, all the while trying to pretend that everything was "normal," even though it wasn't. They must have spent a good hour and a half eating and talking. Everyone finally stood up from their seats and walked to the door, Mick was first. He passed me at the cashier's desk and walked out the door.

My heart was pounding like I was about to ask a girl to the prom. If I missed this opportunity, there wouldn't be another one in the future.

"Excuse me, Mr. Jagger," I said, loud enough for him to hear.

"Yes?" Mick stopped, turned around, and looked at me.

"May I take a photograph with you?" I asked.

"Yes, of course," he said and smiled.

"Thank you!" I shouted and jumped.

I grabbed the disposable camera and handed it over to one of Mick's friends. When I stood next to him, Mick put his arm around me and said, "Here, this is better, yes?" I was immobile.

Mick's friend took one picture, and I was satisfied. I was about to say, "Thank you," and reach for the camera, when Mick said, "Let's take one more."

"Really?" I shouted. I said another big "Thank you" and walked back into the restaurant. One of the customers who was dining at the window seat saw the whole thing, and said, "You were so obvious being excited and calling everyone you know"

The next day, I took the disposable camera to have the pictures developed.

The shop clerk looked at my camera and noticed there were still twenty-two exposures left.

"You only took two pictures. Don't you want to use all of them and bring it back again, so that you get your money's worth?" he asked me.

"Oh, believe me—I got my money's worth. Those two pictures are worth millions to me," I said, grinning from ear to ear.

*****

The former Red Hot Chili Peppers guitarist, Dave Navarro, loved the Seared Tuna *Sashimi* with Avocado and Salsa at Rock'n Hollywood Sushi. He visited us twice, sometimes three times a week, ordering his favorite *Sashimi* every time. Most of the time, he placed a "To Go" order over the phone. He ordered the Seared Tuna *Sashimi* Special so many times that when we saw the order on a ticket, we always guessed it was him. Dave rarely dined in, but when he did, he sat at a corner table with his friends, and remained quiet, hiding from the other patrons in the restaurant. Heath Ledger, Leonardo DiCaprio, Paula Cole, and Anthony Hopkins were exactly the same way. People noticed them only when they entered or exited the restaurant. While they were sitting at a table, almost no one recognized them. Everyone kept a low profile, dressed in regular clothes, and remained quiet. No partying. No *Sake* Bombs. Their behavior was nothing like the weekend Hollywood wannabees.

Celebrities really aren't any different than you or I. They deserve to be treated the same as anyone else, and it would be an insult to treat them differently just because they are famous. Every customer deserves to feel special; every customer deserves to be treated equally. This is what I came to understand after seeing and serving some of the more recognized faces in the entertainment business in LA.

Shortly after Saito-san decided to open for lunch, a middle-aged man started to come in every day.

"I was driving on Sunset and saw your sign saying open for lunch," the man said. "There aren't many places open for lunch in this neighborhood."

The man ordered the same Special over and over. Just like Dave Navarro, he loved the Seared Tuna *Sashimi* with Avocado and Salsa. When I saw him on the fourth consecutive day, I wondered what was going on. While I knew he enjoyed the *Sashimi*, and I knew it was good but was it something I wanted to eat every single day of the week? No.

Then things became more comical. The man started coming in for dinner too, ordering the same *Sashimi*. That was twice in a day. Then, he started bringing his friends with him, "You see, isn't this good?" He often told us that it was the best *Sashimi* he had ever had, which was nice to hear. Since he came in almost every day for a couple of months, we started to prep extra salsa, chopping tomatoes, white onions, and cilantro.

One day, I asked him what he did for a living. He told me he was a musician, and his studio was just around the corner. I didn't think much of it until I saw his CD at the Virgin Mega Store. His first name was Steve, and he was a jazz vocalist. The Billboard Chart on the wall told me that his CD was number one on the chart!

"We saw your billboard on Sunset Boulevard. the other day," I told Steve one day.

"Oh, yes, you did? I am embarrassed. The record company put it up," Steve told me.

"Your CD is #1 on the chart!" I exclaimed.

"Well, yes, it is," Steve said quietly. He blushed.

We congratulated him, and he said, "Thank you." Later, Steve gave each of the Sushi Chefs a signed copy of his CD as a gift. Even though the music wasn't something we enjoyed, we appreciated his kindness. We never told him, some things are just better left unsaid. Looking back now, I wonder, *Is it a coincidence that two different musicians like the same Sashimi Special?* Maybe Steve told Dave, maybe Dave told Steve, or maybe not. Who knows?

STRIPPERS

The neon sign said, "Totally Nude," "Open Late." It belonged to THE strip club, "Body Shop," our next-door neighbor. While Rock'n Hollywood Sushi was the first Japanese restaurant on Sunset Strip, Body Shop was the first all-nude strip club on the Strip. It opened its doors in the 1960s.

Location and convenience. That was what we offered the patrons and employees at the Body Shop. No alcohol is allowed at a totally nude establishment. That's a California law. So, their customers sometimes chose to stop at Rock'n Hollywood Sushi to slam-dunk alcohol before walking into the Garden of Eden next door. They also made sure to have plenty of drinks because the Body Shop had a strict no re-entry policy. If they wanted to drink more, they had to leave, come back to Rock'n Hollywood Sushi, drink more, then pay another $20 cover to go back to the Body Shop again. Bad news for them, good news for us.

"Can we sit at the Sushi Bar? We just want some drinks," two young men asked Toshi. We all knew they were on their way next door, it was written all over their faces, though, they acted like they weren't.

"Of course, no problem," Toshi grinned at them.

They ordered two bottles of Sapporo and a warm *Sake.* They spent less than ten minutes drinking, paid the $25 bill, and left. A quick $5 tip for the Sushi Bar, without making a single piece of sushi.

"Great," Toshi said after they left. "I don't mind more customers like them. More drinks at the bar, the more tips for us. No need to make sushi."

For many of the girls who worked at the Body Shop, we offered a comfortable atmosphere for a quick sit-down meal or a to-go order. Most times, they just sat at the Sushi Bar by themselves, ordered a couple of rolls, ate, paid, and left a good tip.

Most of the girls only spent about fifteen minutes at the Sushi Bar. By sitting there, they knew they could order directly from the Sushi Chefs and have faster service. They were also pretty quiet. They just ate their sushi.

I could tell who they were as soon as they walked in. They typically wore sweat pants and a sweatshirt and always had heavy makeup, perfume, and big, exaggerated hair. After seeing so many of them every day, I started to notice some patterns. They all walked a certain way. They all dressed a certain way. They all talked in a certain way.

"I bet she works next door," Toshi said when a female customer in her twenties walked in.

"How could you tell so fast?" I asked.

"Well, I am not sure, but when you work here every day for eight years, it comes to you naturally," Toshi said, with a grin.

It's interesting how humans adapt to their environment and develop certain senses. We could also tell when a chef walked into the restaurant because of how he talked, how he behaved, and how he spoke. I wasn't exactly sure how we knew, but somehow we did. Similarly, we could tell if a professional escort walked in with a "date," though, we never asked them to confirm it.

*****

"So, have you ever gone out with your customers? Have you ever had sex with any of your customers?" I asked Tammy, a stripper from the Body Shop. She came and sat at the Sushi Bar at least a couple of times a week.

"Wrong idea," she just smiled.

Tammy was a tall brunette. A pretty, 23-year-old girl from Minnesota, who used to dance at Clubs in Vegas.

"I like the customers in L.A. better than the ones in Vegas."

"Why?" I asked, wondering. "Are you suggesting people in L.A. are actually nicer?"

"No, that is not what I am saying. I don't know if L.A. people are nicer than Vegas people. I don't think so. It's just that customers at strip clubs in Vegas are rude and demanding. They have the wrong idea that strippers are easy and willing to do anything for money," Tammy explained, as she took a bite of her Spicy Tuna Roll.

"They also think they can do whatever they want to do in Vegas. They think that if they offer lots of money, we'll meet them in their hotel. You see, only girls who are desperate for extra income would ever visit customers in hotels. It's very dangerous. I never did, and I never will. Here in L.A., the strip club customers are much nicer, they follow the rules, and are gentler, compared to the men in Vegas."

I was shocked. Based on what she just told me, all of the young drunk Valley Boys and Frat House guys that came into Rock'n Hollywood Sushi were actually *nice? Did I have it all wrong? How could it be?*

"So, you have never done a lap dance for your boyfriend, right?" I asked.

"Well, I've done it once or twice, but let me ask you this, do you always make sushi at home for your girlfriend?" Tammy asked me back.

"I don't have a girlfriend, so I don't make sushi at home," I joked. Tammy smiled and finished her Spicy Tuna.

"So, I'm guessing you don't eat that much sushi at home either, right?" Tammy asked.

I liked talking to her because she was quick and intelligent. I never asked about her education, but she was definitely street smart. In our conversations, she picked up on things that most people didn't.

"You are right. I rarely eat sushi at home because I see it and taste it every day here. Other Sushi Chefs are the same. When we go out, we eat Thai food, Ramen, Hamburgers, or Mexican food. I feel as if I don't need to eat sushi. I almost lost interest in eating it. Don't get me wrong. I still love sushi," I said.

"I understand what you are saying, Kaz. You see, it's the same for me. I don't think about sex and naked women because that's what I see every day. So, I don't feel the need to think about it when I'm not working," Tammy winked at me. "Work is work."

She had a very charming smile. I really fancied her.

*****

Every day when I drove into the parking lot at work, I saw the neon sign. Every time I went outside to take a break, I saw the neon sign. The sign was enticing, and I couldn't escape it. I wanted to see *Totally Nude* at the Body Shop after work because they were *Open Late*. So, one day, I casually asked Toshi and Kai if they wanted to go with me. They both showed a complete lack of enthusiasm. As a matter of fact, they both said they weren't interested in going there at all. I couldn't figure it out. It was just like the "I can no longer eat Hamachi" story.

"You can go in there for free because you know the doorman, right?" I asked Toshi.

"Yup, we can. We've been there many times, and you know what? Nothing happens. You look at those naked girls, and then that's it. Nothing. Nada. Zip," Toshi told me.

"I know why you want to go there. I felt the same way before. But I am telling you, If you go there, you will be disappointed. It's like buying a Super Lotto Ticket for $100 million Jackpot. You think you will win, but you never will," Toshi said.

The logical part of my brain understood Toshi's words. Just like a casino in Vegas. The house always wins. Always. I knew he was right, but my testosterone didn't want to listen.

Several months went by, and one day, out of the blue, Toshi and Kai agreed to go with me to the Body Shop after work. I was thrilled! I changed out of my uniform and dashed to the bathroom to wash my hands. I always had to make sure my hands didn't smell like fish whenever I went out after work. Before we left, we each drank a bottle of Sapporo. I felt just like one of the young men we made fun of.

We walked to the front door at the Body Shop. "Hey, fellas. Welcome," the doorman greeted us and escorted us inside. We didn't have to pay the cover charge. I already loved this place! We sat by the stage, ordered two $5 soft drinks, and watched five or six different girls dance on the stage. But that was it. A couple of the girls, including Tammy, recognized us and smiled while they were dancing in front of us.

Tammy stopped at our table to say hello, and we talked for a bit. After a few minutes, she announced, "I've got to go. I have to make some money. I love talking to you, but talking doesn't pay the bills," she said.

She knew I was cheap. She knew I wasn't there to pay $115 for a 15-minute private dance, and so did the other girls. None of the strippers treated us any differently than anyone else. We kept watching the girls on the stage, and all of a sudden, I was bored, tired, and sleepy.

"What's wrong with me? I'm getting bored watching beautiful naked girls," I said to Toshi.

"See? Do you remember what I told you?"

"Yup, you were right. It was not what I expected," I said. But then again, what exactly did I expect anyhow?

After that night, we didn't go to the Body Shop for a long time. The entire experience, however, changed my opinion on a few things. I viewed strippers differently. I viewed women differently. Before I worked at Rock'n Hollywood Sushi, I looked at strippers as an object of desire. I only saw their naked bodies and wanted to have sex with them. I looked down on them. I thought their chosen profession was "dirty." I thought they sold sex. And I was wrong about all of it. When the strippers came into the restaurant, they were just like any other customer, trying to make a living just like everyone else. Just like me. They deserved to be treated exactly the same as anyone else who walked through that door.

In fact, all the girls from the Body Shop liked being treated like everyone else. Sure they were strippers, but only at work, not when they ate at our restaurant. When I was at the Body Shop, they didn't treat me differently. They treated me just like any other customer. I started to understand that every customer deserves respect, no matter who they were or what they did for a living. All of our customers came here for one thing, sushi. Their professions don't matter. It's not my business at all.

*****

Earl was the manager at Rock'n Hollywood Sushi. He was a big Filipino American guy who looked like a big Buddha. So, we called him Big Earl. He reminded us of a famous Hawaiian Sumo Wrestler Champion in Japan, Yokozuna. His official job title was restaurant manager, but we never considered him to be a manager. The only thing Big Earl ever did, it seemed, was to stand by the front door and talk to the valet guys. He also whispered to drug dealers, smoked cigarettes with his so-called friends, and gossiped with other restaurant managers. He even flirted with the strippers. That was it. That was pretty much all that Big Earl did, hung out.

He didn't know anything about restaurant inventory or supplies. He didn't know how many chopsticks we used in an average week. He had no idea what type of dishwashing soap we used, and he couldn't tell the difference between canola oil and olive oil. He also didn't know how to close the register. The only thing Big Earl knew how to do was lock the front door.

"Big Earl doesn't do shit," Kai shouted in Japanese. He must be drunk, his customers bought him a couple of *Sake* Bombs earlier. "He is lazy."

We were all amazed at how Earl managed to hold onto his job. I asked Toshi why they kept him.

"I think Saito-san sees him more like a security guard," Toshi mumbled.

Big Earl was fired several times. But every time he was fired, he was hired back within a week. It was a big mystery to all of us. No one knew why he was fired in the first place, and no one knew why he was hired again. But, everyone knew one thing, Big Earl would be "back again soon."

Earl lived in Pomona, some forty miles east of West Hollywood. He commuted an hour to work at Rock'n Hollywood Sushi and had a girlfriend named Tatiana. She visited Earl every once in a while. She was a petite, cute, girl-next-door type with long brown hair. There was something "innocent" about her that made her different than most of the Hollywood crowd. We had no idea where Big Earl met her, and we never asked. We also didn't know what Tatiana did for a living, and we never asked about that either. I heard a rumor that she wanted to be an actress. Like Emma, I couldn't picture Tatiana as an actress, she just didn't fit into the stereotypical Hollywood image. She seemed too innocent, too naïve.

Earl was pretty serious about Tatiana. He bought her presents and roses each time she came to the restaurant— every single time. A Mexican Flower Lady frequently came into Rock'n Hollywood Sushi to sell long-stemmed roses. She visited all of the couples sitting in the restaurant, present the rose to the guy and slowly say, "That will be $8."

"That's a scam. One rose for eight bucks?" Kai used to say every time the Flower Lady walked in. Kai loved complaining.

"There is nothing you can do when you are on a date and that Mexican lady puts a rose in front of you. She knows you have no choice, if you are a guy, sitting there with your date. She also knows that a guy would never ask how much because it would make him look cheap. So, she can charge whatever she wants, making it pretty fucking expensive like eight dollars, and it's a scam!" He continued.

We used to talk about Big Earl and his girlfriend all the time behind the Sushi Bar. We teased him, saying how even a guy who does nothing can still get a pretty girl like Tatiana. Maybe we were jealous. Toshi, Kai, Jun, and I, all Japanese Sushi Chefs were single, all of the waitresses had boyfriends, and all of the Latino kitchen guys were married.

*****

Tatiana came into the restaurant a lot and followed the same routine each time: Big Earl placed (and paid for) her order, she sat in the very first seat at the Sushi Bar, Big Earl sat next to her, and they talked while she enjoyed her sushi. He also used his employee discount, but he never cheated. That was the only thing that impressed Kai.

"You know some of the waitresses cheat. They try to get free sushi. Big Earl does it right, man," Kai said, looking at the ticket. "I am going to make this order for him."

For the next six months, Tatiana visited the restaurant twice, sometimes three times a week. Then, one day, she stopped coming. We all wondered what happened to her. We all assumed they stopped dating.

"What happened to Tatiana," Toshi asked Big Earl one night.

"We broke up."

"Really?" Kai shouted from the other end of the Sushi Bar.

"Yes, we did," Big Earl sighed.

"How come?" Toshi asked.

"It's complicated."

Even though we were jealous that Big Earl had a girlfriend, I felt sad for him, I thought they made a good couple. They always looked happy together, talking, and eating sushi at the Sushi Bar.

*****

Months went by. One night, a girl came in the front door and sat at the Sushi Bar. She was wearing crystal clear, six-inch heels, the ones you find at a sexy lingerie store on Hollywood Boulevard. I knew she worked next door.

"Spicy Tuna, please," The girl said while I was busy preparing *Ebi*.

"Yes, right away," I stopped my hands and looked up to see her face.

"Tatiana?" My jaw dropped. "What are you doing here?"

"Hey, Kaz," She smiled. "I am working next door now."

Yes, I can see that. It is so obvious. But why? Why work next door to where your ex-boyfriend worked? Couldn't you choose to work somewhere else? The Body Shop wasn't the only strip club in L.A., there were tons of other clubs. Why do you want to work here?

I tried not to show my confusion. I wanted to ask her all kinds of questions, but I decided to keep my mouth shut, it wasn't any of my business. We weren't very close, even when she was still dating Big Earl.

I rushed to make her a Spicy Tuna Roll and handed it to her. She thanked me and told me her new stage name: "Porsche." Porsche ate her Spicy Tuna, drank some green tea, left a good tip, and then left the bar before Big Earl came to work.

"See you later," she smiled. It was the same innocent smile I used to see before she became Porsche.

I couldn't help but watch her walk out of the restaurant in her six-inch heels like a slow-motion scene from a film. I stood still for a minute, trying to digest what just happened.

Later, I mentioned Tatiana/Porsche to Toshi and Kai, who told Emma about it.

"Wow, why would she work next door?" Emma asked. We couldn't agree with her more.

Emma told us Earl was planning to buy her a ring or maybe bought the ring before they broke up.

"A ring?" Toshi asked, with his usual curious tone. "Yeah, what kind?"

"I heard it was an engagement ring," Emma replied.

"Big Earl proposed, and she said no. There was no explanation. She just said something like, not now, maybe later. I don't know exactly what happened," Emma said, as she cleaned up a booth after a large party.

Everyone in the restaurant was talking about Earl and Tatiana. We wondered why she became Porsche after she broke up with Big Earl. The main focus of our discussions, of course, was why she chose to work right next door to Rock'n Hollywood Sushi. If she wanted to get away from Big Earl, wouldn't she work somewhere else? Maybe she became a stripper as some sort of revenge. Making him watch her go to work and take her clothes off right next door.

None of us ever knew why they broke up. Big Earl didn't say much about it, and no one asked him. One thing was certain, Big Earl wasn't happy that Tatiana started working at the Body Shop. For three months, he tried to talk to her every time she came in. But she'd just sit by herself and refuse to speak to him. She still but talked to Toshi, Kai, Jun, the waitresses, and I like she used to. She only ignored Big Earl. Every time I saw her, I wanted to ask her why they broke up, why she became a stripper, and why she worked next door. But, it's my job to treat everyone the same and avoid getting into their personal business too much. At the Sushi Bar, she was my customer, and I was her Sushi Chef. Nothing more, nothing less. And that was all I needed to remind myself.

*****

It was a busy Friday night, order tickets were piling up on top of the *Neta* Case, and the waitresses were waiting for their sushi orders. Lillian switched shifts with Leah, so she was working that night too.

"I knew it. I knew it was going to be busy. I knew I shouldn't work on a Friday night." As usual, Lillian complained, and we ignored her. Once she started complaining, it was best to leave her alone.

"You know what they say? There is no curse when you leave God alone," Toshi said.

Then, a petite girl sitting at the Sushi Bar caught my eye. Every time I looked at her, she looked back and smiled. She already had several bottles of beer with her friends, and Toshi noticed her too, "I think she likes you." he said.

I looked at her again, and she was saying something, but the music was loud, and I couldn't hear her. The stereo was blasting Bon Jovi's *Living on a Prayer,* so I leaned over the Sushi Case and asked, "Hi. I'm sorry. What did you say? I couldn't hear you because of the music."

"Make me something special," she repeated in a loud voice, looking into my eyes.

Toshi and Kai were handling Sushi Bar orders, and I was taking care of the table orders that night.

"Is it okay? Can I make her order?" I asked Toshi. She was sitting in front of him, so technically, the girl was his customer.

"No problem. We can switch, and you can do her orders. I'll take care of the table orders."

"Gee, thanks," I said to Toshi, feeling grateful.

"Hi," I greeted her back. "I think I am going to make you something special. Any fish you like? How about shrimp?" I asked.

"Yes, I love shrimp," she replied with a big smile.

I was excited. It didn't feel like she just wanted food. She was flirting with me, and I quickly picked up on the signs. This was the first time I actually met a girl sitting at the Sushi Bar. I wanted to make her something extraordinary. I wanted to score big on this one.

"Dos Camarones, por favor," I told Javier, the Sushi Bar waiter, who told Alejandro in the kitchen to make two Shrimp Tempura. Javier looked at me with a big grin that said it all, *Yeah, I know what's going on here. I know what you're up to.* I looked over at Big Earl, and he knew what I was up to.

I decided to make her one of my Specials: Double Shrimp Roll.

Each Sushi Chef had his own "Special" roll. Toshi and Kai made the Popeye Roll— Albacore on the inside and Blanched Spinach on the outside with *Bonito* Flakes and *Ponzu* Sauce. Kai's other Special was a Kimchi Roll—Spicy Albacore on the inside, wrapped with Kimchi on the outside. For my Special, I combined a Shrimp Tempura Roll with Spicy Shrimp and called it Double Shrimp Roll. It was beautiful, the Chili Oil Mayo sauce, Orange Tobiko, Fish Egg, and green avocado made it really colorful. It became a popular to-go item among the waitresses, though we never put it on the menu. I wanted to keep it as my very own Special, serving it only to a selected few.

I chopped up some shrimp with my knife, mixed them in a bowl with mayo, masago, chili oil, and shichimi (Japanese seven-chili powder), and waited for the Shrimp Tempura to come out. When Pedro brought out the sizzling hot plate from the kitchen, he glanced over at the Sushi Bar and saw me standing where Toshi usually stood.

"Que Paso? What happened?" Pedro asked Toshi, wondering why he was standing in the back.

"Kaz is busy, you know. Con chica Bonita en Sushi Bar," Toshi said, in his broken Spanish.

I quickly rolled the hot Tempura and cut the roll into eight small pieces.

"Here you go. It's called a Double Shrimp Roll—Shrimp Tempura,

Cucumber, and Avocado inside, Spicy Shrimp on top with Masago, or fish egg. Be careful; it's still hot," I said.

"Wow, this looks great! Nice and orange outside. I love it, thanks!" she replied.

"You're welcome!"

She took one bite and her face light up with a smile.

She asked me how I came up with the Special, "I've never had anything like this before. Did you invent this?"

"Yes," I said confidently.

"It's great. I think you should put it in on the menu."

"Well, okay. I may tell the manager later."

She ordered a couple of other rolls and two more glasses of Sapporo, handing one to me. I stayed at Toshi's station for thirty minutes, making sushi for her and talking. After she stopped ordering sushi, I switched back with Toshi and started on the table orders again.

She noticed I moved away from her seat and had a puzzled look on her face.

"This is my station at the Sushi Bar," Toshi told her. "Kaz stands over there and does table orders."

"What time does he get off?" she asked him.

"Normally, around midnight, but maybe, early tonight."

"Really? That would be nice. I'll wait till he gets off," she said to Toshi, and then looked over at me.

The orders kept coming in, but after a while, things finally slowed down. I was down to the last two table tickets and moved as fast as I could to finish them up. She was still at the Sushi Bar, talking and drinking with the other customers.

It was 11:20 PM. All of the table orders were finished, and there wasn't a line of people.

"I think we'll be fine now. You can go take off now, Kaz," Toshi grinned as if to say, *You owe me one.*

"Thank you!" I smiled back. Without wasting a moment, I dashed off to the bathroom, changed my clothes, and washed my hands and face. I didn't want any trace of fish smell on me tonight. I made that mistake once before. After work, I went out to a bar in Hollywood and met a young, attractive girl. We were talking, and things were going really well, when suddenly she looked at me and said, "Gee, you smell like food. What have you been doing?" And that was it, the end, finito. The girl left, and I smelled my hands; yep, they were fishy. I vowed not to go out after work anymore. Or, if I did, I made sure I washed my hands at least a couple of times after I finished my shift.

As I rushed out of the bathroom, my heart was pounding with excitement. I knew it was going to be my lucky night. I passed by the front door, and Big Earl whispered, "Good Luck!" I smiled back and gave him a big 'thumbs up.' Then I walked over to the Sushi Bar, sat next to the girl, and ordered a beer. Earl brought me a bottle of Sapporo, on the house.

"Thanks, Earl," I said, trying to suppress my smile. He looked at me with the same expression and walked back to the front door.

We drank and did a couple of *Sake* Bombs with the others at the Sushi Bar.

"What's your name?"

"Rosey, I work next door. "

"Oh, really? I don't remember seeing you here before. Many girls come in here and order sushi to go. Is this your first time here?"

"I just started working at the Body Shop, so this is my first time here. I like it. It's nice. You're nice."

"Where are you from, Rosey?"

"I was working in Vegas before I came here."

"Hmm, how was working in Vegas? Did you like it? I heard lots of girls worked there before they came to L.A."

"Yes, the money was good, but I got bored living there. I got tired of all the casinos, you know? So, I decided to move here."

Rosey moved her hands constantly and fidgeted as she talked. I also couldn't tell what she really looked like because she wore a lot of makeup. She seemed nice, and she was attractive, but she really wasn't my type.

My mind was racing, *Should I care if she's my type or not? I'm just trying to score here, and so is she. I've fantasized about this very moment since I started working here.* But, never in my life did I have a one night stand. Never.

I drank another glass of Sapporo.

"Did you get those piercings in Vegas?" I asked Rosey, looking at her eyebrow and nose rings.

"Yes, I have lots of these," she said. She stuck out her tongue, which was pierced with a silver ring. "I also have one under here," she said and pointed the area between her legs.

"Right there? Really?"

"Yup, really, really," Rosey smiled.

"Wow, how does that feel? Did it hurt?"

"No, not really. I mean, it hurt a little when I had it done, but not like screaming pain. Once done, it's not a big deal. It's just there."

"So, what is that for anyway? I mean, how do you use it?"

"Do you wanna see it?"

"Now? You mean now?" That wasn't the answer I was expecting. My heart started to pound again. She was looking directly at me, with her eyes wide open, like holding a biscuit in front of a puppy. I got the sign. I knew she was saying, *Let's get it on!*

"Come on," Rosey said before I had a chance to say anything.

She stood up, took my hand, and we started walking toward the back of the restaurant. I knew where we were going. As we passed by the front door, Earl stood there smiling and gave me a big thumbs up. I gave him a big smile back. Then Rosey pulled me into the boy's room and locked the door behind us.

DRUGS

"Here you go," A customer at the Sushi Bar stood up with a fifty-dollar bill and a small Ziploc bag.

"Thanks," Toshi grinned. His hand moved like a magician's, and before anyone saw it, he hid the bag in his pocket.

The tiny bag contained white powder.

It wasn't something I expected to see, but I did.

"Is that what I think it is?" I asked him. I couldn't hide my shock.

"Yes," he replied calmly.

"But why? Do you do...that?"

Toshi didn't say anything, he just stood there.

Rock'n Hollywood Sushi was the very first Japanese restaurant on Sunset Strip when it opened in the 80s. It was also one of the first rock 'n' roll sushi restaurants in all of Los Angeles, after the infamous California Beach in Hermosa Beach.

The previous owner, Shige, who died of cancer, was a legend, according to Toshi.

"He was energetic and charismatic," Toshi once told me.

Shige was the owner and a Sushi Chef. He came to the restaurant every day, stood behind the Sushi Bar, and made sushi.

"He drank a lot, partied a lot, and did a lot of coke. Shige was friendly, and everyone loved him. Many customers came back to Rock'n Hollywood Sushi because of Shige. He was one of the main reasons this restaurant was so successful," Toshi said. I figured Shige was also the reason for Toshi picking up the drug habit. And then it was Toshi who introduced cocaine to Kai. It was like passing the traditional sushi secrets from one chef to another.

I was confused. I respected Toshi as a skilled chef and as my sushi teacher. He was a good teacher, patient, and gentle, not like some traditional style Japanese Sushi Chefs, who just screamed and threw things at you. But doing drugs while at work wasn't part of my work ethic. I wanted to ignore the drug habit, but it was like trying to hide a cut that was bleeding. I couldn't respect him as a person anymore. In my opinion, frequent drug use is a sign of weakness. Sure, I tried recreational drugs once in a while, but it didn't become a habit, and I would never do it at work every day.

Next, I learned that Juan was a pothead. *What is this?? Am I surrounded by regular drug users and didn't even notice?* I thought.

"You didn't know? Juan smokes almost every day since he started working here. Everyone knows," Toshi told me.

My jaw dropped. I was shocked. Like George Michael coming out of the closet shocked.

"Really? I mean, really, really?" I said. "How can anyone move so fast high?"

"It's a mystery to us, too. We have no idea. If I smoke like Juan, I can never move that fast. In fact, I wouldn't be able to work at all," said Toshi.

"When I smoke pot, I want to be alone. After getting high, I want to stay in my home alone, watch TV or play a video game, so it's quite astonishing how Juan-chan can work after smoking," Kai added.

Since I couldn't figure out how Juan smoked pot every night without slowing down, I decided to just ask him about it.

"It relaxes me," Juan said.

"You never feel fatigued or want to lie down on the floor?" I asked.

"No, not at all," Juan said.

"When I smoke pot, I just want to relax and fall asleep," I said.

"I guess it all depends on your body and chemistry," Juan replied, as he chopped some cucumbers.

"By the way, I heard you used to be in a gang?" I asked.

"You know, I am grateful for Shige giving me the chance to work here," Juan said, looking straight at me." I started as a dishwasher and worked here for one year. Then, Shige moved me to the kitchen. I had never cooked, so they taught me how."

Juan continued. "I learned how to use the knife, how to chop vegetables and make Tempura and Teriyaki Chicken. I learned how to make Miso Soup, too. One day, Shige asked me to help him at the Sushi Bar, and I started learning how to make California Rolls."

"Wow, he actually taught you how to make sushi?" I asked.

"Yes, that's right. He did," Juan said. "If it had been a traditional Japanese Sushi Chef, then I had probably had no chance. But Shige was different. Who would think about training a Mexican to be a Sushi Chef? Without Shige, I wouldn't be here, and I could still be in a gang, and probably would have ended up being shot dead. I owe Shige my life, and now he is gone. I am sad, but I am grateful. I am also grateful to Toshi, who taught me everything I know."

When Juan said he was grateful, I could see he meant it. He genuinely enjoyed everything about the art, craft, and the life of being a Sushi Chef. But smoking pot every day? That I couldn't understand and didn't want to accept, so I just decided to let it go. It was his choice, his life, not mine.

In the two months that followed, I learned that Alejandro, the elderly, petite, dark-skinned Mexican kitchen chef, also used cocaine. He had been working the longest at Rock'n Hollywood Sushi.

"Alejandro was here when I started working eight years ago. The restaurant has been here for over twenty years, so I don't know how long, but I'm sure he has been here a long time," Toshi said.

"I've been working here over twenty years," Alejandro finally told me.

We called Alejandro "Mario" because his mustache made him look like Super Mario. At first glance, Alejandro didn't appear friendly. He was crabby and quiet when I encountered him in the kitchen on my first day. He always looked angry, too, but I couldn't figure out why. I later learned that Alejandro was just a shy and quiet guy. He used alcohol and coke to stay friendly. When he was drunk, he was a lot warmer and more welcoming.

Alejandro did coke at least a couple of times in the evening: once around five o'clock when the restaurant opened for business, and then again after the restaurant closed, around one or two in the morning. On busy weekends, he did it three times a day, sometimes four, Toshi told me

I don't think I ever noticed all of the users at the restaurant because I never did coke in my life. It never sounded fun. So, I never knew how they acted when they were high. Also, no one ever lost control because of the drugs; Toshi, Kai, Alejandro, and everyone else were all professional and did their jobs just fine.

When I asked Toshi why, he told me, "That's because the stuff we take is very, very weak. It's cut quite a bit."

Some of my friends told me how it felt and asked me if I wanted to try it. Every time, I said, no, because instinctively, I knew my body wouldn't like it. My heart wouldn't like it. I have atrial fibrillation, a condition that makes my heart chambers beat irregularly. So, I know that my heart doesn't need an added stimulant, especially cocaine.

Toshi told me it helped him work. It gave him a good vibe, kept him focused and relaxed at the same time. It sounded bizarre. I was unable to comprehend, but that was okay. He did his job. He wasn't mean, he didn't ask me to do unreasonable things, and neither did Kai, Juan, or Alejandro. There wasn't a single reason for me to even remotely suspect that they were doing drugs until they finally told me.

After he told me Alejandro was on coke, Toshi told me about another person who regularly did drugs.

"Did you know Lillian uses coke, too?"

"Lillian, too?" I asked, again surprised.

"Yes, she is high most of the time when she is working here," he confirmed.

"How do you know?" I asked.

"We buy from the same dealer," he said. "Sometimes, she tells us when the dealer comes in."

My jaw dropped again.

"You know she smokes pot at home when she is off. I told you we've been to her house on Hollywood Hills? Her bedroom is Barbie Pink? Well, at home, she is nothing like you see here..." Toshi said.

"Now it makes sense the way Lillian acts, like out of the blue, she just shouts out and screams," I said.

"Yup, that's her," Toshi said.

"Who are the dealers?" I asked Toshi.

"Some of the Latino waiters and busboys, and sometimes the weekend valet and parking attendants, too," Toshi said.

"So, like Javier, the Mexican waiter?" I asked.

"Yes, he is one of the dealers," Toshi said.

"How about Peter, the busboy?"

"Yup, he is too," Toshi said.

It felt like everyone at the restaurant was either buying or selling drugs. Well, everyone except for the managers, the owner, and me. I never looked at any of my coworkers the same way again.

*****

I didn't care if everyone around me did drugs, so long as they did what they were supposed to do, and it didn't affect me. It wasn't any of my business anyhow. But I wasn't going to do drugs on the job because it would change me and my work habits. That was unprofessional. So, I made a rule never to do drugs while working at the Sushi Bar.

But, I guess rules are meant to be broken, and I did do drugs a couple of times at work.

It was Saturday night, a few minutes after midnight. There was a massive pile of order tickets stuck on the check spindle, and the customers already bought Toshi, Kai, and I each three *Sake* Bombs and a large bottle of Asahi. Sunset Strip attracted what we called a "weekend" crowd. Out of towners, Valley Girls, teens, and young males from Pomona, Ontario, Rancho Cucamonga, all drove over thirty miles to come to Hollywood and party. When they flocked in on weekends, it was *Sake* Bomb time. They loved to buy us Sushi Chefs alcohol and drink with us. Some nights, we would be buzzed or drunk by 9 PM.

"It was a busy night, wasn't it?" Toshi said.

"Yes, it looks like things are finally slowing down," I said. I looked around, and there were five large bottles of *sake*, some half full, sitting on the back counter.

"Look at the aftermath," Toshi said. "Those Valley Boys, sure love to buy us drinks."

"I hate *Sake* Bombs," I said. "I don't know who invented them, but they should be punished."

"I agree, but thank God for *Sake* Bombs. The more these Valley Boys drink, the more tips for us without making a single piece of *nigiri*," Toshi said.

"That's true," I said.

I also noticed the *Neta* Case was close to empty.

"We only have one *Maguro saku* left. Should I bring one from the walk-in?" I asked Toshi.

"I bet no more customers are walking in tonight, so let's wait. If we get an order in, then we'll get some," Toshi said.

I agreed. It felt like the night was over, even though we still had two more hours to go. It's funny after you work at a restaurant for a while, you start to foresee the flow of customers. Maybe it's just a hunch, yet, quite often, it's right on the money.

We were all tired and drunk, ready to call it quits for the night.

"I hate this," Toshi said. "Too much *Sake* Bomb and no customers. Nothing is worse than standing here doing nothing for the next two hours. It will only make us more tired."

"I agree," Kai said.

Five minutes of standing at the Sushi Bar felt like an eternity, there were no orders, nothing to do. Emma put a Bob Marley CD in the stereo.

"Hey, do you want to smoke some pot?" Toshi asked. "I got an excellent one."

"Pot?" I said. "I don't know."

"Why not? We won't get any customers in, so we definitely won't be busy. It will be okay. If one of us gets really stoned, there are three of us, so we can cover each other," Toshi said.

We had nothing else to do. We were bored, like passengers waiting for a delayed flight at an airport. *But what about my rule?* I asked myself. *I vowed not to do drugs on the job,* I reminded myself. *Oh, what the hell, most of the customers are drunk anyway. Who's going to notice if we're stoned?*

"OK. let's do it," I said.

We all dashed through the back kitchen and out the back door to the stairs. Toshi took a marijuana cigarette out of his pocket, lit it, and puffed a couple of times. He inhaled deeply, blew out the white smoke, and released an intense smell of weed into the air.

"Wow, it smells great," I said.

"I told you, it's a good one," Toshi said.

We passed the cigarette around a couple of times. I immediately felt my face relaxed. It was uplifting. I felt cheerful, carefree. Before I knew it, everything was in slow motion, I was high. We must have spent ten minutes by the back stairs before we went back inside.

"Hey, where were you guys," Emma asked. "I put a big order in."

We all looked back to the printer—there was a long ticket hanging out.

"Oh shit," we all said. Our voice echoed. Now, I started to panic because I wasn't sure if I could make any sushi at all.

Toshi picked up the ticket, examined it, and said, "I am going to make California and Rainbow Rolls."

Kai looked at it too and said, "Sunset Roll, *Maguro*, and Albacore *Nigiri*."

I was left with four orders of Salmon *Nigiri*.

No problem, I thought. *Thank God all three of us can work on this order together.* I don't think I could do this alone.

I reached out and grabbed one long block of Salmon from the refrigerator, cut a few slices for *nigiri*, wet my right hand in the water, picked up some *shari*, placed a piece of Salmon on top, and formed it all into *nigiri*. The temperature of the rice felt strange.

"*Shari* feels very.... weird. It's kind of warm and cold at the same time," I told Toshi.

"I think you are too high," Toshi laughed.

"I, um, I thi...nk so, so." my voice sounded like poorly digitized music.

Kai heard me and started laughing, too.

"What are you saying, Kaz?" he asked.

"I do..int, know," I said. "I caint maive fast."

I tried to move my hands, but it felt like my body didn't want to cooperate. Like I was at the bottom of the ocean, trying to make Salmon *Nigiri*. After what felt like fifteen minutes, I plated the *nigiri*, looked at my ticket, and made sure I had fulfilled the order. I had no idea how long it took me, but I'm sure I spent a lot longer on it than usual. I hoped Emma didn't notice. That would be embarrassing. Toshi and Kai finished their orders before I did, and after I put the plate on the counter, I went back to drink some hot green tea.

"That wasn't too bad," I thought out loud. "I still cannot believe how fast Juan makes sushi when he is high. I know I can't. It took me like fifteen minutes to make Salmon *Nigiri*."

Emma came around the corner to pick up her order. She picked up the tickets, examined them, and then looked at the plates.

"Hey, there are only four pieces of Salmon here," Emma shouted. "Who made this? It's four orders of *nigiri*, and should be eight pieces, not four."

I turned around and said, "Oh, that was me. I am sorry, I made a mistake."

I quickly picked up the plate and took it back to the Sushi Bar. Even though I told her I was sorry, I must have had a big grin on my face, because Emma looked at me and giggled.

"Kaz, are you drunk?" Emma asked.

"Yes, I am," I lied. "Your order is coming up."

I cut an additional four slices of Salmon and started to make more *nigiri*.

"Gosh, it feels so, so weird," I said to Toshi and Kai, as I grabbed a slice of fish and some *shari*. "It kinda smells strange, like, I don't know, but it just smells strange." Toshi and Kai looked at me and just laughed.

*****

Although I never tried cocaine, I did try some hallucinogenic drugs like acid and magic mushrooms during my college years. After spending three of my college years in Iowa, I enrolled in a small, avant-garde private art college thirty miles north of Los Angeles. The school was known for its wild, out-of-this-world Halloween and Mardi Gras parties, where being naked was the standard costume. For many students, experimenting with drugs was part of their extracurricular activities. It was pretty normal to see everyone 'on' something every day, like seeing your next-door neighbor take his dog for a walk.

I never experimented with drugs on a regularly, unlike my dorm-mate, Greg. He took acid almost every weekend to see what kind of artistic inspiration he would get. I used to see Greg on rollerblades on Saturday afternoons around the swimming pool, giggling, listening to music, and chatting to himself, drawing scribbles in his sketchbook. He told me acid and rollerblading went well together, though, I never saw how that affected his paintings. His graduate thesis piece was a small 300 square foot Gallery, *Suburban Lawn,* filled with green grass, abandoned rusted, galvanized rectangular water tubs, broken bicycles, dirty Barbie dolls, and abstract paintings on the wall. The whole thing made me thing, *Huh??* I had no idea what Greg was trying to express.

Seeing everyone around me doing drugs naturally made me curious. I wanted to try it at least once so I could figure out what everyone was talking about. It wasn't difficult to find drugs at my college. If you asked, you could probably get any recreational drug you wanted within the hour. It was as easy as finding a cup of coffee.

I asked Greg if he could get me some "shrooms," aka magic mushrooms.

"Sure, no problem. I know Vince can get some," Greg said.

"Vince? I know him." I said.

"Are you doing it alone?" Greg said.

"Umm, I don't know. I mean... It's my first time." I replied.

Greg smiled. "If you are doing it for the first time, then you should do with someone. Someone who has done it before," Greg said. "You need a guide because if you don't, you could end up with a bad trip, you know?"

"What do you mean by a bad trip?" I asked.

"A friend of mine went to the desert with her friends and took some 'shrooms, but she drifted away from her friends," Greg started talking. "She couldn't find her friends and thought she lost them, or that they were dead. Suddenly, flowers with her friends' face started to bloom from the sand. She panicked and began to scream until her friends came and found her."

"Really? Flowers with your friend's face? That's scary," I said.

"Yes, that's a bad trip," Greg said. "You need someone cheerful to guide you so that you can have a good, fun trip. You don't want to be negative when you are tripping."

"Ok," I said. "Anything else?"

"Yes. The best temperature for 'shrooms is *78°F*," Greg said.

"*78°F?*" I said.

"Yes, *78°F*. You want a nice and warm place, not too cold. Not too hot, either," Greg said.

"Why not too cold or hot?"

"Because you could have a bad trip," Greg said. I still couldn't imagine what a bad trip would look like.

"One more thing," Greg added. "Be in an open space, not indoors."

"Okay."

*****

"So, that is what happens when you are on a magic mushroom," I explained what Greg told me to Toshi.

"That sounds very interesting," Toshi said. He seemed particularly interested in everything I saw when I was tripping.

"So, You are saying you see things you normally wouldn't?" Toshi asked.

"Yes, sometimes the color of the night sky changes, like purple and pink," I continued. "You start to have funny sensations in your arms and body, and your skin starts to itch, things like that."

Toshi was even more curious.

"The best thing about 'shrooms is that there is very little damage to your body the next day," I said. "When you are on acid, you get exhausted because you cannot sleep all night long. But with 'shrooms, you can if you want to. It's natural, too."

"I want to try it. Can you get it?" Toshi asked me.

"Okay, I will ask a friend of mine."

*****

A week later, I got some magic mushrooms and brought them to work to show to Toshi.

"So, is this it? It looks like dried porcini mushrooms. It smells weird, like a rotten, foul smell. How many should we take? Is this going to work?" Toshi asked a lot of questions, like a kid in a candy store.

"When I tried it, I ate a couple of pieces. Since we don't know how strong they are, we should start with just a few and see how it goes. If we overeat, there is nothing we can do to stop it," I said. "Also, we should wait until we finish cleaning up because once we get going, we won't be able to function normally. We should also go somewhere open, outside."

"Okay, let's wait 'til we are all done," Toshi agreed.

We both waited anxiously for the end of the night, and it was slow. At 10 PM, the restaurant was almost empty, with just two couples sitting in the corner.

"Jesus, cerrado, closed?" Toshi asked the manager.

"No, not yet. If no one walks in within the next half an hour, then we can close," he replied.

"Sounds good," Toshi said.

Five more minutes passed, and no one walked into the restaurant. We sat behind the Sushi Bar and waited, no one put an order in. Toshi started to get anxious.

"Should we do it now?" Toshi asked me.

"Well, we should wait till Jesus tells us we are closed," I said. "We can do it after we are all done."

"How long will it take to kick in?" he asked.

"I say, thirty minutes."

Another five minutes passed, and no customers walked in.

"Should we do it?" Toshi asked again. I looked at the clock, and it was 10:15 PM. I paused for a minute and thought *if we take them now, we should be okay.*

"All right let's do it," I said. I grabbed the small Ziploc from my bag and picked up two of the dried mushrooms. When I was about to hand them to Toshi, Jun said, "Can I try it, too?"

Both Toshi and I looked at Jun, surprised.

"Really, Jun, do you want to try too?" Our voices echoed.

"Yes, I would like to try," Jun said.

We were stunned. Jun didn't drink, he didn't do drugs. He was a hard-working Sushi Chef, and we never thought he wanted to try magic mushrooms.

"Umm, okay. Here..." I handed Jun the ones I was going to give to Toshi.

"Thanks," Jun said.

I picked two more pieces, gave them to Toshi, and took two for myself. After we ate the magic mushrooms, we sat at the end of the Sushi Bar, waiting for Jesus to say, "Cerrado, closed."

After ten minutes, I started to feel a familiar tingling sensation in my arms.

"Hey, I feel it. I feel something. Do you?" I shouted.

Toshi looked at me. He seemed excited.

"Yes, I am feeling something."

"Me, too," Jun said.

I knew what came next, a big wave of happy, uncontrollable laughter. But it would probably be another five minutes or so. I looked at the clock. It was 10:40 PM.

"Hey, Jesus, cerrado?" I asked.

Jesus looked at his watch, looked outside, closed the front door, and locked it.

"Cerrado," he said.

"Okay, let's go," I said. I knew we had less than ten minutes before we started getting out of control. Thank God no customers walked in; we were in no shape to make sushi.

Toshi, Jun, and I started to clean up the Sushi Bar as fast as we could. We only cared about putting the leftover fish back into the walk-in. We knew we did a horrible job of cleaning the *Neta* Case, but we also knew there was nothing we could do about it. By that time, we were all being careless.

While we cleaned, I felt more tingling sensations spreading through my body. I felt funny, but a good kind of funny. I looked at both Toshi and Jun and said, "Don't you feel funny? Isn't this fun?"

As I looked at them, they looked back at me, and then I burst out laughing. When I started laughing, they started laughing, too. We were out of control.

"Yes, I see you, it's funny. I know it's not funny, but it's hilarious. It's hysterical!"

Our laughter filled the empty restaurant. Luckily, Jesus was outside, smoking cigarettes, and talking to the valet guys. Music played loudly in the restaurant. Emma counted her tips. *No one noticed*, I thought.

"Let's go see Alejandro in the kitchen," Toshi said.

"That sounds like a plan," I said, still laughing hard.

We walked down the side pathway to the back kitchen and approached Alejandro by the stove.

When we looked at him and laughed uncontrollably for a few

minutes. Alejandro looked at us with a blank face.

"What are you guys laughing at," Alejandro asked. He did not look amused.

"Alejandro, say the line, that funny Japanese line we told you," Toshi said.

"No," he said. He looked at us and realized we were 'on' something. He lit his cigarette and started smoking.

"Oh, look! He's smoking!" I shouted. Toshi, Jun, and I started laughing again, pointing our fingers.

"Oh, come on, say it, say it please," Toshi asked again, still laughing.

"Yes, of course!" Alejandro said in Japanese. It was a line from a famous TV comedy show.

We all started laughing, so he repeated the same line one more time, "Yes, of course!"

We laughed and laughed and laughed for a good five minutes. I was laughing so hard that my stomach hurt. I tried telling myself to stop laughing, but I couldn't.

Another few minutes of uncontrollable laughter echoed in the kitchen. When we were finally able to gain control, I told Toshi that we should go outside, somewhere open, like Santa Monica Beach.

"We could drive there and be there in thirty minutes. It's a good place to be because no one will be there, and it's a wide-open space. No bad trip when you are in a wide-open space, my friend told me. We'll lie on the beach and look up the sky. It'll be beautiful," I said.

"Okay, let's go there, then." Toshi agreed.

We weren't laughing anymore, which was a sign that we started a different stage of tripping. I knew the next stage would contain some visual hallucinations and altered emotional states.

We dashed upstairs, changed, and hopped into my car. At that time, I drove a convertible and put the top down. It was a beautiful drive down Sunset Boulevard. It was a little chilly that night, and my body started to shiver. I thought, *what if we get in an accident?* I quickly told myself that everything was going to be okay. *Everything is going to be okay.*

All of the neon signs and streets were shining, sparkling like jewelry, everyone walking down the street looked cheerful. When we finally arrived at Santa Monica Beach, it was a lot darker and quieter than on Sunset Boulevard. No one was walking around, and I started to feel lonely and sad. We parked in a residential neighborhood and walked over to the beach. Once we got out of the car, I thought I was having a panic attack. *Someone's going to notice us. Someone's going to find out we're on 'shrooms. What if that someone is a cop?* Toshi stood by the open car door, and I shouted, "Hurry, hurry, close the door, close the door!"

Toshi looked distressed.

"Close the door," I kept yelling, "It's melting! Close it before someone comes and sees us! You see, everything is melting!"

Of course, the door wasn't melting. I didn't even see the door melting. I had no idea what I was saying.

Toshi closed the door and shook his head.

"Hey, are you okay?" he asked. I came to a halt, looked around, and saw that no one was around, just us. Nothing was melting. Everything was quiet. Everything was fine. The only thing that wasn't quiet was me shouting, "Melting, melting!"

"I am okay now. Sorry," I said.

We walked around the beach and saw flashing colorful lights in the sky: purple, orange, yellow, and red. We laid down on the sand, but it wasn't the 78°F I hoped it would be. It was more like 60°F, with a cold Pacific Ocean breeze blowing in from the dark ocean. After about ten minutes in the sand, we were so cold. We decided to walk back to the car, and that was the end of our magic mushroom night.

SAKE BOMBS

"*Sake* Bomb! *Sake* Bomb! *Sake* Bomb!" Six young men and women seated at the back of the restaurant shouted, slammed the table, and each chugged a large glass of beer.

When they slammed the table, it made a loud noise that caught everyone's attention.

"What the hell was that?" I looked at the table.

"Oh, it's just young college kids, getting drunk," Toshi said.

After all six of them finished emptying their glasses, they cheered. Some of the other customers joined in, and they all started clapping like someone just scored a touchdown.

"What are they doing? What are they cheering for?" I said.

"It's called *Sake* Bomb. It's kind of like a drinking game," Toshi explained.

"What is a *Sake* Bomb?" I asked.

"It's really awful. It tastes awful. I have no idea who invented it, but whoever did should be shot," Kai said.

"How does it work? Why were they banging the table?"

"They put a glass of warm *sake* on top of the beer glass," Toshi said. "They drink it together with the cold beer."

"Warm *sake* with a cold beer? It does sound awful," I said. "How do they keep the *sake* glass on top of the beer glass?"

"You place chopsticks on the beer glass and put *sake* glass on top of the chopsticks. Slamming shakes the table, which causes *sake* glass to drop into the beer," Toshi explained.

"It sounds pretty stupid," I said.

"Well... yes, but then people do lots of stupid things when they are drunk," Toshi added.

"How was it?" Emma asked one of the young men.

"It was awesome," he said. "We are going to do another one. Do you want to join us?"

"No, no. I am sorry. Waitresses aren't allowed to drink while we're working," Emma said. It was a total lie but a good one. I'd seen her and the other waitresses get drunk many times before.

"Okay," the young man said. "How about those three Sushi Chefs over there?" He pointed to us, standing at the Sushi Bar, watching.

"Let me go ask them," Emma smiled.

"Oh, no," Toshi whispered, shaking his head. "I think we just got a *Sake* Bomb coming."

Emma came up to the Sushi Bar and asked Toshi if we would accept the offer for a *Sake* Bomb.

"Why not," he said reluctantly, looking at Emma. "I prefer just Sapporo, but hey, it's all for the tips, right? *Sake* Bomb is more expensive, so we'll go with *Sake* Bomb."

Emma looked back to the booth and raised her thumb.

"Yay!" all six of them raised their hands in the air and ordered another set of *Sake* Bombs for themselves, plus one for Toshi, Kai, and me.

"Well, Kaz, this is your lucky night. You get to taste your first *Sake* Bomb," Toshi giggled.

"Oh, boy. I can hardly wait," I said.

"I wish I had your job," Big Earl chuckled.

"Shut up," Toshi said.

Within a minute, Emma brought out nine sets of *Sake* Bombs on her small, black round tray.

"Here you go, guys," Emma handed us three sets and took the rest over to the booth.

Toshi and Kai split their chopsticks and placed them carefully on top of the beer glass. "So, who invented the *Sake* Bomb?" I asked.

"No one knows. Some say a soldier in Japan during WWII came up with the idea. Others say some Japanese businessmen watched several New Yorkers drinking Boiler Makers and tried it with *sake*," Toshi said.

"We all know it's an American invention, just like a California Roll," Kai said. "No Japanese would think of putting cheap, warm *sake* into cold beer. Americans don't know the difference between good *sake* and bad *sake*."

We all carefully placed our beer glasses on top of the *Neta* Case so that everyone could see. We then put the cup of warm *sake* on top of the chopsticks, ready to make its dive into the beer.

"Ready?" Emma shouted loud enough, so everyone in the restaurant could hear her. All six college kids were standing on the seat of the booth now, ready to hit the table with their tightly closed fists. All the other customers were watching.

"*Sake* Bomb," Emma said.

"*Sake* Bomb," Toshi, Kai, and I said.

"*Sake* Bomb!" The six kids shouted, and everyone banged the table.

As the *sake* cup dove into the beer, we all lifted our glass and poured the golden liquid straight down our throats. I felt the cold beer first, followed by the uncomfortable warm feel and taste of cheap *sake*. I emptied the beer and raised my glass first. Toshi was next, and then Kai, then the three boys, and finally the girls.

"Sushi Chefs win!" Emma shouted as the entire restaurant stood up, cheered, screamed, and started clapping.

"Ahh, this tastes terrible," I said to Toshi, who had a very sour look on his face. "You look just like how I feel right now."

*****

Fridays and Saturdays were our busiest nights at Rock'n Hollywood Sushi. I called the weekend "amateur night" because, on weekends, the restaurant was flooded with all of the Hollywood wannabees. Partying, drinking, and eating sushi, like that's what all the celebrities do. Anyone who worked at a restaurant or bar in L.A. knew that's not how the stars liked to party. If and when they did, they went somewhere else, like a private mansion somewhere on top of Hollywood Hills. A place where none of the Orange County chicks, San Fernando Valley Boys, or Inland Empire Latino *amigos* would ever go. Even if they knew where the celebrity parties were, they wouldn't be able to get in. So, they drove over 30 miles from Orange County, down to Sunset Strip, just to get a taste of Hollywood.

I'm not sure why, but for some reason, the weekend amateurs think that buying a drink for the Sushi Chefs is a Japanese custom. It is not.

Some customers order drinks for the Sushi Chefs as soon as they walk in the door, even before they have a chance to sit down and order their own.

"Here you go; these are from those guys over there." Emma brought us two bottles of Sapporo.

"What do you mean? They just walked in," Toshi said, looking perplexed.

"They wanted to buy you a drink," Emma smiled.

"When did they order this?" Toshi asked.

"Before they sat down," she told him.

"That's fast. Why are they so anxious to buy us a beer? Are they looking for something in return? We won't give them extra sushi just because they bought us a beer," Toshi said. He had a big table order and four customers at the Sushi Bar. Kai was busy serving a table of six, and I had a medium-size table order too. We were all busy and not in the mood to drink, at least not yet. The night was still young.

"They're just being nice, I suppose," Emma said. "Why are you so surprised? Don't you want to drink beer?"

"In Japan, not every customer offers the Sushi Chef a drink. Only regulars offer a drink to the chef," I explained to Emma. "You see, it's like buying a drink for your friend. Unless you are a friend, it's considered impolite and inconsiderate to offer a drink to a chef. We don't know them, and they are not regulars. Besides, we are considerably busy with orders right now."

"So, you are saying they shouldn't have ordered you a drink," Emma said.

"No, what I am saying is they should have asked, that's all," I said. "Now we have to stop our work, drink with them, and say, *kanpai*. It slows us down."

"I see," Emma said. "Do you want to send it back?"

"No, we'll drink it now," Toshi said. "Let's do *kanpai*, Kai."

Kai was busy taking orders from customers at the Sushi Bar, so we had to wait a few minutes before he was ready to grab his glass full of beer. We all looked at the two guys who bought the drinks and shouted, "*Kanpai*," or cheers, chugged the beers, and get back to work.

"Thank God it was Sapporo, not warm *sake*," Toshi sighed.

"I agree," Kai said.

"How come you prefer Sapporo over warm *sake*?" Emma asked.

"Because the *sake* we have is so cheap, it's bad," Toshi explained. "All the warm *sake* is cheap and gives you a bad hangover and a headache. This Sapporo is brewed in Japan, so it tastes better than. this Asahi, which is brewed in Canada."

"I will make sure to tell the customers you like Sapporo than Asahi and *sake*," Emma smiled.

"Oh, and no *Sake* Bombs, if you can," I added.

"Well, that's a tough one," Emma giggled. "They all want to do *Sake* Bombs, and they want to do them with the Sushi Chefs, so I can't stop that one."

On weekends, we worked until 2 AM, and working at the Sushi Bar is a physically intense job, ten-hour shifts, always on your feet. Sure, it's nice to be able to drink for free, but when you do it for three, sometimes four nights a week, you just get tired. We always had to pace ourselves to avoid being drunk before midnight.

Kai wasn't a strong drinker and had trouble pacing himself. He did, however, drink more often than anyone else did at the Sushi Bar. It only took about three or four drinks before Kai started talking "shit," like a rapper from South Central Los Angeles.

It was funny listening to Kai talk when he drank. None of it made sense a bit of sense to anyone else, but he didn't care. He'd look at an order ticket, start mumbling, then shout, laugh, and imitate what he thought was a brother from the 'hood talking to his homeboys.

"This is da shit, you know what I'm sayin'," Kai used to say. He used the phrase, 'you know what I'm sayin,' more than anything else, and for a while, I thought that was all the English he knew.

On a good day, when customers bought us a drink, we'd say, "Yes, excellent. We were thirsty!" On a bad day, we'd say, "Oh, no. We had too much to drink last night." Good days came when we were awake and felt great. Bad days happened when we drank too much the night before. Usually not because we chose to, but because too many of our customers bought drinks, *Sake* Bombs included.

"We have to do something about this," Toshi said. "We are getting too many drinks again tonight. We will be wasted before 10 PM."

"Here you go," Lillian said, bringing three large bottles of Sapporo and a bottle of warm *sake* to the Sushi Bar.

"Do you have to do this?" Toshi asked Lillian.

"Come 'on," Lillian tapped his shoulder, obviously amused. "You can do this. You are a strong Sushi Chef." she giggled.

We all raised our glass in the air, smiled, and looked to the customers who had bought us drinks.

"I sometimes feel like a monkey in a cage, you know?" Toshi said.

"I know what you mean," I said to Toshi. "I don't want to drink this."

"I don't either," Toshi said. "To entertain the customers is one of our job duties. They are watching us, so we have to drink it."

"Oh, boy," I said.

I started to sip the beer and closed my eyes, but I just couldn't swallow it. When I opened my eyes, I still had beer in my mouth. Since no one was watching me, I squat down and spit the beer into the sink.

"What are you doing, Kaz?" Kai asked.

"I am not drinking tonight," I said.

"Did you just spit out the beer into the sink?" he asked.

"Yup, that's what I did," I said. "No one can see me when I am down inside of the Sushi Bar. Besides, they are too busy drinking."

"That is brilliant," Toshi said. "All we have to do is say, '*Kanpai*,' with them, raise the glass, drink, and hold it until they get busy drinking their beer, and then, we can spit it out when they are not looking."

SHIGE

Shige was a legend and ahead of his time. He opened Rock'n Hollywood long before sushi was popular among Los Angelenos. He came to work and drank with the customers and with the staff every night. He drank Sapporo and did *Sake* Bombs. A lot of them.

Toshi always told me Shige was an energetic, affectionate, and charismatic person. Everyone loved him. A lot of customers became regulars at Rock'n Hollywood Sushi because of him, and it quickly became the *hot spot*, even for celebrities.

"It was very popular back then," Toshi explained. "I have been here only eight years, but I heard many stories like people having sex in the back parking lot and about drug dealers. People partied a lot harder back then."

The success of Rock'n Hollywood Sushi brought lots of money to both Shige and Saito-san. One day, they decided to buy another sushi restaurant: Sushi Suzuki in Beverly Hills.

*****

To say the least, Sushi Suzuki was an interesting, unique place. "It is more like a problem child because of the working conditions, the ambiance, the service, the people, the chefs, and the waitresses." Kai told me, "The food doesn't have a good reputation, either."

Both Toshi and Kai filled in there on several occasions. They both told me that it was a horrible experience. The Sushi Chef, Hachi, always argued with the customers, waitresses, kitchen staff, and even the owner.

"Quite frankly, I don't think he should be working at the Sushi Bar," Toshi said. "Hachi would use his *Sashimi* Knife to point at you when he gets angry. He uses his knife like the pointing stick during a business presentation. He reminds me of my high school teacher. It's scary. I mean, imagine you are sitting at a Sushi Bar, and the Sushi Chef points a sharp knife at you, toward your face."

"Really?" I said, shocked.

"Knife is not a weapon. It's not a pointer. It's for cutting fish. You should never point it to anyone, especially when you are upset."

"What exactly is wrong with Sushi Suzuki?" I asked Toshi.

"Well, now Shige is gone, and no one listens to Saito-san at the Sushi Suzuki. They just do whatever they want to do. You know here at Rock'n Hollywood Sushi, we listen to Saito-san's directions, even though we don't always agree with them," he offered.

Toshi said Saito-san both used to share recipes and Specials with the Sushi Chefs at Suzuki, but no one ever made any of them, not even once. Well, technically, they made them once, in front of Saito-san, when he told them to try, and that was it. After Saito-san left the restaurant, it was back to the same old menu and the same old Specials. They did keep things on the menu and pretended like they were serving them when Saito-san walked in.

"What do they do if and when a customer orders that Special?"

"Very simple. They just say, 'Sorry, we are out,' or 'Oh, that Special? We don't make it anymore."

How could a restaurant function like that? I wonder.

Sushi Suzuki, however, was a popular place, with a lot of regular customers. It ran entirely on its own, like a plane on autopilot. All the stories Toshi and Kai told me were horrible, but somehow it was still in business, something had to be working.

"Hey, I just remembered I did visit Suzuki, a couple of years ago with my friends," I told Toshi.

"Really? Why did you go there?" Kai shouted across the Sushi Bar.

"I did not choose. It was my friend who called me to meet him there," I told him.

"Did you meet Hachi, and did he point at you with his *Yanagiba*?" Kai asked.

"No, I don't think so. I did not see any chef like that. I sat at a table," I said. "I don't even know who Hachi is now. I only hear about him from you and Toshi."

"Oh, I'm sure you'll meet him someday," Kai said.

JUAN

It was a Wednesday evening, at 7 PM.

As I was looking down at the cutting board, putting *shari* on a sheet of *nori,* I heard someone in. When I looked up, I saw Juan.

"Hey, Juan. What are you doing here on your day off?" I asked.

"I thought I would come here for dinner. I brought my family," he said.

"What family?"

"My children."

"Your...children? What? You have one, two... oh my God, three children? When did that happen?" I asked.

When I looked back down at my cutting board, I saw that the *nori* and rice were all soggy. *Well, that's no Bueno*, I mumbled to myself.

"I don't believe it. You're a father? You didn't tell me for the last six months, and now you tell me?" I asked.

"Hey, kids, let's eat some sushi," he shouted with a grin.

*****

Juan was a Mexican Sushi Chef at Rock'n Hollywood Sushi. He was twenty-five, short, with a mustache and short dark black hair. Everyone loved Juan because he worked hard. He did exactly what he was asked to do and was dedicated to mastering his craft. He was also friendly, got along with his co-workers, and never caused any problems.

Mainly, I liked Juan because he respected both Toshi and Kai. He understood the seniority culture of the Japanese kitchen, he probably learned that from Shige years before. He didn't just use words like 'Sensei' (teacher), and 'Senpai' (Senior), but he meant them. He had respect for anyone who knew more than he did in the kitchen. That type of respect doesn't come easy to everyone.

It amazed me how quickly Juan made sushi, too, especially once I learned about his drug habits. He could make a California Roll faster than anyone else at Rock'n Hollywood Sushi. In fact, he may be the fastest sushi roller I've ever worked with.

Juan also called me Kazu instead of Kaz. I liked that about him too. I found it charming.

MIYAKO SUSHI

After six months of working at the Sushi Bar, I was used to doing all of the prep work and setting up the Sushi Bar by myself. I learned how to serve the customers at the Sushi Bar. I still couldn't make great *nigiri* or *Sashimi*, but I was slowly getting better.

"Hey, Toshi, did you hear the rumor that Saito-san bought another sushi restaurant, Miyako Sushi of Tokyo?" Emma asked as she set the tables.

"Miyako?" Toshi asked back to Emma.

"Yes, Miyako on Ventura Boulevard. You know, the one on the other side of Hollywood Hills in Studio City?"

"I know where it is," he replied.

"You know Miyako?" I asked.

"Yes, of course," Toshi mumbled.

"What is the matter?"

"I cannot understand it. Why Miyako?" Toshi squinted his eyes.

I had never heard of Miyako, but it was obvious that both Toshi and Kai knew. Something was wrong with this picture.

"Why Miyako" Kai shouted. His voice echoed in the empty restaurant.

"I know," Toshi said. "It doesn't make sense."

"Why it doesn't make sense?" I asked.

"Miyako is a totally different restaurant from us. It's not a rock 'n' roll sushi place. It's a place to eat. It's quiet. It's nothing like here," he explained.

I was shocked and surprised all at the same time. Shocked because we just learned the news casually from a waitress, not from Saito-san himself. I also felt like he was hiding something, even though we all know he wasn't the best communicator. I was also surprised to learn that our newly-acquired sister-restaurant was so much different from

Rock'n Hollywood Sushi. But the idea of having a new sister restaurant was intriguing.

For the next few weeks, the mystery Miyako Sushi became the center of our conversation. Since Saito-san hardly came into the restaurant, no one got a chance to ask him about it. Kai asked the manager, but he didn't seem to know anything either.

*****

Miyako had a high ceiling with dark wooden beams and white walls. It reminded me of an old-style Japanese house. It was cozy and a quiet, a perfect spot for a sit-down dinner for couples on a date. Customers expected good food and good service. No *Sake* Bombs. No dancing. No drugs. No rock 'n' roll, and definitely, no strippers.

Saito-san walked in during a slow night and told Toshi about the new restaurant.

"Yes, we heard," Toshi said, without changing his expression. The air became tense.

"I decided to buy it because the previous owner is retiring."

"Isn't it old?" Toshi asked as if he didn't know.

"Yes, thirty years, I think. But it's a good place. It does good business. We are going to make it better." Saito-san sounded confident. Toshi didn't look convinced.

Saito-san then looked over at me and said, "So, Kaz, do you want to work at Miyako?"

I froze. I was stunned.

"Ummm, you want me to go to work there and not here?" I liked working at Rock'n Hollywood Sushi. I liked working with Toshi, Kai, Juan, and the waitresses. I didn't want to leave, but I didn't want to tell that to Saito-san.

"I want you to go there a couple of times a week. You can still work here too," Saito-san replied.

Toshi looked like he had something to say, but he kept his thoughts to himself.

"Okay, but why do you want me to go there? What do you want me to do?" I questioned Saito-san.

There were a lot of *why's* in my head, and nothing made sense.

Why me? Why not Toshi or Kai? Am I qualified? No... I'm still learning, I only have six months of experience. I still can't slice Sashimi well enough, and I don't know how to fillet fish. Is that okay?

"I want you to watch and learn what they do and inform me of what they are doing. You will be a Sushi Chef and an assistant manager there," Saito-san said.

"An assistant manager?" I asked, shocked again.

"Yes, assistant manager."

"How about a Sushi Chef?"

"That, too."

Saito-san turned around and looked at Toshi, who was prepping some shrimp.

"Toshi-chan, would that be okay? Kaz can work two days over at Suzuki, and three days here?"

Toshi didn't look up from his cutting board, "I suppose that is fine. I need to work out the schedule, shift things around."

"That's fine." Saito-san agreed.

"We need him on the weekend, so can we send him on Tuesday and Wednesday, and he can work here on Thursday, Friday, and Saturday?"

"Yes, that works," Saito-san nodded. Then he turned back to me, "I want you to get more training over there. You let me know everything that happens at Miyako."

"Are you asking him to be a spy?" Kai giggled from the other end of Sushi Bar.

"No, not a spy. As an assistant manager, your job is to oversee the restaurant's operation and report to me. This way, the old employees at Miyako don't get suspicious."

"That is spying," I said.

"Well, it depends on the perspective. Either way, there will be a lot to learn. The menu, Specials, prep, ordering, POS systems, and so on. We need to make it better."

Why fix it when it is working just fine? I wondered but refrained from asking.

Then, I suddenly remembered something Saito-san said to me during my interview, "Rock'n Hollywood's destiny depends on you."

I never understood why he said that to me, someone without any sushi experience at all. I always wondered if he was serious or just joking with me, but I never did ask.

Everything happened so fast. I was excited about the new opportunity and my new title. But, at the same time, I was nervous. *Can I meet Saito-san's expectations? Am I carrying the restaurant's destiny on my shoulders?* I wasn't exactly sure how to react.

After my shift, I went home and reflected on all the events of the night. I tried to make sense of things and only came to one conclusion: *nothing made sense, but everything felt right.*

I felt excited about my new job title. I felt excited about a new restaurant. I felt excited about my new co-workers. I felt excited about learning all of the new and different ways to prep. I felt like I was starting a new job without quitting my old one. Chances like this are very rare, I felt lucky.

These last six months here at Rock'n Hollywood Sushi prepared me to work at Miyako Sushi.

*****

I met Akio, Mako, and the kitchen chef, Roberto, on my first day at Miyako. I also met a Japanese waitress, Miki, who happened to be Hachi-san's wife. I automatically expected Miki-san to be rude because of the stories I'd heard about her husband.

I was pleasantly surprised to find that Miki-san was a really nice person. *Don't make snap judgments,* I reminded myself. I never asked Miki-san about Hachi, or their relationship, or any of the stories I heard about Hachi-san's behavior. I figured it had nothing to do with us working together at Miyako. She was a professional worker, and I respected that.

Miki-san was, without a doubt, an excellent waitress. She kept her eyes on her customers, anticipated their needs, and watched and expedited her orders smoothly and efficiently. I could count on her to do her job, and when she was working, everything went smoothly. She had been there for over six years, and she gave me great advice and suggestions.

I enjoyed working with Miki-san, and I knew the customers did too.

*****

Miyako's two Sushi Chefs, Akio and Mako, appeared to be extraordinarily good at their job. They were nice on the surface, seemed to be cooperative, and were always polite and attentive. While Saito-san thought everything was okay, but I always sensed that something was off.

Saito-san planned to change Miyako, once everyone started figuring that out, things looked a lot more like a hostile corporate takeover. The staff was uncertain. They were used to the old ways of Miyako, and I understood that. And even though I worked in the same restaurant with them, under the same new owner, I was on a different side of the fence. I was on the new owner's side, and they were on the old owner's side. Akio and Mako became defensive and weren't open to all of the sudden, radical changes Saito-san proposed.

I was in an awkward position. On the one hand, I disagreed with most of Saito's ideas, but on the other hand, I couldn't share my thoughts with Aiko or Mako because it would only create confusion.

I knew Saito-san wanted Miyako to be more like Rock'n Hollywood Sushi. He suggested new dishes, a new menu, new décor, new fish, new Specials, new music, and almost everything new.

My job was simply to learn how the old staff ran the restaurant and report back to Saito-san. Akio and Mako knew I was watching them, so they were careful, following all of Saito-san's requests, at least when I was around. I have no idea what they said or did behind my back. Instead of worrying about it, I decided not to care, which made me feel better.

*****

Later, I learned that Akio and Mako kept their emotions to themselves. They agreed to our requests, but when we left, they didn't always follow through.

Saito-san wanted to make Miyako more profitable, increase sales, bring in more customers, and sell more sushi. More of everything. I disagreed with all of it. I thought we should do exactly the opposite: simplify the menu and have only one signature dish. I always thought to have the 'Best Spicy Tuna' in town was enough, but Saito-san didn't agree. He pushed his ideas, and it was frustrating to me. I'm sure it was also frustrating to Akio and Mako.

Saito-san wanted to add a new Sashimi Special to the menu—Crispy Albacore Sashimi: slices of seared Albacore Tuna, with Fried Red Onions and Orange Spicy Citrus Ponzu Sauce. It was already a very popular dish at Katsuya, just a few blocks down the street on Ventura Boulevard.

"I don't think it's a good idea," Mako said. "It's a Special from Katsuya, isn't it? We are stealing it, so that's not good."

"Well, let's try to see if we can change something, "Akio said. Akio seemed more open to new ideas, but I wasn't sure if he was just pretending to be cooperative.

He took out a small notebook and started to flip through the pages, "I think it's somewhere here..."

"There, here it is!" Akio exclaimed. "Spicy Ponzu Sauce. I think this will go well with Albacore Sashimi. It has soy sauce, rice vinegar, sugar, mirin, orange juice, chili sauce, and red peppers."

"It sounds good," Mako said. "Let's make one right now and see how it tastes."

To me, Mako appeared to be merely following whatever Akio said because Akio was the Head Chef.

Saito-san watched us mix the sauce. In a matter of minutes, the hot Orange Ponzu Sauce was ready. Akio then seared the Albacore, using a handheld torch, sliced the fish, and we had a small plate of Sashimi that smelled incredible. We all dipped into Akio's sauce.

"This is good," Saito-san said first.

"I think so too," Akio said.

"I agree," I said.

Mako, however, didn't say a word.

"Very good. We are going to put Seared Albacore Sashimi with Spicy Ponzu Sauce on our new menu," Saito-san declared.

*****

Every time Saito-san suggested something new, the Kitchen Chef, Roberto, fought back. "Oh, that is not good. It won't work." When asked why he felt that way, he always answered, "Because we've been doing it this way for over fifteen years, so there is no need to change it."

Roberto was a Mexican chef who worked at Miyako since it opened some fifteen years earlier. From the outside, Roberto looked like an ordinary Mexican chef in a Japanese kitchen. But, he reminded me of a typical stubborn, old Japanese chef - very loud, outspoken, emotional, and angry. There is a Japanese word, Ishi Atama (Stone-Headed), or someone who is headstrong. I assume that the Japanese chef who taught Roberto was Ishi Atama, too.

Roberto was an excellent kitchen chef. To this day, he is the most skilled Japanese kitchen chef I've ever worked with. He expedites every order, and all of his dishes come out perfectly. He rarely makes a mistake, and his food always tastes great. In fact, his food is better than most of the Japanese restaurants I visited in L.A. His Miso soup has a good dashi broth base, and his Kakiage (shredded carrots, onions, vegetables, and small Shrimp Mix Tempura) is the best I've had outside of Japan. After taking one bite, Saito-san screamed, "Wow, this is dynamite! How come it's not on the menu? We should put this on the menu!"

Roberto simply said, "No."

One Thursday afternoon, after we closed for lunch, Roberto made soba noodles with Kakiage for makanai. Saito-san was watching Roberto, and we all sat down to eat.

"Roberto, this Kakiage tastes wonderful. Who taught you this recipe?" Saito-san asked.

"The previous kitchen chef, Shin-san, taught me."

"I think it's great. I know I asked you before, but why don't we put it on the regular menu? "

"It has always been a makanai dish, not for customers."

"What? Makanai only? It's a sin not to put it on the menu. Let's put it on the menu," Saito-san insisted.

"No, it is not for the customers!" Roberto suddenly yelled. He looked angry.

I didn't understand why Roberto raised his voice. If something tastes this good, why not put on the menu? There are so many stories about employee meals becoming signature dishes at restaurants. This Kakiage could be one of those stories. I knew it would become a hot lunch item. Why not try it? We had nothing to lose. This time, I agreed with Saito-san. It was a good idea, no, it was a great idea. We'd have more customers. We'd get busy. We'd make more money. Everyone would be happy. Why not?

"I think we should put this on the menu, " I said to Roberto.

"We will never put it on the menu because it's makanai." Roberto remained adamant.

Saito-san looked angry and frustrated. He, too, raised his voice, "Roberto, we'll put this on the menu, and you will be making this!" Saito-san stood up from his chair and walked out of the restaurant.

But then, a few weeks went by, and Kakiage didn't go on the menu right away.

Saito-san visited Miyako frequently to eat Roberto's makanai. Each time, Saito-san complimented how delicious everything was. Roberto made excellent Tempura, Chicken Kakiage, and even some Chinese dishes, like MaPo Tofu.

By this point, Saito-san must have tasted Roberto's Kakiage at least ten times, and each time he asked Roberto to put it on the menu. Each time, Roberto said, "No," and became angry.

A few days after the last argument, I finally asked Roberto why. "How come you don't want to put Kakiage on the menu?"

"Because it's messy. It makes my frying oil dirty. I have to change the oil more often. I already have a lot of work in the kitchen. I don't want to change the oil during our business hours, especially when we are busy."

Now, I understood why Roberto got so angry. Now I understood his perspective. He worried about the kitchen operation, something Saito-san would never understand. Roberto knew that when it was busy, he might not have enough time to change the oil, and that would lower the quality of the Tempura and other fried dishes. To him, it wasn't acceptable because he took pride in his work. He cared too much about the quality of his food.

Regardless, Saito-san put Kakiage on the menu, and as we suspected, it was an instant hit, ten orders in the first week, and twenty in the second week. Now, Roberto changed his frying oil between lunch and dinner, just another task he had to do. It can take fifteen-to-thirty minutes to drain the fryer. Once it's drained, it has to be cleaned, that's another ten minutes. Finally, the new oil needs to be added, another five minutes. While Roberto works on this for 30 minutes and longer, the rest of us have nothing to do, we can even take a nap. But, for Roberto, by the time he finished changing the oil, half of his nap time was already gone. Therefore every time he got a Kakiage order, I heard him groan in the kitchen, "Uhhhhh!"

*****

"How come we freeze Salmon here?" I asked Akio one day.

"So that we can keep it fresh, longer."

"Doesn't freezing affect the taste?"

"Well…" Akio squinted his eyes. Is he hiding something? I wondered.

"Some, but not too much. As long as we don't keep it like over a month, it's okay. Besides, we go through so much Salmon that it's gone within a week."

"I see," I said.

Toshi once told me he never froze Salmon because it changed the taste. He said that freezing sacrificed that nice, fatty, Salmon flavor. Technically, I'm not sure who's right, but it didn't seem like freezing was a better option judging by Akio's response.

"What do they do at Rock'n Hollywood?" Akio asked me back.

"They never freeze it," I said simply. I sensed Akio wanted to know more about the prep work at Rock'n Hollywood Sushi, but I kept my lips closed.

So each night, the Sushi Chefs at Miyako took some Salmon from the freezer and put it into the fridge to thaw overnight. Ebi was also frozen after they cooked it. The chefs would deshell and butterfly the Ebi, separate it into ten-piece bundles, wrap them in plastic, and store the bundles in the freezer with bamboo sticks to keep everything straight.

I learned that Akio's saba curing method was slightly different too. They also bought fresh, whole Anago (Sea Eel) instead of frozen. Filleting *Anago* was a lot different than filleting Tuna or Salmon.

*****

"What's this tiny hole on the cutting board, Akio-san?" I asked.

"Oh, that hole? It's for prepping *Anago*."

A hole for prepping Anago? I thought. Then, I realized that they bought fresh *Anago*, not frozen.

"You buy fresh and cut it open?"

"Yes, we do."

"Wow, isn't it difficult?"

"Yes, it is. It takes some getting used to because *Anago* is so much different from other fish."

Sea Eel looks like a white-colored snake. The very first thing you need to do with your *Anago* is pierce it in the eye with an ice pick to prevent it from moving around on the cutting board. This is the reason for the tiny hole on the cutting board. You then cut it open from the backside to remove the intestines and the bones. Since *Anago* is shaped so different from other fish—round, an inch thick in diameter—it takes some experience to locate the spine. It's also extremely slippery, you have to rub Anago with salt to remove some of the slippery texture.

I watched closely as Akio prepped the *Anago*. When he was ready to cut it open, he carefully placed his knife and slid it all the way from the tail to the head. His knife made a clicking noise the whole time, a sign that his knife was exactly where it was supposed to be.

"Are you cutting above the bones like we do with other fish?" I asked.

"Yes, the same idea. It is really hard to locate the bones."

Akio cut the *Anago* open with only one stroke. Next, he placed his knife just below the bones and let it slide again. I heard the nice clicking noise again, but there was something different.

"How come you are moving your knife from its tail?

"It's easier to remove the bones this way."

There were ten pieces of filleted *Anago* in the bowl now. Akio sprinkled them with salt, rubbed the eel hard, and then rinsed it with water. He then took the bowl of *Anago* into the kitchen and put it in a large pot filled with water, soy sauce, and sugar. The *Anago* cooked in the pot for 15 minutes when Akio removed it and let it cool, that was it. Freshly cooked warm *Anago*: there is nothing like this on earth, it's so soft and aromatic. It's one of my favorites, but I've only tasted it while I was working in a kitchen. I always wished that every sushi restaurant would serve warm, freshly cooked *Anago*, but I know it's not possible.

*****

"Why is this called #3?"

"That is because it was the third item on the Specials Menu," Akio told me. "It did not have any name, just Special Menu #3."

Special #3 was one of the most popular items on the menu at Miyako Sushi. A cucumber-wrapped roll with Snow Crab, Salmon, and avocado, but no rice, and cut into five pieces. On a typical day, we got five or six orders for #3. We always pre-cut extra cucumbers during our prep time for Special #3 to make sure we had enough for all of the orders.

Katsuramuki is a cucumber peeling technique that I learned how to do my very first day at Rock'n Hollywood Sushi. It's also how I cut my finger during my first shift as a Sushi Chef. I looked over at Akio and Mako's cucumbers, they were even and a lot thinner and nicer-looking than mine. I started to feel intimidated. I thought practicing *katsuramuki* at Rock'n Hollywood Sushi worked well, but here at Miyako, it required more cutting skills. The slices had to be a lot thinner so we could wrap *nori*, Crab, Salmon, and avocado with the cucumber at least three times.

I picked up another cucumber, placed my knife over it, and started to move it up and down, as I rotated the cucumber. My first incision looked good, and I continued to move along the same way. After my first round, I noticed my peeled cucumber looked wobbly.

"How come mine is looking wobbly and not yours? Your cucumber looks nice and even," I asked Akio.

"I know it's really tough. When I started, mine looked just like yours. It takes practice."

I knew that already. That wasn't the answer I was looking for. I needed technical advice, not a personal story of struggle. I was frustrated. *Okay, I need to regroup,* I thought to myself. Let's look at this logically. Akio and Mako have been Sushi Chefs for more than ten years. They've been practicing *katsuramuki* for a lot longer than I have. They also make sushi faster and better than I do. At this point, if I were doing everything as well as they do, I'd be a prodigy. Unfortunately, I'm not. I've only been a Sushi Chef for six months. It's okay that I'm less skilled than the tenured chefs. Instead of getting frustrated, I just need to practice. This is a great opportunity to improve my knife skills. I need to use this opportunity to accelerate my learning curve so that someday

I can be a better chef. I will not be defeated.

RUBIO

"Hey, who the hell is that?" Mako shouted, and we all looked outside. We saw a dark-skinned man getting out of a white GMC cargo van in the parking lot. It was Tuesday afternoon, around 3 PM, just after we closed for lunch.

"Is that a customer, who thinks we are still open?? Why don't you go and tell him we are closed, Kaz?" Mako told me.

I walked out the front door and met the man in the parking lot.

"Do you need Tuna?" The man said.

"What? Tuna?" I responded. I wasn't expecting that.

"Yes, Tuna. Do you want to buy some Tuna? I have a lot in my van. I sell them. Would you like to take a look?"

The man didn't look or sound suspicious, but I couldn't seem to figure out what was happening. *Is there really a man in our parking lot selling Tuna out of his van? What's going on?*

"Who are you?" I asked.

"My name is Rubio. My brother and I sell Tuna we get from San Pedro."

Okay, this is starting to make more sense now. I thought to myself.

"No need to buy, just to look and see if you like them. No pressure." Rubio continued.

"I see. Let me ask the Head Chef if he is interested. Please wait here."

I walked back inside the restaurant to tell Mako about Rubio and his Tuna.

Akio and Mako both looked at each other, shaking their heads.

"I dunno," Akio said, looking at Rubio and his van through the large window.

"Well, what we've got to lose? I'm sure it's not something we can use, but we can take a look," Mako said.

Akio was quiet, thinking. After a few seconds of silence, he agreed, "All right, why not?"

I knew it. I knew they'd be excited to see something new and wouldn't miss the chance to look at fresh fish. After all, Tuna is the "star" of the Sushi Bar, so if there's a chance to find a better Tuna supplier, we definitely shouldn't miss it. I was glad I got a chance to look at the Tuna as well.

We all walked back to the parking lot and asked Rubio to show us his *Maguro*. When he opened the back door of his van, we saw four large coolers, all neatly stacked. As promised, the coolers were filled with Yellowfin Tuna and lots of ice. Rubio pulled out one of the *Shibuichi*. Akio and Mako examined the Tuna, like a mechanic checks over a car. No one was talking.

"What are you looking for, Akio-san?" I asked since I wasn't yet skilled at *mekiki*. *Mekiki* is the ability to tell the quality of a fish by just looking at it.

"Ummm, color, texture, shininess," Akio mumbled. I was disappointed by his answer. I knew what we were supposed to be looking for, but I wanted to hear what kind of color and texture he was looking for in good *Maguro*. He looked serious. Then, he looked over at Mako, and they both nodded their heads.

"You know, these are not bad," Akio told Rubio.

"Oh, really? Thank you. I am glad you like them," he smiled.

"Can we take a look at other ones, too?" Akio says.

"Of course," Rubio responded. He opened another cooler in a flash. "Here they are." The second *Maguro* was about the same size as the first. Nice and firm, and a translucent dark red color. From what I know, these are all signs of a quality Tuna. Obviously, I couldn't tell how it tasted, but I assumed it was packed with a nice Tuna flavor.

"I go to San Pedro to buy some *Maguro* every morning. My brother and I both have been in this business for a while. I can give you a good price, too," Rubio added.

"How much is it?" Akio asked.

"They are around $12/pound."

"That's not bad. That's cheaper than IMP," I said.

"Yes, that is right," Rubio says. "You are...?"

"My name is Kaz. I'm an assistant manager here. I work at Rock'n Hollywood Sushi, also."

"Oh, that's good. Could I go there and meet the head Sushi Chef as well?" Rubio asked.

"Sure, you can. His name is Toshi. You can mention I sent you."

"Brilliant. Thank you!"

"We'll think about it and call if we want to use your Tuna. Thank you," Akio says.

Rubio gave me his business card and drove away in his van. "What do you think? Should we try?" I asked Akio.

"His Tuna is not bad, and the price is good. He said around $12 per pound, right? That's a good price. We could do a test order of one *Shibuichi* for this weekend. The price is better than IMP, a couple of dollars per pound cheaper, and the quality is good. Let's try it and see what happens," Akio repeated what we already discussed.

Not bad? I said to myself. I thought it was better than "not bad," but I refrained from saying it out loud.

I didn't think Akio would go for it, so I was presently surprised. I just assumed he was old-fashioned, hard-headed, *ishiatama* like Roberto, but I'm glad I was wrong.

*****

Two days later, Rubio delivered us beautiful Tuna, better than anything we got from IMP.

"Here you go, Akio-san. This is the best Tuna I have today, so I am giving it to you," Rubio handed over the Tuna with a big smile.

He probably said the same thing to all his customers, who knows?

But hearing it made us feel better. Akio and Mako were both delighted with Rubio's Tuna. I could see their excitement, like children opening a box of GI Joe toys on their birthday. Akio immediately took out his Yanagiba, sliced a small piece from the tail, and put it in his mouth. "Oh, yes. This is excellent."

From that point on, we bought all of our Tuna from Rubio. He brought us good Tuna every single time. Occasionally, we tried ordering from IMP to see if we'd find something better, but Rubio consistently delivered a better product. Sometimes, Rubio would even find us a Big Eye Tuna, which is a bigger fish and more flavorful than Yellowfin. As an added bonus, Big Eye Tuna has the occasional Toro (fatty tuna belly), which is seldom the case with Yellowfin. We sold Toro for more, but having a bonus Toro made us, as Sushi Chefs, even more excited because customers love Toro, and we didn't always have it. Personally, I like Chūtoro (medium Tuna belly) from a Big Eye the best. I find the Otoro (fatty Tuna belly) from Bluefin to be overwhelming, even though it's considered better and priced higher. Big Eye cost us only a dollar or two more per pound.

I liked Rubio because he was hardworking and honest. He always did his best to find us the best fish, and he gave us fair pricing. I'm glad Rubio decided to drive into the Miyako parking lot that first day. I'm also happy that Saito-san had sent me here to work. Otherwise, I may never have met Rubio at all.

*****

Rock'n Hollywood Sushi was a fun place to work, and Miyako was my training ground as an assistant manager. They were two completely different work environments, and I enjoyed working in both places. I gained a lot of experience and felt lucky to be able to train with a wide variety of chefs. My workdays were busy, I hadn't had a day off in three months, and I didn't get a raise or overtime pay, but I loved it. I learned all about the restaurant business, from the back of the house to the front of the house. I didn't know if I'd ever own a restaurant, but I was certain that the entire experience would help me one day.

I spent Monday, Tuesday, and Wednesday nights at Miyako, the quiet, cozy restaurant in a residential neighborhood on Ventura Avenue and Laurel Canyon Boulevard. The rest of the week I spent at Rock'n Hollywood Sushi on Sunset Strip, the brighter, more glamorous side of Hollywood Hills. It's incredible what a difference just a 15-minute drive could make. After spending the beginning of the week at Miyako, it felt nice to end the week at a busier place. You just can't help but embrace the energy of a younger, more energetic crowd.

Saito-san asked me to start working Sunday nights at Miyako, too, so I could learn how to close the register.

"After you write down everything on this spreadsheet, you put all the cash here," Saito-san explained, as he pointed to a small round black metal cover in the floor that resembled a manhole.

"This is the safe. You need these two keys to open it. You will find one in the register, and the manager has the other one."

He inserted both keys, turned, and lifted the cover.

"You know this cost $2,000 to have it installed," he mumbled.

I guess that's expensive, but I'm not sure why he decided to share the information with me. I said nothing.

"You put all the cash and spreadsheets in and close the lid. That's it." Saito-san handed me the manager's key.

When I started working at Miyako it closed at 10 PM, but Saito-san wanted to extend the hours to 11 PM on weekdays and midnight on weekends.

"I don't think that's a good idea," I told Saito-san.

"Why not?"

"Because it will be another burden for the employees. I don't think we will get a late-night crowd in this neighborhood."

He extended the business hours anyway.

Owners like to extend business hours to maximize profit. The rent doesn't change whether they open early or close late. So logically, they may as well stay open longer to get more customers.

In my opinion, longer business hours don't always translate into more profit. It can actually be harmful. Everyone wants to make more money, but no one wants to work longer hours. Ask anyone if they want to go home early on a slow night, and you'll find that most of them will say "yes.". It's boring when things are slow. Even the clock seems to move slower. Plus, slow nights are a lot more tiring than busy nights. It's strange. You get tired when you are busy, but it's sort of a good tired. Slow tired is bad tired. It feels heavy, physically, and emotionally. No one likes to work when it's slow. No one. And longer business hours could mean more "slow" hours— bad idea.

Initially, no one came into Miyako after 10 PM. But after about a month, customers started to realize we were open longer and started to pop in.

During lunch one afternoon, Miki told her customer that we were open till 11 PM now.

"Really? That would be great on the weekends," the customer became excited. "You see, most of the other sushi restaurants in the neighborhood are open late until 11 PM, too. I always thought you closed too early, so I am glad now you are open late."

I told Saito-san about Miki's customer. He said, "That's great! We should keep staying open late." I never did tell Saito-san how everyone hates working longer hours and slower shifts. I knew he just wouldn't understand.

*****

One Sunday night, I closed the register at Miyako and took the 15-minute drive over to Rock'n Hollywood Sushi. When I walked in the door, everyone was surprised to see me in black pants, a white-collared shirt, and a tie.

"Wow...Kaz? Is that you? What's happening? You look so...different." Emma's eyes were wide.

"Oh, I am coming from Miyako, you know, from working as an assistant manager. I have to dress like this," I explained.

"You look really nice," Emma winked at me.

*****

Just like the *Ten Little Indians* song, one by one, all of the old employees started to leave Miyako, until no one was left. Ricardo was the first to go. I wasn't surprised. Day after day, I could see how unhappy he was . Everyone knew it, and it was only a matter of time. Ricardo just didn't get along with Saito-san. They always argued, and there wasn't any trust. He was too close to the original owner. Ricardo liked the way the old owner managed the restaurant, and he didn't agree with any of the new changes. Saito-san, too, did what he thought was best for the restaurant, he wanted to make it better, but he just wasn't a good owner because he failed to listen to anyone.

Toshi once told me that Shige managed both Rock'n Hollywood Sushi and Sushi Suzuki. Saito-san just stayed in the office and took care of the books. Saito-san was never involved in the daily operations of either business. This explained why a lot of his ideas didn't make any sense. He lacked ownership experience and, therefore, couldn't gain respect from his employees. Ricardo included.

Saito-san never asked for anyone's opinion or bothered to take an interest in different perspectives at Miyako. For example, putting Kakiage and Crispy Albacore *Sashimi* on the menu put more of a burden on Ricardo because of the extra time it took to prep the additional ingredients and clean the fryer. Quite often, we'd even run out of Fried Onions, and Ricardo had to make more during the busiest hours, and he always complained about how "dirty" his oil was.

After Ricardo, the next to leave was the Head Sushi Chef, Mako.

"I found a position at another sushi restaurant," Mako told Saito-san, handing him a two-week notice. Miki didn't say anything about Mako's departure, but after he left, she confessed, "I never thought he was a good Head Chef. He was indecisive."

Shortly after Mako's departure, Akio quit too. He was going to work at Momoyama in Beverly Hills. It was a new restaurant where a renowned Sushi Bar, Katsuya, used to be.

Even though I never really got along with Mako or Akio, I remain grateful for everything they taught me. It had to be challenging to teach and work with someone with barely any experience. Someone who didn't follow tradition and was disorganized. Someone who had a hard time keeping his cutting board clean. Someone like me. Mako never pointed it out, though, or asked me to keep my workstation clean. I'm sure he wanted to. Akio, on the other hand, was superb. He had great knife skills and was always very tidy, and I tried to imitate his style, but I wasn't successful.

After Mako and Akio's left, Saito-san hired a new Head Sushi Chef, Jimmy, who was an old friend. Jimmy-san is quite a character. He loved drinking *sake* and gambled on his day off. He was a kind, friendly, and experienced Sushi Chef who got along with all of the staff. Jimmy-san was usually warm and calm, but occasionally lost his temper for no apparent reason, and no one could ever understand why.

When most of the original Miyako's staff left, it was time for me to go back to Rock'n Hollywood Sushi full-time. After all, working there was only temporary, and it had been about four months. It was quite a ride - a challenging, exciting, and outstanding learning experience. When I came back, Saito-san sent Juan over there permanently to fill my spot. Although I was glad to be back, we all missed working with Juan. Looking back now, maybe that was the plan all along, get rid of all of the old employees so Saito-san could bring in a whole new staff.

I briefly met with Juan at Miyako before I left for San Francisco. He told me he loved working there because the customers were more into the food, and they respected his art. I was happy to see Juan so happy. He found his small place in the world of Sushi Chefs and understands the Japanese work ethic of *kaizen*, never-ending improvement.

To this day, whenever I think of Miyako, I think of Juan and wonder if he's still working there. I only worked there for a few months, but it became a special place for me. It's where I met Akio and Mako, Miki, Ricardo, and Rubio. And, of course, Miyako is the place where I met my biggest rock 'n' roll hero: Mick Jagger.

YOSHIDA SUSHI

"Do you want to work with me at Yoshida Sushi?" Akira asked me, out of the blue, at his office on La Cienega Boulevard.

"Yoshida?" I said. The name sounded familiar, but I couldn't figure out where I'd heard it before.

"Yes, Yoshida. It's right next to my apartment on Highland Street. I go there for dinner a couple of times a week," Akira said. I closed my eyes and imagined driving on Highland Street, north to Hollywood Park. A vague image of an old apartment building and strip mall started to appear in my head.

"I think I know where you are talking about," I said.

"Food is okay at Yoshida, nothing spectacular. I go there because it's close to where I live, and there are no other Japanese restaurants in the neighborhood. Lots of families living in the Hollywood Hills go there, too," he added.

I was still working at Rock'n Hollywood Sushi when Akira called me and asked me to meet him at the office. He exported motorcycle parts to Japan.

"I know you are still working at the sushi restaurant, so I am asking you to quit and work for me at Yoshida."

"Aren't you still in the motorcycle business?" I asked.

"Yes, I am. It's been ten years since I started, but the business is slow because of Japan's economy, you know. Now, it's not doing so well, and people aren't buying parts from me anymore because anyone can find and order them online. I will probably close this office soon, so I need to find a different way to make a living," Akira said, looking determined.

"I see."

"That is when I met the owner of Yoshida, who asked me to work for him," Akira smiled.

"The owner is Japanese. He told me about the problem he's facing. Sushi Chefs don't listen to him. Waitresses don't care about the service, and the restaurant is running on its own without a manager." Akira sighed.

Restaurant employees not listening to the owner? That sounds familiar. I thought.

"The owner doesn't know what to do," Akira said. "So, that's why he decided to hire me to change everything. I think this is an exciting opportunity, don't you?"

I wasn't sure what he meant by exciting. Yoshida sounded like a bad restaurant. Why do you want to work for a bad restaurant? But where I saw a problem, Akira saw an opportunity.

"Here is the thing. The owner at Yoshida is thinking about closing the restaurant for a few months, remodeling the interior, hiring new staff, making a new menu, and reopening fresh. What do you think?" Akira said. "He asked me to be the new manager."

"The new manager?" I said.

"Yes, the new manager," Akira said.

"Are you going to take the job?"

"Yes, because, like I said, my business isn't going anywhere, and I need to find something to make a living," he answered. "It's perfect timing, so I decided to take it."

"My first job as the new manager is to find new staff," Akira said. "You're the very first person I am interviewing."

I was speechless. I didn't know what to make of everything he just said.

"Um, I just remembered I've been to Yoshida Sushi before. It was long before I became a Sushi Chef," I replied hesitantly. "I went there with my friend, Noah. He said the same as you. Yoshida is the only sushi restaurant in his neighborhood."

Right after I said that out loud, it hit me. *Yoshida is the only Japanese sushi restaurant in their neighborhood.* I guess it might be a good business opportunity, there wasn't any competition.

"How was it?" Akira asked. "What did you think of Yoshida back then?"

"Well..."I hesitated to answer. *Should tell him the truth?* Then I thought, *Why not? He's not the manager yet, and I'm not an employee*

"We sat at the Sushi Bar and ordered some food. They had Spicy Tuna as the Special on the menu, and I thought, who would put Spicy Tuna on a Specials Menu?"

"Yes, I know about the Spicy Tuna Special. It's been there for over a year," Akira giggled.

"Having Spicy Tuna on Specials Menu, is like having a Cheeseburger on the Specials Menu at McDonald's, right?" He asked.

"I agree," I responded. I'm glad I told him the truth.

"I ordered the Sushi Combination Dinner, which had some *nigiri* and California Rolls. I wouldn't go there unless there is nowhere else to go," I continued.

"That's exactly why I think this is a great opportunity," Akira said. "There is nothing else in the neighborhood, so that's why many neighborhood folks, including families, come to eat at Yoshida, even though the food is mediocre."

Akira sounded more convincing now.

"That's why we are going to be a success. It will be much better food, service, and everything," he explained. "It will be like opening a new restaurant. Most of the things will be new: new fish, new menu, new equipment, new staff, and new customers," Akira said, looking excited, like a small boy who just opened a box of model sports cars.

When Akira first asked me to work at Yoshida, I was skeptical. The restaurant was on the corner of Hollywood Boulevard and Franklin Street, in between a liquor store and a dry cleaner. There was nothing special to catch the customer's attention, and there was no pedestrian traffic. It was also in a shady part of Hollywood, behind the glamorous Kodak Theater and Hollywood & Highland Shopping Mall. It just didn't feel right. But after talking with Akira for a while, I started to think that the success of Yoshida depended on the location. Instead of looking at it as a disadvantage, Akira planned to use it to his advantage. I started to think, *Maybe this isn't such a bad idea.*

I didn't decide right away. I didn't see it the same way Akira did at first. I had some personal debt and couldn't afford to miss a payday. I could only afford to take a couple of weeks off if I decided to quit. I felt loyal to Saito-san, Toshi, and everyone else at Rock'n Hollywood Sushi. When I shared some of my concerns, Akira understood my hesitation, "Why don't we meet with the owner, and then you can decide what you want to do."

"Yes, that sounds good. Let's meet the owner," I agreed.

*****

It was 1995, five years before I became a Sushi Chef when I met Eiji, the manager of the Tiki Lounge, a trendy bar in Hollywood. It was a Hawaiian-themed Bar, famous for its delicious Mai Tai, the annual Luau Party with Hawaiian dancers tossing torches, and the young, hip, Hollywood "in" crowd.

I went there with one of my friends, Jenny, who introduced me to Eiji. He became my very first Japanese friend in L.A. Until I met Eiji, I only had American friends. I didn't really have an interest in hanging out with any of my Japanese colleagues. In college, I intentionally avoided Japanese students because I didn't want to speak Japanese. I rarely called my parents in Japan. Since I wanted to improve my English, I thought speaking Japanese would just interfere with my English-speaking skills. All of my roommates in college in Iowa were American and from the same places, Nebraska, Illinois, and other Mid-West states. I became friends with them to improve my conversational skills. I wanted to learn all about American culture.

It was hard to talk to my Mid-West friends about sushi. Like My friends' idea of seafood was limited to Long John Silvers and Red Lobster, or the Fillet-O-Fish sandwich from McDonald's. They grew up on these types of foods, so it wasn't exactly their fault, they just had no other choice. In Ames, Iowa, for example, where I spent three years, the closest Japanese restaurant I could find was in Des Moines, over 30 miles away. Even then, they only served cooked items like Tempura and Teriyaki Beef. I had to travel close to four hours to Kansas City, Kansas to find anything that even resembled *Sashimi*. But the only time I went to Kansas City, I ate Mexican food. Turns out I was too scared to eat raw fish in a town where the nearest ocean is almost 1,400 miles away.

I started going to social functions and parties, learning how to socialize and talk to people. It was difficult for me in the beginning since I was shy and had trouble talking to strangers. It was hard to find a common subject we could talk about. Everyone talked about radio and TV shows, celebrities, and local news, none of which I was familiar with. I used to stand and listen to the conversations but had no idea what they were talking about when they said things like, "Did you watch *Days of our Lives* yesterday?" Later, I learned it's a popular daytime soap opera on TV. I knew I had a long way to go to master my conversational skills, so I forced myself to find as many opportunities as possible to practice.

*****

When I met Eiji, it seemed like he shared the same values as I did about living and working in this country. He was married to an American girl. They had a son. He had a house in North Hollywood. He had lots of American friends, and he was working at a local bar under an American owner. He wanted to be part of the community, to be equal to other folks living American lives. He wanted to be an American, and so did I.

Eiji hosted a Sunday BBQ party at his house at least four times a year. He loved to cook. He cooked everything from scratch: from Deviled Eggs and Coleslaw to Japanese dishes like *Nikujaga and Sashimi*. He invited his co-workers and good customers from the Tiki Lounge to his BBQ. Eiji also had some Japanese friends who also had similar interests. They worked in American companies and hung out with American friends. At his parties, we spoke both Japanese and English.

Eventually, his BBQ party evolved into a New Year's celebration (*Osechi*) instead. Eiji invited all of his Japanese friends. At the first celebration, Eiji cooked. The next year, I decided to cook and bring some of my *Osechi* dishes to celebrate the New Year. I asked my mom to send me some recipes, including *Kuromame* (Black Beans) and *Nishiki Tamago* (Two-Layered Egg Cake). Everyone at the party complimented my *Osechi* dishes, saying they were the best they've ever had. It was a good time for all of us, and we loved it, we couldn't wait for the next one. Eiji and I even started talking about what dishes to add for the following year's party early. We watched Japanese TV, had some *sake*, and feasted on a special meal once a year.

I received more compliments for my Two-Layered Egg Cake than any other dish I made. Nothing made me happier than someone complimenting my food. I loved watching my friends eating, smiling, and laughing together. I loved that my food helped bring all of these people together, sharing a special moment of life.

*****

The Two-Layered Egg Cake was the most time-consuming dish, but the result was always astonishingly beautiful. Every year, the cake always made me think twice, *should I make it this year or not?* It just took a lot of time. But the rewards were always happy smiles and compliments from my friends. It was worth it, every year I encouraged myself.

The first step is simple. You make hard-boiled eggs. After that, you need to crack them and separate the cooked whites and yolks into separate containers. Then, strain each through a fine strainer, which turns the cooked eggs into a powder. Boiled yolks go through pretty fast, but the whites need more pressure and time. I used to spend a couple of hours just straining the whites while watching TV. Once the straining is done, you season both containers with salt and sugar. Finally, you build the cake, layering the whites first, then the yolks on top in a square pan. Steam the pan for about ten minutes, let it cool, and your Two-Layered Egg Cake is complete.

I also added some sushi dishes to the menu, like *Battera Oshi-Zushi*, a dish of pressed sushi with cured Mackerel. Even though I only get a chance to make most of these things only once a year, I become better at prepping, scheduling, and cooking every year. I've found that the most important part of cooking is planning ahead: making a list of the dishes I want to cook and the ingredients I need to buy, then planning out when to shop, when to prep, when to cook, and so on.

It was at Eiji's *Osechi* Party, where I first met Akira. Akira and Eiji used to work at California Beach in Hermosa Beach, a rock 'n' roll sushi restaurant. The restaurant was legendary, known for selling more bottles of Sapporo than any other place in the U.S. Akira was the manager at California Beach. Once, he said that they used to deliver Sapporo in a 20-foot container, which sat in their parking lot. They were one of the original rock 'n' roll sushi joints in L.A that made *Sake* Bombs and chugging a large bottle of Sapporo famous, all before Rock'n Hollywood Sushi and Tokyo Delve's opened their doors.

When I first met Akira, he owned a motorcycle export business. Akira was a biker and owned a custom chopper made by Jesse James. Apparently, Akira and Jesse were friends long before Jesse and his shop, West Coast Choppers, became famous on the Discovery Channel. Akira never mentioned how much he paid, but he did tell me that the bike was worth more than $50,000.

*****

A few days after Akira and I met in his office, we were at Yoshida meeting the owner, Den-san. Den-san was in his sixties. He had thin, gray hair, was of medium height and wore a light blue sweater and glasses. If he were wearing a business suit, he would look like a Japanese "Salary Man," commuting to work every morning in a sardine-packed subway in Tokyo. He looked calm, gentle, and friendly. Den-san recounted what Akira had already told me about closing the restaurant. He mentioned that he would leave everything to Akira because he trusted him to make things right.

That was it. That's what I needed to hear. At that moment, I knew the new Yoshida would be different, transformed, a brand new restaurant, just like Akira said. Den-san's words took all of my concerns away, and I saw Yoshida as an opportunity, just like Akira did. The thought of being apart of the opening staff at a new restaurant excited me.

"I will do it. I'll work for you," I told Den-san and Akira.

"I know Akira is going to be a great manager because he is great with people. I know it will be fun to work with him. This is very exciting. I'm so grateful to you both for giving me such a wonderful opportunity. Thank you!" I spit out as many words as I could think of.

Den-san and Akira both nodded and smiled.

Now, I had to think of a way to make my transition from Rock'n Hollywood to Yoshida Sushi run smoothly. I didn't have any savings because everything I earned went toward my personal debt. After payday, I didn't have a lot of money left in my bank account. Thank God for the cash tips, it was the only way I survived. I wanted to give at least a two-week notice to Saito-san. After some calculations, I decided I could manage no more than a month without income.

"When do I start working?" I asked the Den-san.

"Well, maybe in a month or two months. I don't know exactly, but I think it's going to take at least two or three months before we can reopen the restaurant," he replied.

I told him about my financial situation.

"You can take one month off, and then start helping Akira after that. Why don't you help him create a menu, choose dishes, change the interior, get new equipment, and so on?" Den-san asked.

*****

The following day, I gave my two weeks' notice to Saito-san.

"Why? You are going to work at Yoshida Sushi?" he exclaimed.

"Why? It's not good there," I asked.

Saito-san looked puzzled.

"I'm not mad about your quitting. It's just that what if the place is not good? Will you be okay?"

I nodded and explained the whole closing and re-opening plan. He seemed to understand but remained skeptical about the future of Yoshida Sushi.

It was going to be okay. I was determined, just like when I walked through the door at Rock'n Hollywood Sushi for an interview. I was grateful that Saito-san gave me this opportunity, but it was time to move on.

I spent only a year and a half there, but I learned a lot more than I ever would have in a sushi restaurant in Japan, I thought. I learned the basics of sushi-making, how to fillet fish, how to set up the Sushi Bar, how to organize my thoughts and my work station, how to tell the quality of a fish just by looking at it. I also learned how to serve and entertain the customers, how to respect and educate them, and how to anticipate their needs. I learned how to serve celebrities, how to treat every customer equally, how to work with waitresses and busboys. I learned the importance of music in a restaurant. I learned that everyone's taste buds are different, how to expedite multiple orders efficiently, how to own up to a mistake. I learned how to think and plan ahead, that teamwork is more important than any skill set, and that co-workers are there to help, even though it may not always seem that way. I learned how to manage a restaurant staff, communicate, prepare for the unexpected. I also learned that if you always serve great food, the customers will notice. I learned that one small change can make a big difference over time, how to be alert, but calm, to not raise my voice, and to arrive at least ten minutes before my shift started. And most importantly, I learned that love is the best ingredient of all.

I didn't tell anyone that I was leaving because I knew they would make a fuss. A week before my last day, I decided to tell Toshi. I wanted him to be the first person to hear the news.

"Really? Yoshida Sushi?" Toshi exclaimed, with his eyes wide open.

"I know, I know," I told him and then explained why.

Toshi told Kai, and Kai told Jun, and now all of the Japanese Sushi Chefs knew. I asked Kai not to tell any of the waitresses, but Emma found out two days later.

"So, I heard you're leaving, right?" she asked.

"Yup, that is correct," I said.

"Oh, that is sad. When is your last day?" Emma asked.

"Next Saturday," I told her.

*****

I clocked out at the end of my last shift, when Emma appeared with a whole German Chocolate Cake from the famous bakery, Sweet Lady Jane, on Melrose Ave. It had candles and, "Thank you; we'll miss you," written on a small piece of chocolate.

"How did you know this is my favorite cake?" I asked Emma.

"Toshi told me, so we ordered one for you," she replied.

"You didn't have to that, but thank you!" I smiled at Emma, trying to hold back my emotions.

"We'll miss you," she continued.

At that moment, I was moved by the gesture but then realized that no one was really going to miss me, except maybe the Sushi Chefs. In a week or two, life would just go on as if nothing happened, just like it did before I came along. I'm sure most of the Sushi Chefs and waitresses who came before me experienced the same feelings too. *Is there anyone here who misses Shige?* I wondered.

For the two weeks after I gave my notice to Saito-san, I felt anxious. I didn't know if I made the right choice. *What if Yoshida doesn't work out?* I had to keep telling myself that everything was going to be okay, things work out the way they're supposed to. After a while, a sense of hope replaced my fear. I knew Yoshida was going to work out. It would be a great success, a new beginning, a new adventure. My experience as a Sushi Chef at Rock'n Hollywood Sushi, as an assistant manager at Miyako, were all steps. Steps leading me to Yoshida Sushi.

After we closed for the night, Big Earl bought us bottles of Sapporo, two for me, and one for each Sushi Chef. We grabbed the bottles, raised them in the air, and yelled, "*Kanpai!*" Our voices echoed in the empty restaurant.

I emptied the *Neta* Case for the last time, cleaning the inside with a soapy sponge, and drying it with a towel. And that was that. I ended my last shift at Rock'n Hollywood Sushi. All the waitresses were already gone, so I sat down in an empty booth and took one last look around the restaurant. It looked exactly the same as it did when I walked in the first day. Empty, quiet, filled with an aroma of soy sauce, vinegar, Sapporo, *sake*, perfume, raw fish, tempura oil, and leftover sushi. But it felt different to me now. I love being in an empty restaurant. Sitting in the quiet, I always find satisfaction in a job well done. It's nice to be able to silently reflect on the orders I made, the customers I served, the drinks I drank, the conversations I had, the mistakes I made, the skills I learned, and all the fun I had. I knew, in time, no one would remember me, but that would be OK because I WILL remember everything. The party will go on.

Looking back, I realize that this was the perfect place to start my sushi career. As someone without experience, I learned the art of sushi. I know I was clumsy, but I learned. And for that, I will be forever grateful.

Toshi, Kai, and Jun joined me in the booth. We all shared a final glass of Sapporo and raised it in the air together, *Otsukaresama,* a job well done.

*****

My one-month vacation flew by.

On my first day at Yoshida, I met with Akira and Toru, the new Executive Chef.

Toru graduated from the prestigious Tsuji Culinary Institute in Japan, trained in fundamental Japanese cuisine. He was in his early 40s and held a chef's license issued by the Japanese government.

Toru and Akira were discussing the menu when I walked in. I noticed some interesting appetizers, like Pumpkin Fried Sticks.

Akira told me about the new menu. It was ambitions and a lot different from Yoshida Sushi's old menu. Akira's goal was to include more authentic *nigiri* and fish, but also be modern with *izakaya*-style, small bites. It was challenging to find a balance between sushi and small plates. *Is this a Sushi Bar with Japanese fare or, is this a Japanese restaurant with sushi?* The old Yoshida was a Japanese restaurant with a Sushi Bar, and most customers ordered from set dinner menus - like Chicken Teriyaki and Tempura Combination. Each dinner also came with a bowl of rice and Miso Soup. No beer, no *sake*, Yoshida was a family dining destination. Customers came between 5 and 7 PM, and the restaurant was empty after that.

Restaurants generally make profit from selling drinks, so that's what Akira aimed for; sell more alcohol. He wanted to shift the restaurant's focus towards the younger, Hollywood crowd, which meant staying open late, offer dishes that would encourage drinking alcohol, and no more set dinner menus.

Akira and Toru also discussed the types of fish they wanted to serve. They decided on interesting, unusual fish, like *Bonito* (or *Katsuo*), *Kohada* (Gizzard Shad), and *Ika* (Squid). I didn't know how to fillet or prepare any of those fish. They also had *Tamago* (Egg Custard) on the menu. This was another dish I didn't know how to prepare, but I always wanted to learn.

Akira also brought a few sample plates and platters from a restaurant supply store. We talked about plating and dish pairing. We looked at the menu and thought about serving portions and prices. There were so many things to consider that I never thought of before. Do you like the color? Is it heavy, easy to carry? Would *nigiri* look on this plate? Is it durable enough for restaurant use? Can we use this plate for multiple dishes? It just wasn't as simple as, "Hey, this plate looks good; let's use it."

When we removed all of the Japanese decorations from the inside of the restaurant, it looked empty and cold. Akira decided to put up a huge picture of Ryoma Sakamoto, a historical figure who revolutionized modern Japan. There was only one picture of him, so Akira contacted the city office where Ryoma was born. He asked for permission to digitize the photo and make a large canvas print to hang inside of the restaurant.

"The city officials are so thrilled that we're displaying Ryoma at a sushi restaurant in Hollywood," Akira beamed. "They are letting us use it with almost no fee."

I couldn't understand why Akira was so excited. I didn't know why he chose this picture as the only artwork in the restaurant. What is the tie between Ryoma and the restaurant? Maybe Akira just thought it was 'cool' that Ryoma was dressed in a traditional Samurai kimono holding a Japanese sword. I never bothered to ask because it wasn't my place to question his decisions. But every day, we made a little progress. One day the menu, another day, the kitchen layout. We had construction crews remodeling the kitchen, fixing the pipes, adding electric outlets, and creating a new Sushi Bar counter.

Akira always said, "We moved one step forward today." It sounds obvious and simple, but it's also true, something that we always need to remember. There are thousands of things that need to be done before you can open a restaurant. Breaking everything down into smaller chunks, and accomplishing each chunk one by one helps you move forward and get things done. It's a lot like making *Nigiri*, you need to prep all of the smaller ingredients first. I still try to remember Akira's words of wisdom whenever I tackle a big project.

*****

"Let's open six days a week," Den-san said to Akira. Toru calculated that he should hire five Sushi Chefs. Three main, full-time chefs to work five days a week, and the other two chefs could come and fill the rotation. This also meant that Akira and Toru would have to work six days a week, at least for the first few months, until things settled down. We all anticipated that the first few months would require a lot of adjustment.

Toru decided not to hire a Head Sushi Chef. This was a radical idea. The Head Sushi Chef at a traditional Sushi Bar is responsible for ordering fish, checking the fish inventory, and deciding on the Specials.

"I think all the Sushi Chefs should be equal at the Sushi Bar," Toru said. "If there is a Head Sushi Chef, then, the restaurant will become his style. We want to make Yoshida a more open, free, hip, and fun place for us to work, and for the customers to come and enjoy."

"I've seen many senior Head Sushi Chefs, and I don't like it. It doesn't help to create a healthy work environment. We are in Hollywood, not in Japan. No one is saying we should follow the tradition. I want everyone to be the same: friendly, and to exchange opinions freely and openly, regardless of experience and age," Toru explained.

I thought it made sense. Everyone always followed the style of the Head Sushi Chef, from filleting to making *nigiri*, to slicing *Sashimi*, to seasoning fish. It's great for quality control, but it tends to limit everyone else's creativity and freedom.

So, we decided to take turns. Every day, one chef would be responsible for ordering, inventory, choosing the Specials and setting their price, and making all of the Sushi Bar decisions. It was like assigning a Head Sushi Chef for the day.
We also decided that the Head Sushi Chef of the day would stand in the Head Chef position at the Sushi Bar.

At a Japanese Sushi Bar, the "Head" position is where a head or star chef stands, similar to the head of the table in a Western dining room. The place where the head of the family or the host of the evening sits. What defines the head position at a Sushi Bar, however, can be rather tricky.

In Japan, the head position is decided based on the flow of the restaurant, similar to Feng Sui. When we looked at the Sushi Bar, we decided that the position closest to the main entrance was the Head Chef position.

Toru chose to hire all Japanese waiters and waitresses referred by friends. The only non-Japanese staff was the dishwasher, Jesus, and the host, Geoffrey.

When it came to choosing a fish supplier, Toru decided to go with IMP, the biggest sushi fish supplier in Los Angeles. "They have the most variety of fish, and they are steady."

I also told Toru about Rubio, the Tuna dealer, that I met at Miyako Sushi.

"He is excellent, and I am sure you'll like him too," I said, and Toru asked me to set up a meeting.

"Hello Rubio, how are you doing? I am at a new restaurant and would like you to come and meet our Executive Chef."

"Hello Kaz-san, it's so nice to hear from you. I will be there tomorrow." He sounded excited.

*****

Rubio came to Yoshida Sushi the next day and brought some of the best Tuna he had. I felt confident referring Rubio. Toru looked at the Tuna and seemed impressed with both the quality and the price.

"Hello, Kaz-san. Very good to see you again," Rubio smiled, just like he did the I first met him.

I thought back on our first encounter. I was skeptical at first because he was selling Tuna out of a van and because he was Mexican. My stereotypical beliefs about Mexican people told me that he didn't know much about Tuna *Sashimi*. But Rubio convinced me otherwise. He changed my entire point of view, just like Juan did at Rock'n Hollywood Sushi.

"We'll call you for Tuna, but we'll be using other vendors, also," Toru told Rubio.

"Thank you, Toru-san. I am glad you told me that. Please give me a call whenever you need Tuna, and I will deliver it anytime," Rubio was grateful.

We called Rubio with most of our Tuna orders. If we needed extra Tuna in the morning, we had it by the time we started our afternoon prep. We all appreciated his hard work, commitment, and the quality of his Tuna.

*****

Freshly painted walls. A brand-new Sushi *Neta* Case. New wooden chairs and tables. A four-by-two-meter canvas of a historical Japanese figure on the wall. It was the grand opening day for the new Yoshida Sushi.

"Who should stand at the Head Sushi Chef position?" was the question of the day.

Since I was the very first employee for the new Yoshida Sushi, I became the first Head Sushi Chef of the day, standing at the head position, the closest to the entrance, at the beginning of the Sushi Bar. The Sushi Bar was an L-shaped wood countertop, with three long silver glass sushi refrigerator cases, one for each Sushi Chef.

We thought it would take the three of us about two hours to prep every afternoon. Since it was our opening day, we decided to give ourselves a total of five hours, just in case.

Toru placed the fish order the previous day. We had *Tai* (Snapper), which I never filleted before. And while I had some experience filleting fish, I was still learning. I knew how to fillet the Salmon, the *Saba* (Mackerel), the *Aji* (Spanish Mackerel), the Striped Bass, and the *Hamachi,* but I didn't know how to fillet the rest of the fish.

I probably could have asked Toru and the other chefs for help, but I was embarrassed. I didn't want them to know how little experience I really had. I was also intimidated by the other two chefs, Ko and Akagi-san. They both had at least five years of experience.

Nervously, I placed the *Tai* on my cutting board and started removing its scales. I moved the fish scale remover back and forth, causing the scales to fly all over the place - on my cutting board and on all of the freshly painted walls around me.

"Shit," I panicked. I grabbed some paper towels and quickly wiped the scales off the walls. Then I looked around to see if anyone saw. Luckily, they didn't, they were too busy prepping. I paused for a moment, trying to calm myself down, *Kaz, you can do this.*

I took a deep breath and placed my knife over the gut and cut it open. I removed the intestines, washed the fish in the sink, and put it back on the cutting board. When I wiped off the skin with my towel, I accidentally pierced my finger with one of the spikes on the back of the fish, which caused a little bleeding. *Stay calm, panic only on the inside.*

When I tried to cut the fish's head off, my knife stuck and wouldn't go through the bones. I pressed harder, but it still wouldn't move. I was frustrated, I tried and tried for three full minutes and still couldn't cut his head off.

I pressed down hard on the knife one more time. This time my it went through the bones and hit the cutting board, but I almost lost control. It was terrifying, *I could've cut my fingers off.* I looked down at my cut, it was terrible, and some of the bones were visibly smashed.

I didn't have time to worry about that, now I had to fillet. I already spent about ten minutes scaling, gutting, and removing the head. I had no idea how long it took the other chefs to fillet *Tai*, but I was sure it was faster than this.

I was getting agitated. This was taking too much time, and I still had a lot more to prep to do: fillet the *Hamachi* and the Salmon, cure the *Saba* and cut *Maguro* and *Hirame*. I also had to prep some giant clam.

In the end, I spent close to twenty minutes with the *Tai*, and it looked horrible, I wasted a lot when filleting. I sighed and looked at my wobbly pieces of *Tai*, embarrassed and disappointed. This was not what I imagined. We weren't even open yet. We still had three hours to open, and I had a lot more prep to do.

At five o'clock on the dot, the new Yoshida Sushi finally opened. Luckily, I somehow managed to finish all my assigned prep work.

Many of the old-time regulars and a few new customers walked in right away. Akira invited some of his friends. Eiji, too, had brought some of his friends, co-workers, and Alex from Tiki Lounge. Alex was a friendly and lovable character from England. He dressed just like a 70's punk rocker in black leather and chains.

All our hard work was finally paying off, and we were off to a good start. The filleted fish in front of me was a constant reminder that I had to get better. I silently apologized to Toru and Akira for my awful filleting skills. Prep was a complete disaster for me that day, but I couldn't share it with anyone else. But seeing all of the happy customers made it better.

Just like Akira said before, today, we moved one more step forward.

KATSUO & KOHADA

"I miss seasons," Ko said one night at Yoshida Sushi.

"I don't mind the warm weather here in L.A., but it would be nice to have some seasons so we can enjoy seasonal fish."

"Let's see what kind of fish they have," Toru looked at the price list from the fish company. One page was dedicated to "Fish from Tsukiji," which had both premium and seasonal fish.

"Look, they have, *Katsuo*. That's seasonal. The First Catch in the spring is great. I haven't had it for a long time. It'd be nice," Ko said. "What do you think, Toru-san?"

"It's not that expensive, about $8 per pound for the whole. That's about $16 per pound when filled," Toru said.

"Do you think customers are going to like it?" I asked him. "It's not something they're used to eating. Also, it has a distinctive, strong, iron flavor. It's not fishy, but definitely, more *fish* flavor."

"It's true," Toru squinted his eyes. "But it's worth trying. They may like it. The only way to find out is to try, so let's get some."

The following day, a beautiful torpedo-shaped fresh *Katsuo*, weighing seven pounds, arrived from Japan. It looked like an Albacore or a small *Maguro*.

Ko was the only one who knew how to fillet the *Katsuo*. I stood right next to him to watch and learn. He picked up its long fin, which reminded me of the fin of a Flying Fish. Ko looked excited, and so was I. I couldn't remember the last time I had a fresh *Katsuo*.

"The first part is the same as other fish, you gut it and remove the head," Ko explained. With his large *Deba*, he cut through the head, opened its gut, removed the intestines, and cleaned its stomach with water. The dark blood looked a lot like the blood from a *Maguro*, but the meat was a lot darker, more of a deep burgundy red, but still had a translucent.

"The next step is very different from other fish," Ko continued. "You need to cut the fin. It's a bizarre knife movement. Well, it's not strange, but more unique, and only done for *Katsuo*."

Ko placed his *Deba* by the top fin, circled it once, then inserted the tip of the knife to scoop out the fin and some skin adjacent to the fin. He left the rough, uneven cuts on top of the fish. It looked like someone just grabbed it and removed the fin by hand.

"It may not look like meticulous knife movement, but that's okay," Ko said. "After removing the fin, it's the same as any other fish. In fact, it's the same as *Maguro*, *Sanmai-Oroshi*, three-piece filleting."

Also, since *Katsuo* has such a powerful and distinctive aroma, it needs to be smoked to soften it. Traditional smoking requires a straw, but if you don't have one, you can alternatively sear it with a torch or over a stove.

When Ko finished prepping the *Katsuo*, he cut a few slices, then seasoned them with *ponzu*, lots of scallions, and grated ginger.

"This is good," I said. Toru had one bite, but he didn't seem satisfied. I went into the back kitchen and came back with a can of ground garlic.

"I think this is better," Toru poured some of the garlic over his slice of *Katsuo*. "Garlic goes well with *Katsuo*."

I tried another piece and thought it was better than the one with the ginger alone. The garlic seemed to enhance the whole taste of the *Katsuo*.

Now, we could serve *Katsuo* to our customers.

A couple of months went by, but *Katsuo* never became a hit, even with our regular customers. Overall, people seemed reluctant to try it because they'd never heard of it before. A few adventurous customers, however, did try the *Katsuo*, but even they had mixed reviews. In the end, we took *Katsuo* off the menu.

*****

"Let's try *Kohada* this time," Ko said, looking at the price list again. At

Yoshida, we received a fax every night from IMP. Thanks to the popularity of sushi restaurants in L.A. and Orange County, they received air shipments from Tokyo twice a week. One page of the fax was always dedicated to special items available from the Tsukiji Market in Tokyo.

"*Kohada*?" I said. "I don't think anyone would be interested in it. Besides, no one knows what it is."

"We can try ordering a small amount first and see how it goes," Ko said.

Toru didn't look amused. *Kohada* wasn't cheap. The fish was only about the size of a large Goldfish and cost $20 per pound - way over budget, even as a Special. Plus, only two Sushi Chefs at Yoshida know how to prep *Kohada*, Také-san and Ko, and they only worked on Friday and Saturday.

Toru-san, however, agreed to give it a try. We scheduled our first shipment of *Kohada* for a Friday delivery, so Ko could teach me how to fillet it.

*****

Kohada is definitely one of the most classic e*domae neta*. The day *Kohada* hits the Tsukiji Market in Tokyo indicates the arrival of summer, when all of the Sushi Chefs fight to get the first catch.

Kohada is an unusual fish, having four different names, all dependent upon how old or how big they are. The smallest fish are called *Shinko*. *Kohada* is next, followed by *Naka-Zumi*, and finally, *Kono-Shiro* when it's all grown up. For sushi, only *Shinko* and *Kohada* are used, while *Naka-Zumi* and *Kono-Shiro* are used in cooked dishes. There are some other fish that have different names based on size. *Hamachi* is one of them, referred to as *Buri*, when grown.

At the beginning of the season, the price of *Shinko* can get pretty high, even several hundred dollars per quarter pound. And, the smaller the fish is, the higher the price. Despite the cost, many Sushi Chefs still buy it because they have to have it at their Sushi Bar. Having the first fish of the season is tradition, and chefs will do anything to get it. If you don't serve *Shinko* in the summer, then you are not considered an e*domae* sushi restaurant. It's like having a Sushi Bar without *Maguro*. Of course, it's not like the Sushi Police are checking every restaurant in Tokyo to look at their menu. But it is about a Sushi Chef's pride: being an e*domae* sushi restaurant requires having the *Edo* spirit.

Prepping *Kohada* requires many years of experience; it's a tiny fish and takes meticulous attention and technique to fillet. Cleaning and removing the scales and bones are difficult without tearing its flesh. Once filleted, you have to cure it with salt and vinegar (*shime*). Curing times can vary greatly, depending on the size of the fish, its fat content, and the season. Determining the perfect curing time requires extensive training, and cured fish usually tastes the best the day after it's prepped, so a chef has to estimate the change in flavor at the time of curing. Some people even say that if you want to test a Sushi Chef's skill, let him prep *Kohada*.

*****

"First, you scrape off the scales using the *Deba*." Ko began when we received our *Kohada.*

He was using a miniature version of a *Deba* knife. I'd never seen such a small *Deba*, so I asked him about it.

"This is called *Ko-Deba*, a small *Deba*, and it's perfect for small fish. I use it for *Kohada, Saba*, and things like that. I bought this while in Japan."

"Really. I did not know such a knife would exist."

"I know. I hardly used it until now, so I am glad I have a chance to use it here."

Ko looked excited and enthusiastic when he told me about new things. He knew way more than I did about sushi techniques and fish. I was thrilled Toru had hired him.

"After the scales, cut the edge off the stomach like this, moving the knife alongside the stomach. Then, using the tip of the knife, gut it, scrapping out everything from the stomach. Then cut it open, butterfly it, remove the small bones, and then wash it in water. Gently, very gently."

"Ok thanks. I will give a try," I said.

I picked up one *Kohada*. It was the smallest fish I ever filleted, and it looked like more like a pet fish than a meal. It may have been a little bigger than a Goldfish. I only had a regular *Deba* knife, which seemed entirely too big to use on the *Kohada*, but I didn't have much of a choice. I slid the tip of my *Deba* into the fish. I cut more than half off the stomach.

"Whoops. That did not go well," I said. "It's so soft, and when I cut it, its stomach just falls apart."

"I know. It's really, really soft, and you need to handle it carefully and gently when you cut it."

I felt stuck, at a loss. I looked at my sad-looking half filleted *Kohada* for about thirty seconds and then decided to keep going. I scraped out the intestines from its small belly, and then slide my knife alongside the tail to butterfly it, or split it in half. By this point, the fish was a lot smaller than when I started.

That was even worse.

"Not to worry, Kaz-san. You will get used to it," Ko said, kindly.

Half of the *Kohada* I filleted wasn't even servable, but neither Ko nor Toru seemed upset. We cured them all in salt and vinegar to finish prepping.

"Just like *Saba*, the second or even the third day is the best time to eat *Kohada*," Ko said.

"Really? How come?" I asked.

"I don't know. Letting them *sleep* makes them taste better," Ko said.

TAMAGO

"If you want to know how good a sushi restaurant is, you should order *Tamago*," my mother used to tell me.

My mother's explanations always puzzled me. How could *Tamago*, a non-fish dish, test a Sushi Chef's skill? Shouldn't it be fish?

"Why *Tamago*, not fish?" I once asked my mother at a Kaiten Sushi restaurant.

"That's because it's difficult to make a good *Tamago*," she said.

"That's it? Is that the only reason?" I asked back.

"Yes, that is it," she answered.

Was that the answer I was looking for? Tamago is difficult to make? Maybe, but it still didn't make any sense to me.

A quarter-century later, I finally came to understand the meaning behind my mother's wisdom.

*****

I spent over 500 days watching Toshi make *Tamago* at Rock'n Hollywood Sushi. Every time he did, I wanted to make it too. I wanted to learn, and I wanted Toshi to teach me. So, I waited.

Finally, I thought I waited long enough. I knew Toshi decided my training, but one day I just asked him to teach me how to make *Tamago*. He said nothing. Not even a 'no,' just plain silence. I felt sad and betrayed. Even though I was frustrated, I respected Toshi. He was my teacher. There has to be a reason.

*****

My *Tamago* training started abruptly at Yoshida Sushi, 150 days after I left Rock'n Hollywood Sushi.

It was a slow Wednesday evening, around 6 PM. Ko, Ryo, and I were standing at the Sushi Bar, waiting for the evening crowd to come in. Toru came out from the kitchen to check on things.

"It's slow tonight, isn't it?" he asked.

"Yup, Toru-san, looks like it's going to be a slow night," Ko replied.

He walked up to my station to look at the *Neta* Case, "Kaz, it looks like you are doing a lot better than a couple of months ago. All the fish look great," Toru said. "Did you cut them?"

"Yes, not all, but some of them," I said. "I've learned a lot since I came here. I did not know how to cut *Tai* properly. I did not know how to prep *Katsuo* before. And I never prepped *Kohada*."

"You learned a lot," Toru nodded.

"Thanks to Kai and Také-san," I said. "They taught me well. I really like working here. Everyone is nice and teaches me a lot of things I don't know," I added.

"That's fantastic," Toru nodded.

He started to look around the Sushi Bar and noticed a warm, fluffy *Tamago* that Ko had just made.

"Look at this *Tamago*. It looks beautiful," Toru said. "Who made it?"

"I did," Ko said.

"I thought so. Ko, you are very talented," Toru's voice filled with pride.

Toru turned around and looked at me, "Kaz, have you ever made *Tamago* before?"

"No, I have not," I replied.

"Didn't they teach you at Rock'n Hollywood Sushi?"

"They never did."

"How long were you there?"

"A year and a half," I said.

"I think it's time you should start a new training."

"A new training?" I squinted my eyes.

"What do you say if I teach you *Tamago*?" Toru said.

"*Tamago*? Really?" I was surprised. In fact, I almost gave up on the idea of learning *Tamago* at all. After the way Toshi reacted when I asked him to teach me, I never dared to ask anyone else.

I felt like a kid with a free pass to Disneyland.

"Yes, really? Really, really? That would be great," I exclaimed. I wanted to raise my fists, and swing them in the air, but held back. I didn't want to offend Toru.

"Okay, then. Let's start your training soon," Toru said. "Ko made one for tonight. So, how about we start tomorrow?"

"Tomorrow?" I asked. "But, Ko's *Tamago* is enough for tomorrow. There will be plenty," I said.

"That's silly," he smiled. "Yours won't be servable for at least a month or two."

"Oh, that's right," I said. "So, what are we going to do with all of it? It will be such a waste, even for practice."

"Not to worry. We'll eat it for *makanai* every night," Toru said gently. "I don't think anyone will complain. It'll be one of the side dishes anyway."

"Thank you, Toru-san," I said, my heart filled with gratitude.

*****

The next day, I finished all of my prep work in an hour and a half. We had thirty minutes before we opened, so I went to the kitchen to tell Toru I was done.

"Good, you finished all your prep, right? Come over here, then," Toru told me. He had a small notebook in his hand.

"This book has some secret recipes," he whispered. "I am trying to find one for Tamago to teach you. It's a recipe I got from a friend at another restaurant. Where was it...?" Toru flipped through the handwritten pages in his notebook. There were so many recipes in that notebook, *dashi* broth, sushi vinegar, salad dressing, sauces..., everything.

"Ah! Here it is. I found it," Toru exclaimed.

"I am going to show you how to mix the egg first," he continued, as he walked to the refrigerator and grabbed a carton of eggs.

"You need to put ten eggs, sugar, salt, a small amount of soy sauce, and *dashi* in a bowl," Toru explained. "Which means you need to start making *dashi* first. But, look here. I made the *dashi* already for you. The *dashi* needs to be cold to mix with eggs. If it's hot, it will harden the eggs. So, be careful." Toru started to crack the eggs into a bowl.

"Soy sauce is for the flavor, not for the taste. Just add a little bit, like one tablespoonful. When you add too much soy sauce, the color becomes brown. You want to keep it nice and golden yellow," Toru said.

"I see."

Toru picked chopsticks up and started to stir the eggs. The chopsticks made a rhythmical sound as he circled them inside the bowl.

"When mixing with chopsticks, do it slowly to avoid too much air getting into the mixture. Too much air in the egg makes holes in cooked egg," Toru explained. "Just like this, gently move your chopsticks in a circular motion."

"After mixing, you want to strain it to remove the egg whites, so that the finished mix will only have the yolk." He picked up a strainer and poured the egg mixture through the sieve and into another bowl. The strained mix had a smoother texture without white spots. Now, we were ready to start cooking.

"Oh, by the way, the recipe is in my book, so write it down and keep it with you," Toru said.

"Thank you," I said. "May I taste the egg mix?"

"Sure, sure, of course," he said.

I picked up a tasting spoon and dipped inside of the bowl. The mixture was sweet with the flavor of the *Bonito* flakes from the *dashi*.

"It's quite—dashi flavored," I said. "Dashi is very predominant."

"Yes, that is why it's called *Dashi Maki*," Toru said.

Then he grabbed the wooden handle of a square copper *Tamago* pan from the shelf above the stove. He placed the pan on the stove and turned the flame up high. He grabbed a bottle of vegetable oil and poured some into the pan.

"The temperature is the most important and difficult part. You need to adjust the temperature constantly; otherwise, you will burn your eggs."

Toru was paying close attention to the size of the flame. He kept the pan over the heat for two minutes, until white smoke started to come out from the oil.

"Why do you put oil in the cooper pan first?"

"It will help to heat the pan evenly," Toru said. "When heating the pan, make sure to tilt it so that the oil touches both sides of the pan. To find out if the pan is hot enough, dip your chopsticks in the egg mix and run the tips on the pan, like this," he continued.

As he ran the chopsticks on the pan as if to scratch the surface, he made two thin lines of cooked egg with a sizzling sound.

"You see that? That means the pan is hot enough. Now we are ready to go," Toru said.

"Okay. Wait, I am going to write all this down. I'll be right back." I rushed to the Sushi Bar, grabbed my small notebook and a pen, and returned to the kitchen.

"Sorry, now I am ready," I said.

"An experienced chef can cook it in less than five minutes. That's how long you should aim for. Just five minutes," Toru said.

"Okay, five minutes," I agreed.

Then, Toru started to pour a small amount of egg mixture into the pan. Immediately, the egg mix began to harden, making some bubbles, but most of it was still liquid.

"Speed and heat control. That's the key. The faster, the better, but when the pan is too hot, you will burn your egg. The *Tamago* needs to be free from burnt brown spots," Toru said, as he moved the pan up and down, then side to side to spread the mix evenly.

Rhythmically, Toru poured the egg mix into the pan, flipped it, rolled the egg in layers, then poured in more of the egg mix, and rolled it again. As the egg started to harden, it formed into a round, like an omelet. The process looked like a choreographed dance, like watching experienced Sushi Chefs make *nigiri*.

"At this point, the inside of the egg is not completely cooked," Toru said. "We want to keep it half-cooked, so it stays nice and juicy."

Pour, roll, and repeat. Toru must have done it six or seven times until the egg became the same depth as the pan.

"It's looking good. We are done," Toru reached out for a plate and placed the finished, steaming hot, juicy *Tamago* on it.

Now it was my turn.

I looked at my notebook and made the egg mix according to the recipe I just wrote down.

"Are you sure it's fine to copy your friend's recipe?" I asked Toru.

"That's fine. He probably copied it from someone else, too," he smiled.

When I started to stir the mix with my chopsticks, Toru told me to stop, "You are moving the chopsticks too hard and too fast."

"Really?"

Yes, do it more gently," Toru advised.

I returned to my chopsticks and slowed down.

"That's good, "Toru gave me a thumbs up.

I placed the copper pan on the stove, added some oil, and waited until I thought it was hot enough. When I poured the egg, it didn't make a sound.

"You forgot to check the temperature," Toru said.

"Oh, I forgot," I said.

I poured out the now half-hardened egg from the pan and put it back onto the stove. After two minutes, I placed egg-dipped chopsticks on the pan and ran them along the inside. The egg hardened right away.

"The pan is hot enough now," I said.

I poured some of the egg mix into the hot pan and tilted it right and left to cover the entire surface. The egg started to bubble quicker than I expected.

"Now the pan is too hot," Toru said.

"What should I do?" I panicked.

"Roll it fast, and then pour more egg mix. Hurry, do it quickly."

When I flipped and rolled the egg to pour more mix, it was burnt and brown.

"What should I do now?" I asked Toru.

"Just keep making. Don't worry, and this is a practice," Toru said. "I am not expecting you to be successful right away."

I poured in more of the egg mix, and then I had to flip it. When Toru did it, he flipped the pan using his wrist; he didn't need to use chopsticks. The movement was similar to an experienced Chinese chef tossing ingredients from a wok into the air. So, I grabbed the wood handle firmly, lifted the pan from the stove, and then moved my hand backward to flip the egg inside. But the egg didn't flip; it just stayed in the pan. I tried it again, this time, with more force. This time the egg flipped halfway over and became a lump, not a nice roll of cooked egg. Also, by this time, I had spent entirely too much time trying to complete the flip. Now my egg was starting to brown. I rushed to try and turn the heat down.

"No, keep the heat. You need to practice with high heat. Lowering the heat is not the way to do it. If you need, you can remove the pan from the heat, or raise it up to control the temperature of the pan, and not the heat itself," Toru said.

There were so many things to pay attention to at the same time: temperature, flipping, moving the pan side-to-side, pouring, and mixing the egg. I was not that good at multitasking.

"When you flip the pan, you only need to use your wrist, not the whole arm. Just quickly flex your wrist, and you should be able to roll your egg," Toru said.

I poured another mix and tried to flip the egg, but I failed miserably. The whole egg became one broken, deformed lump.

"Oh, no," I said.

My first *Tamago* came out brown instead of golden yellow like it was supposed to be. It looked like someone dropped it on the floor. Some parts were torn and had holes. It was bulky, dried up, and sad-looking, but it tasted good.

"Hey, everyone, it's dinnertime!" Toru shouted. "Oh, we have an extra dish, *Tamago*, thanks to Kaz."

We couldn't serve my first *Tamago* to customers, but at least we were able to enjoy it, so I didn't feel so bad. After all, it was only my first try, and chefs can spend years mastering a dish.

I practiced *Tamago* every day for the next thirty days, and Toru served it for *makanai* every night. Everyone enjoyed my *Tamago*, and it looked better and better every day. After just two weeks, it wasn't a broken lump anymore.

While I practiced, Ko shared techniques with me that he learned in Japan. I had more control over the temperature, and I was able to flip the pan (or egg) better.

After thirty days of training, Toru looked at my *Tamago* and said, "Who made this *Tamago*?"

"I did," I said.

"Really?" Toru looked surprised. "I think this one is almost servable."

"Are you sure?" I asked, stunned.

"I said almost," he laughed.

It took another month before I was allowed to serve my *Tamago* to the customers at Yoshida Sushi. It took another year to achieve a level of perfection. Now, I can say that I can consistently make a good quality *Tamago*.

I found the most important key to a great *Tamago* is controlling the temperature, which isn't something a Sushi Chef is trained to do. I once overheard a French chef talking about how difficult it is to make an omelet. He, too, said the key element was temperature control.

I finally understand why my mother told me about *Tamago* at a sushi restaurant. To be able to make a great *Tamago*, a Sushi Chef has to spend several years, if not more, before he is allowed to learn how to make it. It signifies discipline, devotion, and patience. Learning about fish and *nigiri* is a given, and should always come first. A chef who can make a great *Tamago* is someone who's already spent years mastering everything else.

GO–SAN

The ordinary sign at the corner strip mall store was nothing fancy. Just large green letters on a white background, "SUSHI."

"Is that it?" Toshi asked me in doubt.

"I think so," I replied.

We both looked at each other as if to say, *Should we go in, or should we not?*

"This must be it. That's the correct address," I said. I remembered what Ko told me—it doesn't look like a sushi restaurant from the outside. He was absolutely right; it did not.

"Let's go in," I said.

I parked my car in front of the store, and both Toshi and I got out. He still looked skeptical, which made me nervous. But, at that moment, I trusted that it was going to be good. But, I never expected it to be such a memorable dining experience.

*****

"Go-san is great. I miss going there. Oh, I want to go there so badly," Ko said, one evening at Yoshida.

Ko was talking about a small sushi restaurant, *Go's Mart*, that no one ever heard of. There were a lot of new sushi restaurants popping up in Hollywood and Beverly Hills those days, such as Sushi Sushi, White Lotus, Katsuya, and Katana, but not Go's Mart.

"It's a tiny place with only four seats at the Sushi Bar and a couple of tables. It's my favorite place in L.A. I think might be the best Sushi Bar in town and a well-kept secret," Ko said.

"How come it's a secret place?"

"Not very many people know about it, even the Sushi Chefs. Go-san doesn't advertise. Only those who love sushi go there," he explained.

He was talking a lot faster than usual. "Slow down," I interrupted him, laughing.

"It's not really a sushi restaurant. It's a fish market with tables. That's how Go-san started. There's nothing fancy about the place. If you see it from the outside, you wouldn't even know that it's a sushi restaurant."

"Is it a place we can just walk in? No reservation or anything? Should we call ahead and make a reservation?" I asked.

"I think you should definitely make a reservation. Oh, I'm jealous you are going. I'm so busy with other work and the music band, I cannot go," Ko said, as he banged the wall with his fist. "Go-san is a very nice person, gentle, and friendly. You'll like him, Kaz-san."

*****

During my break, I called Go's Mart to make a reservation for Toshi and I. We had Sundays and Mondays off, and Go's Mart was closed on Mondays. We both knew that Sunday wasn't exactly the most ideal day to visit a Sushi Bar because all the fish suppliers are closed on Sunday. But, we had no other choice.

"Sunday is the only day we can go," I told Toshi over the phone. Ever since I left Rock'n Hollywood Sushi, we remained friends.

"Okay, that's fine," Toshi said.

"So, where is this place? Did you say, Canoga Park?" Toshi said, with a sarcastic tone.

"Yup, Canoga Park. It's all the way out there," I said, with the same sarcastic tone. "I know, but it's a good place. One of the Sushi Chefs at Yoshida said it's his favorite place, so I know it'll be great," I said, confidently.

"All right. If Go-san turns out to be great on a Sunday, that's good because he will be even better on weekdays," Toshi said.

Later, I checked the location of Go's Mart in my Thomas Guide, a map of the greater Los Angeles area. The Thomas Guide was owned by virtually every single resident of the city, and everyone kept a copy in their car. This was a time before Google Maps and smartphones. Los Angelenos knew where they lived using a combination of a page, letter, and number, like "Page 237, A-3." Go's Mart was on page 457, a back section of the map I never opened before.

*****

We drove an hour from Hollywood to Canoga Park. It had been ten years since I moved to L.A., and I was living in Santa Monica at the time. In all those years, I'd never been to Canoga Park.

Canoga Park is located in a suburb of Los Angeles in the San Fernando Valley. An area with lots of strip malls, single-story suburban houses, and two-bedroom condo complexes with swimming pools and a courtyard. No trendy clubs and bars. No Hollywood stars. No movie studios. No stylish houses. No slender, tall, beautiful men and women are walking around— no highly Zagat-rated restaurants. One thing Canoga Park was infamously known for was for being the adult entertainment capital of the world, aka Porn Valley.

Go's Mart was situated in the corner of a shopping mall with a big plastic sign.

Upon arrival, Toshi asked in the car, "How could we ever have known this place existed if you or Ko did not tell us?"

"I know. So, this is the best sushi place in L.A., better than Urasawa in Beverly Hills, according to Ko, so what's wrong with exploring?" I mumbled.

*****

When we arrived at Go's Mart, the parking lot was empty, and there wasn't a line to get in. It was quiet, very quiet. I was hesitant, but I tried to remember what Ko said, this place is just a hole-in-a-wall. As we walked inside the store, we noticed a small refrigerator with some fish and a sushi counter with only four bar stools. There were also two tables with two chairs each. It was like walking into a Mom and Pop ice cream parlor in a small town.

Behind the Sushi Bar stood a tall, skinny Japanese man with short hair and a stiff, rigid-looking face. We figured it must be Go-san. Ko already told me that Go-san didn't look friendly, at least at first sight.

"Hello…? We made a reservation for two people, under Kaz," I said to the man.

"Oh, yes…," the man paused for a moment. "Are you Kaz-san? We have a reservation for…two?"

"Yes, that is correct," I said.

"Good. We were expecting you. Here, please have a seat," he was looking down at the cutting board, moving his hands.

"Thank you," I responded with a bow.

We sat at the bar, observing the restaurant. Toshi and I were both a little anxious because we'd never been to a place like this before.

"*Irasshai*," Go-san said, handing us two cups of *ocha*, green tea. "What can I do for you?"

"*Omakase*, please," I told Go-san.

"Okay," Go-san nodded.

"Anything you cannot eat or don't like?"

"We eat everything," I replied.

"I understand. Thank you," Go-san said.

"I work with Ko, a Sushi Chef at Yoshida Sushi. He told us about you. That's why we came here today."

"Ko?" Go-san looked puzzled.

"Yeah, he has very long hair, plays guitar," I added.

"Oh, yes, Ko. I remember now. He's been here a couple of times. You work with him, huh?" Go-san said. "Well, today's Sunday, so we are a bit short of fish, you know. If you came on Tuesday, it would have been better, but, oh well, I'm sure you already knew that, right?"

"Yes, when Ko told me about you, we couldn't wait. We'll come on Tuesday the next time. At the moment, we both have Sundays and

Mondays off. We wanted to come here as soon as we heard about you," I told Go-san.

"I understand now why you come here on Sunday. Hope you like my sushi and come back on Tuesday the next time," Go-san smiled.

I felt relieved as soon as I saw him smile. It was the first smile since we walked. I ordered a bottle of Sapporo to drink while we waited for the first course.

Five minutes later, Go-san handed us two plates, "Here is an appetizer, *Nasu Dengaku*, baked Japanese Eggplant with some Sweet Miso. It should go well with your beer."

"Thank you," Toshi and I replied.

The eggplant was sweet and moist, just out of the oven, and it matched perfectly with the Sweet Miso Paste.

"This is delicious. What kind of eggplant is this?" I asked, observing the small round shapes.

"It's *Kamo Nasu*, Kyoto Eggplant," Go-san explained.

"Where did you get Japanese eggplant from?" I was surprised.

"My wife grows it in our backyard."

*****

Go-san's eggplant was sweet and creamy. It melted in my mouth. When I looked over at Toshi, his eyes were half-closed, and he looked delighted. We then knew that the next course was going to be just as good, if not better than the eggplant. Ko was right. This was going to be the best sushi.

I watched Go-san while we waited for the next course. Using his *Yanagiba*, he picked up a white fish fillet from the refrigerator case and made two slices. He picked one piece up in his right hand and then grabbed a small amount of *shari* with his left. He moved slowly, squeezing the fish and rice together, gentle and firm. Go-san's style was completely different from my nigiri-making style. Toshi and I worked in a fast-paced environment. The faster we made sushi, the better it was.

"Here is Hirame." Go-san placed each piece on our plate. We noticed it looked different from the Hirame we usually made. I served it with Momiji-Oroshi (Grated Daikon Radish with Hot Red Peppers and Ponzu sauce).

"What's this red topping?" Toshi asked.

"It's Goji berry," Go-san replied.

"Goji Berry?" I asked, beaming and looking at the red topping one more time.

"Yes, try it. It goes well with Whitefish," Go-san smiled.

I never thought of using Goji berry for nigiri. Whitefish has a very subtle sweet flavor and umami. Goji berry has a slightly stronger sweetness than Whitefish. It wasn't overwhelming but just enough to give depth to the whole flavor. It was brilliant.

"Here is Toro." Go-san's Toro looked different from the ones we were used to seeing too.

"This Toro is fantastic. Nice medium Chu-Toro. It's not overwhelmingly fatty, but good and pleasantly fatty," Toshi said.

"Where is this from?" I asked.

"It's from Spain. These are farm-raised," Go-san replied.

"I did not know they could farm raise Bluefin Tuna?" Toshi's voice was filled with excitement.

"Well, it's half farm-raised. They catch the adult Bluefin and put them inside of a large fishing net in the ocean. Then, they feed the Tuna and let them grow until they are nice and fatty. So, it is part farm-raised."

"Everything is fantastic," I said.

"Thank you," smiled Go-san.

We had some Kohada, Saba, and Uni. Each thing we tasted was new, and like we'd never eaten them before. In fact, it was the best sushi I ever ate.

One of the most striking differences about Go-san's sushi was the wide variety of toppings he used. He used Goji Berry, Gold Leaf, and Yuzu Peel. His finishing touches, though small, distinguished his sushi from others and made our dining experience extraordinary.

It was mesmerizing to watch Go-san making his nigiri, calm but energetic like he was putting all of his energy into each piece.

He took his time, which was completely opposite of what we were used to. It was considered a skill to be "fast-handed," at least according to every Sushi Chef I ever worked with.

Go-san had his own philosophy. He used, "one squeeze at a time," and looked like he was making a perfect Origami Paper Crane. He was very meticulous in an excellent, calming way.

Toshi and I both loved our dinner. The taste was incredible, but the whole dining experience was superb. I learned a lot from Go-san that night. He was inspiring. I wanted to be like Go-san, making one sushi at a time, while also making my customers happy. Someday I will, I told myself. Someday.

JIN–SAN

"Three years on a stone." That's what a Japanese proverb says. "Be patient. Spend three years devoted to something, and it will pay off." Just like a traditional Sushi Chef's training in Japan.

For the older Japanese generation, it's quite acceptable to go through rigorous training. The Japanese see value in hard work, devotion, and determination. To be a true master, it's crucial to master ourselves at every step of our training. Little things matter, too. Though one millimeter of difference in a day seems like nothing, in five years, that equals 1,825 millimeters, which is about the size of your foot, mastering the Art of Sushi is an accumulation of daily practice and never-ending improvement, focusing on efficiency, discipline, and attention to the tiniest details.

I once heard a story about a Sushi Chef's training in Japan, an apprentice who spent his first three years doing nothing but errands, cleaning the restaurant, and doing the dishes. Then, he made rice for another three years. He was finally allowed to touch the fish after five years. But he still didn't know how to make *nigiri* or *Sashimi*. He wasn't allowed to stand at the Sushi Bar and make sushi for customers.

I never met a Japanese Sushi Chef who went through such training until I met Jin-san.

*****

By now, I had two years of experience as a Sushi Chef. You could say I had an intense two years of training. You could also say I had only two years of training. I knew how to fillet basic fish, like Tuna, Salmon, and *Hamachi*. Unlike some of the Japanese Sushi Chefs who went through traditional training in Japan, I started to practice making *shari* during my first week, making rolls the following week, and *nigiri* and *Sashimi* after three months. I was allowed to touch and fillet the fish after ten months of training.

Working with other Sushi Chefs who had more experience made me want to improve my skills. I still didn't know how to fillet a lot of different fish, and I made rolls, nigiri, and *Sashimi* slower than most of the other chefs. I figured the only way to improve my skill was to get more practice. I was already working full-time at Yoshida Sushi, five days a week. So, I couldn't work anymore even if I wanted to. The only way to get more practice was to work at another sushi restaurant on my days off. I decided to look for another restaurant job.

It was 2002. I looked at the classifieds in the paper and found a place about an hour away in Long Beach called Sushi of Naples. When I called, I interviewed, and got hired. They decided to give me shifts on Sunday and Monday. The restaurant was on a street filled with shops and close to the beach. The neighborhood felt like a small resort town. Since I only had to go there on the weekends, it felt like a mini summer beach vacation. It was perfect.

*****

On my first day, I met Jin-san, the Head Sushi Chef at Sushi of Naples. He was a small, soft-spoken and energetic person. The Sushi Bar stretched from the entrance all the way to the backside of the restaurant. Above the Sushi Bar was a second floor with more tables. Behind it and below the second floor was the kitchen, where they made Tempura, Teriyaki Chicken, Teriyaki Salmon, and other cooked dishes. They also had Latino chefs who made sushi for the tables. Four other Sushi Chefs took care of the Sushi Bar orders. They were all Japanese, and the restaurant had about 70 seats.

Jin-san started his sushi training when he was fifteen, as an apprentice at a sushi restaurant in Tokyo. He lived in the owner's house above the restaurant. He slept, worked, and ate with the owner's family and other employees from the restaurant. Jin-san's story was similar to the ones I've heard before, but he was the very first Sushi Chef I met who had gone through the actual training in Japan.

"Is it really like the story I heard?" I asked him.

"Yes. My day started at six in the morning. The first thing I did was clean the restaurant floor, the dining area tables, Sushi Bar, bathroom, and the kitchen," Jin-san said in his soft tone. "The first year, my job was to take care of errands and deliver sushi orders. I was sent for shopping, and just about any small or big chore around the restaurant. The most important thing was to keep everything clean. Not only the restaurant but the tools, knives, uniforms... Everything must be perfectly clean."

"When did you practice making sushi, then?" I asked.

"Almost never for a long time because I was so busy doing chores. I had no time to practice sushi. Well, even if I had time, I was not allowed," Jin-san suddenly started to laugh. I didn't understand why he laughed, but I noticed Jin-san laughed a lot, sometimes with no reason. I found it to be charming.

A non-Japanese person might think, "Why would you become a sushi apprentice only clean and do small chores like forced labor?" The answer is simple, the Japanese value tradition, devotion, and discipline.

All of the small chores have nothing to do with real sushi training, but they will strengthen your discipline. And discipline helps build a solid foundation for lifelong learning. It's simply a test. *If you can't take care of the small things, how are you going to take care of the big things?* That's how the Japanese view others. They say: "The way you do one thing is the way you do everything."

*****

Whenever I had a chance, I asked Jin-san more questions. I wanted to learn as much from him as I could. I didn't want to miss this opportunity.

"Jin-san, when did you practice your sushi skills?"

"Whenever there was time. I didn't know when they would allow me to touch the fish. They didn't tell me. I didn't want to wait, so I made time to practice. Mostly on my day off, I would go to the fish market and buy leftover fish with my money. Sometimes, I got them for free," he explained.

"How?" I asked, wondering who was generous enough to give away fish.

"I befriended some of the fishmongers at the fish market. They saw so many other sushi apprentices doing the same, so they understood what I was going through. They were generous and encouraging. I used to take the fish to the restaurant and practiced filleting, making *Sashimi* and *nigiri*," Jin-san said.

"Did the usual training continue?"

"Yes. For the first several years, my main job, besides cleaning and small chores, was cutting vegetables and learning how to make *shari*. I worked from six in the morning, throughout the day without breaks, and went to sleep at midnight."

"That is a very hard and long workday," I said, feeling immense respect for him.

"It was all worth it," he smiled. "After several years of training, I started working as a Sushi Chef at a different restaurant in Tokyo. One day, I was asked to come to Los Angeles to help open a restaurant called Sushi Roku, the number six in Japanese. They named the restaurant after the six original chefs and partners who opened the restaurant. After working for Sushi Roku, I decided to leave and start working in Long Beach."

"I see. Did you want to come to America?" I asked.

"I never thought of coming to America. I planned to stay here for three years, help Sushi Roku, and go back to Japan. I did not want to stay here forever. But, for some reason, I ended up staying here for eleven years now," Jin-san told me.

Jin-san suddenly shouted, "*Irasshaimase*!" when he saw a customer walk into the restaurant. A middle-aged man sat at the Sushi Bar, right in front of Jin-san.

"Hello, Jin-san. It's so nice to see you again."

"Yes, me, too," Jin-san said and laughed.

"*Omakase*, please," the customer told Jin-san.

"Yes, one *Omakase*. We got a nice *Aji*, Spanish Mackerel, for you. I think you are going to like it," Jin-san said, with a smile

"I cannot wait," the man smiled back.

*****

At the Sushi Bar, Jin-san always looked happy. He engaged with his customers, made jokes, and entertained them. There wasn't a single moment when he wasn't smiling while in front of his customers. Just like Také-san at Yoshida Sushi, Jin-san was efficient, organized, and kept his workstation very clean. He was also fast, faster than any Sushi Chef I ever worked with. Twice as fast as Také-san and four times as fast as me.

After he finished serving his customer, Jin-san said, "I'll be doing some prep in the back," and left the Sushi Bar. It was a Sunday afternoon, and the restaurant wasn't busy, so I asked him if I could watch.

"Of course, it is not a problem," Jin-san smiled, inviting me to the back.

"I am going to fillet *Hirame*." Jin-san picked up a medium-size piece, weighing about two kilograms. He placed his knife on the edge of the fish and moved in a circular motion along the side fin. He then filleted the whole fish and did the same on the other side.

"This is *Sanmai-Oroshi*," Jin-san said. "Have you seen this? It's faster than *Gomai-Oroshi*."

"No. I only know *Gomai*, a five-piece fillet. Never seen *Sanmai*, three-piece before," I said.

"Really? It's very simple. Three-piece is a lot faster than five-piece. It's easier, too, when you get used to it," Jin-san smiled.

When you fillet a whole fish, the Japanese count the bone piece as one of the number of fillets, *Sanmai*, the three-piece fillet, is standard for most fish. Halibut is done as a five-piece, four fillets, and one bone piece. You don't count the head as a piece.

Jin-san moved so fast, yet so graceful. I had never seen anyone fillet a fish so quickly. I kept my eyes on Jin-san and stood completely still with my mouth wide open. It was like watching Clark Kent change into Superman in a telephone booth, right before your eyes. Before I realized what was happening, Jin-san was finished. It took him less than three minutes to fillet a whole Halibut.

"I'll teach you how to do *Gomai-Oroshi* later," Jin-san said.

*****

I noticed he was using an ordinary chef's knife with a white plastic handle. Something you would see in any restaurant kitchen. It wasn't a *Deba*, the fish-filleting knife, or a Japanese knife.

Jin-san noticed me staring at his knife and smiled. "You want to know where I got the knife?" he said,

"Yes," I nodded.

Jim-san smiled and said, "This knife is not *Deba* or *Yanagiba*. I got this knife from a restaurant supply store for $15. I have two of them, one to fillet fish, one to use at the Sushi Bar."

"$15?" I asked. "Really?"

"Yes, really," Jin-san smiled. "I do have an expensive *Yanagiba* at home. One of them costs over $2,000, but I never use them here. I could, but here it's casual sushi dining. If it were a Michelin star restaurant, then it would be a different story. There is no need for such an expensive knife here," Jin-san paused for a moment.

"Besides, you see, it's not so much about how expensive or how great a knife is. Many Sushi Chefs think it's the hard steel and the make, like Masamoto. But, it's how you sharpen it," Jin-san said.

"How you sharpen it," I repeated his words.

"Yes, it's how you sharpen it, how you take care of it that matters. I can tell what kind of a chef he is by looking at his knife. The knife will tell me everything," Jin-san said, as he looked at me.

I felt embarrassed because I knew my knife wasn't in great shape. Toshi taught me how to sharpen my knives, but that was it. That was the moment I decided to hang onto my inexpensive stainless-steel $60

Yanagiba from Rock'n Hollywood Sushi and improve my sharpening skills. I had so many opportunities to buy better a *Yanagiba*, but for some reason, I never did.

During my break, I borrowed the whetstone at the restaurant and sharpened my *Yanagiba* as best I could. I thought about getting the same knife as Jin-san used to fillet Halibut, but it would not be right for me. *I should hang on to my knives and learn to master them*, I thought.

I wound up working with Jin-san for less than twenty shifts during my three months at Sushi of Naples, but each time I worked with him, he taught me something. I learned more valuable lessons from him than anyone else.

Like Go-san, Jin-san inspired me, not just as a chef, but also as a person. He was warm, gentle, and patient. He taught secrets and life lessons, and he loved sharing his stories, knowledge, and experience. Nothing like the traditional hard-headed Sushi Chefs in Japan I had heard about in stories. I wanted to be able to tell other Sushi Chefs the same thing Jin-san told me, "I can tell what kind of a chef you are by looking at your knife." I didn't know when that would happen, but I knew someday I would.

TAKÉ–SAN

I didn't like Také-san when I first met him, but he taught me a lot. He was one of the original Sushi Chefs that worked at the Yoshida Sushi before it re-opened with a new owner.

Také-san seemed arrogant. I didn't think we could trust him. During our first meeting, I didn't know what to make of his facial expressions. He was quiet and didn't share his opinion like the other chefs did. *Why didn't he want to share his ideas?* I thought. He had more experience than any other chef in the room, 15 years. But Toru trusted Také-san, and never questioned him or forced him to speak.

I thought back to my experience at Miyako Sushi. The chefs were uncooperative and didn't want to accept any new ideas. I didn't want to go through that again. I thought Také-san was distancing himself from us the same way. We were new employees. He was an old employee. I tried to tell myself that everything would work itself out.

During the day, Také-san worked as a Head Sushi Chef at a big sushi restaurant in the Universal Studios Hollywood Shopping Mall. After he finished his day shift, he came and worked at Yoshida, three nights a week. We started to prep at 3 PM, and Také-san's shift began at 4:30 PM after most of our prep was done.

Také-san checked the fish in the Sushi Case as soon as he came in for his shift. He'd pick up each tray, open the plastic wrap, look at the fish for a few seconds, put the plastic back on, and put the tray back into the case. He checked everything, the Crab Mix for California Rolls, the Spicy Tuna Mix, and the vegetables. After checking all of the fish and vegetables, he'd open the small refrigerator under the Sushi Bar and look inside. Each time he found a container without a label, he asked, "What's in this?" It was usually some sort of garnish, scraps, or leftovers. Také-san also rearranged his workstation. He used the Crab and Spicy Tuna mix the most, so he moved them right in front so he could reach them easily. He also changed the order of the fish trays in the Sushi Case so that the Tuna was the closest to, *Hamachi,* next, followed by Salmon. Again, in the order he used them.

After observing Také-san during several shifts, I noticed he was able to make sushi faster than anyone else, but he wasn't exactly moving faster than anyone else. In fact, to me, he looked like he was moving slower than the other chefs. Still, he finished his orders quicker than anyone. *Why?* I wondered. *What is the magic?* I just couldn't figure out how he did it. Since I knew it wasn't magic, I started to observe him, and pay attention to every small move he made.

It took me roughly three to four weeks of careful observation, until I realized his not-so-secret secret: Efficiency.

Making a California Roll can be a messy process. The mayo in the Crab Mix and the avocado can make your hand and cutting board dirty very easily. Instead of grabbing the Crab Mix with his hand, like I did, he used a spoon instead. He also used the same spoon to spread the Crab Mix on the *nori,* whereas I used my fingers. As a result, Také-san's hands stayed very clean, so he didn't need to wash them as much. Me? I had to wash my hands every time I made a California Roll. I'd leave my station, walk to the sink, wash my hands, dry them off, and then walk back to my station. This whole process only took about ten seconds, but ten seconds after every single California Roll can really add up. That was the difference between Také-san and I.

Also, I noticed that Také-san made less of a mess than I did overall. Toru once told me that I was the "dirty" Sushi Chef.

"Your workstation is dirty," Toru shouted as he walked into the Sushi Bar one evening. "You must keep your workstation clean. Look at these food scraps, fish pieces hanging around on your cutting board, and the edge of your station, Kaz! You need to wipe them off with your towels."

Keeping my workstation clean wasn't something Toshi taught me about at Rock'n Hollywood Sushi. I thought I kept my work station relatively clean. I never thought I was a messy Sushi Chef until I started working at Yoshida with other experienced Sushi Chefs like Ko and Také-san. I knew I wasn't exactly clean, but it was humiliating when an

Executive Chef called me a "dirty" Sushi Chef.

So again, I observed Také-san carefully to see what I was doing wrong.

I noticed there was almost no debris left on Také-san's cutting board after he made a California Roll. When I made one, there was Crab Mix, avocado stains, and *shari* all over the place. I had to wipe the cutting board off with my towel and walk it over to the sink to rinse it off every single time. Again, the whole process only took about ten seconds, but that was more time I lost after every single roll I made.

By observing Také-san, I also learned that he picked up the perfect amount of Crab Mix each time, so nothing fell off his roll. He picked avocados up with the tips of his fingers, making as little contact as possible, and placed them on top of the Crab Mix. This made the avocados stable. When he rolled his roll, he made sure to keep all the ingredients intact, so that they didn't fall off of his *nori*.

When making a *nigiri*, Také-san casually placed the *saku* blocks in front of him and quietly slid his knife to make a slice. The whole movement looked calculated and well-choreographed— not a single moment of hesitation. Everything looked automated.

Me? I always had to stop and think about what to do next. I had to look for the grain on the Tuna *saku* once I placed it on the cutting board. If I put it down wrong, I'd have to pick it up and flip it over. Then, I'd examine it one more time to make sure I got it right. When I placed my knife over the Tuna *saku*, I usually stopped to decide how long and how thick I should cut it. By the time I cut one Tuna slice, Také-san would be finished making a whole *nigiri*.

I tried not to get frustrated. Instead, I decided that one day, I would be just as efficient as Také-san. One day, I would be a fast Sushi Chef at the Sushi Bar.

*****

One Thursday evening, Také-san walked in at 4 PM.

"Hello, Také-san. Aren't you early today?" I asked.

"Yes, it was slow at Universal City Sushi Bar, so I finished all the morning prep and left early," Také-san said.

That day, I was working at the Head Chef position, and Také-san was right next to me. He pulled out his knives from his bag and placed them on top of the cutting board.

"Is there any prep I can help you with?" Také-san asked.

"I think we need to do *Hirame*," I told him.

"All right," Také-san said, as he picked up one of his knives.

The knife he held was about ten inches long and curved at the tip. It looked like a smaller version of the knife the pirate in a movie would use during a battle.

"That is quite a knife you have there, Také-san," I said. "What is that for?"

"Yes, isn't it an odd-looking knife? It's actually a fish filleting knife," Také-san responded, with a smile. It was the very first time I saw him smile. "I saw a Mexican guy at the Wholesale Fish Company use this knife. I asked him how to use it, and he showed it to me. I thought to give it a try, and you know what? It's terrific. It makes filleting fish a lot easier than a *Deba* or long chef's knife."

"Really?" I was curious, "How would you use that curved tip?"

"Let me show you," Také-san said.

"When filleting Halibut, I use the tip to cut the skin like this." Také-san moved his knife along the Halibut's side fin and made an exact cut in line with the fin.

"You see, it's effortless like this."

"Wow!" I exclaimed. He made it look so easy. For a moment, I thought about getting the same knife but then realized that it's Také-san's skill, not the knife that made it possible. Having the same knife wasn't going to make a difference.

"By the way, where did you buy that knife?" I asked, anyway.

"At a restaurant supply store in Van Nuys. It only cost me $30," Také-san replied. I thought about Jin-san's $15 knife. Curious how two experienced sushi chefs, both used inexpensive knives.

"Can you show me how I can fillet Snapper better? I have minimal experience and always have difficulty separating the gut bones," I said. "We have one *Tai* here."

"Yes, Kaz-san, no problem. I'll show you," Také-san smiled at me again.

I handed him the whole *Tai* Snapper. He put it in a plastic bag and placed the entire thing in the sink. Then, he started removing the scales in the sink instead of on the cutting board.

"When you do it this way, scales don't fly all over the Sushi Bar, and you have less mess to clean up," Také-san explained.

"Wow, that is brilliant. I never thought of that," I replied. "When I scrape the scales on the cutting board, they fly all over the place and make it hard to clean. I sometimes find scales stuck on the back wall, and that is embarrassing."

"I know. That is why I use a plastic bag. It makes cleaning so easy," Také-san smiled.

The way he cleaned the fish was so simple but so brilliant. He was a magician, showing me the secrets behind his tricks.

That moment, something changed. I no longer looked at Také-san the same way I had looked at him before. I liked him. Maybe he was holding back before. Maybe he's shy. Maybe he's the type of person who needs time to get to know someone before he opens up. He wasn't anything like Mako from Miyako. He wasn't defensive or holding back. He wanted to talk to me. He enjoyed sharing his knowledge with me, and he wanted to, he liked to. It seemed like he enjoyed teaching me. I was the one holding back. I was intimidated by his experience. I was the one who didn't feel confident. I was wrong about Také-san. When I realized I could learn from him, I was no longer afraid. Now, I just wanted to learn as much as I could.

Later, I asked Také-san why he was so quiet in the beginning, he said, "Because I am an old employee, I did not want to interfere with you, Akira, Toru, and other new staff, so I was careful not to say anything. I just wanted to observe first and see how it goes," he explained.

*****

One day, during our evening prep, we were discussing a variety of techniques to keep the fish fresh in the refrigerator. Our goal was always to maximize freshness, color, and taste. The most standard way was to wrap the fish tightly in plastic wrap. Tuna, however, was wrapped in a paper towel first, and then in plastic wrap. The paper towel kept Tuna a nice, bright red. They even sell paper specially designed to preserve the Tuna color. Without the paper towel, it turned an unattractive, unappetizing darker red, faster.

"How should we keep *Tai* in the fridge?" I asked Toru.

"I think you should keep it whole, not filleting, tightly wrap it with plastic," Toru replied.

"I agree with Toru," Ko said.

Then, Také-san walked into the Sushi Bar to start his shift.

"*Ohayo Gozaimasu*," he said. "What are you guys talking about?"

"We are discussing what's the best way to keep *Tai* in the fridge," I said. "Could you share your opinion with us?"

"Well," Také-san took off his leather jacket, revealing his white chef's coat. "For white fish, it's better to fillet and store in the refrigerator. That way, it will age and taste better," Také-san said.

"Really? Fillet and plastic wrap?" I asked.

"Really?" Toru questioned him too.

"Yes, really," Také-san replied. "For most Whitefish, the prime is about five-to-seven days. You store in the fridge and let it age like they do with beef. It ages better when filleted."

We were all shocked.

"Wouldn't it better not to fillet the fish because of discoloring?" I asked.

"I know. It's hard to believe, right? I don't know exactly why, but from my experience, for white fish, it works better if you fillet it," he answered.

"Also, it's better to remove the skin before you store it," Také-san added.

Asking Také-san questions was like opening a treasure chest and finding a precious little jewel each time. I loved it. Now, all I had to do was to look for more opportunities to open that treasure chest.

FRESH FISH DOESN'T ALWAYS TASTE THE BEST

A Sushi Chef once told me about *Ama-Ebi*, Sweet Shrimp. He said it starts to taste better after two-to-three days in the fridge. When fresh, the texture is nice and plump, like cooked shrimp, but there's less *umami*. When aged a couple of days, Sweet Shrimp develops a sweeter *umami* flavor. The tradeoff is that the texture becomes different as time passes. The flesh gets softer, which affects the overall taste.

I guess I didn't know much about fish. I always thought the fresher the fish, the better it tastes, but I learned that's not always the case.

Paul Johnson, the owner of Monterey Fish Market in San Francisco, taught me that Salmon is at its prime five days after it's caught. Tuna, like Yellowfin, Bigeye, and Bluefin, can take anywhere from five days to two weeks to get that nice, savory taste. It's the same concept as aging beef to increase amino acids, glutamine, or *umami* in the meat.

At Kanpai Sushi, where I worked in L.A., I remember having "live" Halibut from a fish supplier. It was dead when it arrived at the restaurant, but the owner told us it was alive and fresh when he picked it up. We filleted the Halibut and sampled it to see how it tasted. The "live" Halibut had almost no taste and was tough like rubber, not edible at all. So, we decided to let it sit and age, or "let it sleep" in Japanese. We kept it wrapped tightly in plastic, over ice in the commercial refrigerator. On the third day, we tried it again. The meat was a lot softer, but it still lacked *umami*. On the fifth day, it finally started to taste like Halibut, tender meat with sweet *umami* flavor. Now that the Halibut was servable, we made *Sashimi* and *nigiri*, but we never told our customers about aging thinking, it might confuse them.

I later watched a documentary, *Jiro Dreams of Sushi*. Jiro's oldest son talks about aging Bluefin Tuna for up to two weeks to maximize its taste. It's a Sushi Chef's experience and skill that determines when to serve the fish. As such, aging is a crucial task for a Sushi Chef.

I always hesitate to answer certain questions from my customers like, "What's fresh today?" or "When did you get this fish?" because fresh fish does not always taste the best and, in the case of Halibut, it might be inedible.

Some restaurants carry live fish in a fish tank. The tank is usually displayed in the restaurant and filled with Spot Prawns, Crabs, and Lobsters. We tend to think that a live fish is fresher and tastes better than a dead one. But, those fish probably aren't in the best of health.

Fish swim in the open ocean and catch their prey. Imagine how you'd feel to being taken out of your home and placed into a small fish tank, not getting enough exercise, and not getting enough food. The change in the environment can cause stress for the fish. So, can we really say that the fish in the fish tank are as healthy as when they were swimming in the ocean? Probably not.

We tend to think automatically that a live fish is fresher and tastes better than a dead one. But, they're not always at their optimal health, even though they're alive. The fish in the fish tank usually taste inferior to the properly stored, aged, dead fish.

So, the next time you are in a Sushi Bar, don't ask, "What's fresh today?" Instead, ask, "Which fish is at its prime today?"

KANPAI

I'd been working at Yoshida Sushi for over a year when Miho, a Japanese acquaintance, came in for dinner. Miho was friends with Akira and Toru, so she and I were always friendly and spoke often. She told me about a new sushi restaurant she was opening, Kanpai, and asked me if I wanted to work for her. I was happy at Yoshida, but I figured it wouldn't hurt to go and take a look.

The restaurant was close to the LAX airport in Westchester, a neighborhood in Los Angeles. Westchester isn't exactly your typical L.A. hot spot. It has more of the suburban, small-town feel. And it was just a few doors down from Alejo's, my favorite Italian restaurant in the city.

The restaurant space was still under construction when I got there. The walls needed paint, and the refrigerator was missing. The floors also needed tile. But unlike Yoshida Sushi, everything at Kanpai was going to be new - the sushi bar, the plates, the refrigerators, the chairs, the windows, and the new storefront sign. Everything. It looked like they had a really long way to go, but I was excited to see what it looked like when it was finished.

I was also a little skeptical about the location, *A suburban neighborhood? Can we really open a successful sushi restaurant in suburbia?* I thought. But, the idea of working at a brand-new sushi restaurant excited me. After my experience re-opening Yoshida Sushi, I saw this as a significant step forward in my career.

I decided to join Miho and her partner, Shoji, in their new adventure.

I told Akira and Den-san my decision to leave Yoshida Sushi to work for Miho at Kanpai. They both understood my decision and wished me luck.

It was fun and exciting to be part of the opening staff at Kanpai. I helped create the menu and the dishes, and I even got to taste test the ingredients. Shoji was looking for new ideas, so I told him about some of the Special rolls Tom made at Rock'n Hollywood Sushi. Just as I hoped, the experience helped me explore a more creative side of sushi and gave me a deeper glimpse into restaurant ownership.

A week before opening day, Shoji came back from IMP with a variety of fish.

"Look what I found!" He had a huge, kid-like smile on his face when he walked in the front door. Shoji was carrying a long Styrofoam container packed full of fish.

"I got there early in the morning, and I saw all of the other 'big players' like Nozawa-san and Hiro Urasawa." Shoji named some of the famous chefs he met at the market. I thought back to my amazing *Omakase* experience with Nozawa-san. I knew Hiro Urasawa through Akira, who helped him open the Beverly Hills restaurant after Masa Takayama left for New York. It must have been quite the outing at the fish market.

We got busy prepping all of the fish Shoji brought back and made some of the dishes off of our new menu. We all got to taste them and then discussed the flavors. We were all very excited to open Kanpai and share our creations with our customers.

Opening day was incredibly busy, despite everyone's low expectations. And the second day was just as busy. In fact, for the first two weeks, from the time we opened at 5 PM until we closed at 10 PM, a constant flow of customers poured in, and out of the restaurant, there was never a dull moment. We even had customers waiting outside at 4:50 pm, anxiously waiting for us to open every night.

The unexpected popularity shocked us all. No one could figure out how it happened.

"Did you placed an ad?" Peter, a headwaiter, asked Shoji.

"No, I don't think Miho did," he replied.

Shoji, then asked one of the customers at the Sushi Bar, "How did you hear about us?"

"We shop at the supermarket across the street and saw the 'opening soon' banner when we walked by. You see, there's nothing out here. We have to drive around the city to go to nice restaurants, especially if we want fresh, quality sushi, so we are so glad you opened!" The man explained.

Word of mouth. Even though we had to push our timeline back a couple of weeks, people saw the banner. They were excited. They waited.

For the first several months, business was good, exceptionally good. Miho was happy, and Shoji looked extremely happy when the restaurant was full of customers. Kanpai was going to be successful.

Kaz Matsune

SAN FRANCISCO

LOS ANGELES TO SAN FRANCISCO

I met Yoko, chef, and owner of Minako Organic Japanese Restaurant during a visit to San Francisco. I really liked San Francisco, and Minako was located right in the Mission District, so I asked Yoko if I could work part-time at her restaurant. Yoko agreed and asked me to work on Sunday and Monday each week.

It was exciting for me. For some unknown reason, I always wanted to work in two different cities. Commuting between Los Angeles and San Francisco gave me exactly the experience I was looking for.

Luckily airfare was relatively cheap at the time, so every Sunday afternoon, I flew from LAX to SFO. Once I arrived in San Francisco, I hopped on the subway to 16th Street and then walked the final two blocks to start my shift at Minako at 4 PM.

I'd stay at Yoko's house for the two nights I worked in San Francisco and then turn around and fly back to L.A. on Tuesday afternoons. I'd make it back to L.A. just in time to start my evening shift at Kanpai.

*****

My real move to San Francisco happened in April of 2004. I heard about the San Francisco Zen Center from a Japanese Zen Priest that I met when I still worked at Yoshida Sushi.

It sounded like a fantastic opportunity for me, so I sent in my application to become a resident there. It was accepted, and I moved to San Francisco.

The three years I spent living at the San Francisco Zen Center (SFZC) were incredibly busy. As residents, we were required to participate in various practices, temple cleaning, and we each had to complete one kitchen prep shift each week.

During the day, most of the residents worked outside of the Zen Center, myself included. I continued to work for Yoko at Minako for a while, but I wasn't making enough money there.

Luckily, I found a job working at another restaurant, Ozumo. I mainly worked the lunch shift, but sometimes took evening and weekend shifts when they were available too.

I also knew that the SFZC owned the Greens Restaurant nearby at the historic Fort Mason Center, less than an hour north of the city. The restaurant had been open for 25 years and was started by the Zen Center's practitioners. As soon as a position opened up, I took a job there as a line cook in the evenings.

Between working two restaurant jobs and my responsibilities at the Zen Center, I didn't get a lot of sleep during those years. But my "five-hour sleep working at two restaurants, Zen Center life" is something I wouldn't trade for the world.

HOSTELS, COUCHES, AND FRIENDS

It was March 2008. I had no money, no savings, and no place to live. I was staying at a Youth Hostel in the Mission District of San Francisco, but they only let guests stay for two weeks maximum, and my two weeks was almost up. I needed to find another place to stay. I already exhausted my stay at the Youth Hostel in downtown San Francisco. There was one in Berkeley I could go to, but I didn't have the $15 round trip to spend commuting to work on the subway every day. I had $115 in cash, and I didn't know when my next payday was going to come.

One day, I was riding the bus when a familiar face hopped on and sat in front of me. It was someone I hadn't seen for two years.

"Janice?" I said.

"Kaz?" the girl answered. "What are you doing here?"

"Well..." I told Janice all about my situation, broke, and nowhere to go. Then, something miraculous happened. She asked me if I wanted to stay with her in her Nob Hill/Tenderloin apartment for a couple of weeks.

"That would be great!" I accepted with excitement. I can't even explain how grateful I was for her generosity.

Janice's apartment was tiny. One bedroom, with a small kitchen, and a living room. The first night, I slept on the couch in the living room, but it was small and uncomfortable. Plus, Janice worked in a downtown office and woke up at 6:00 AM to shower and eat breakfast so she could make it to work on time. She made so much noise in the morning that it was impossible to sleep through.

After that first night, two things were certain:

I had to find my own place to live as soon as possible. Two weeks would be entirely too long to stay at Janice's

The couch in the living room wasn't going to work. I had to find somewhere else to sleep. *But where?*

I looked around the apartment after Janice left that morning to see what else I could do. The kitchen was a decent size, but there was no way I could sleep in there. Besides, Janice used it every morning and every night to cook. I could sleep in her bedroom, but I didn't think Janice would approve. I mean, we were friends and all, but we definitely weren't that close. Then, I found a little closet-like room, long and thin, just big enough for a Yoga Mat. *I can make this work.* I thought. When Janice got home, I asked her if I could sleep in the closet. Even though she was surprised, she agreed. I wound up sleeping in her closet for ten days before moving in with another friend, Tom, in Oakland.

*****

Couch-hopping from friend to friend was difficult. I knew I desperately needed a place of my own, but that required money and a job. At that point, I didn't have either one. I decided to sign up with a temporary staffing agency doing on-call event catering because I thought it would be a quick and easy way to make some much-needed money.

The first job the agency sent me to was in a café at the *de Young Museum* in San Francisco's Golden Gate Park. As soon as I walked into the kitchen on my first day, I saw about thirty chefs rushing back and forth, carrying sheet pans full of potatoes, sliced chicken appetizers, and large bowls of salad. It was chaotic, like nothing I'd ever seen before.

The kitchen manager saw me and shouted, "Can you make whipped cream?"

"NO," I shouted back.

Next, he asked me to cut the bread, but I didn't own a bread knife.

"Have you ever cooked Roast Beef?" the manager asked.

"No, not really," I replied hesitantly.

Frustrated, he finally asked, "What CAN you do then?"

"I can make sushi and cut fish," I said confidently.

He looked confused, paused for a second, and said, "Well, sushi isn't on the menu. I need to find something for you to do."

So I chopped onions. I was a little embarrassed, but I didn't care. I was willing to do whatever it took to make some money.

After the Museum, the agency sent me to work in a cafeteria at a biotechnology company, Genentech. The campus was located in South San Francisco, and my shift started at six in the morning. To get there on time, I woke up at 4 AM and caught the very first subway at the Ashby Station near Tom's apartment. I'd take the subway to the Colma Station and then ride a bike for 30 minutes to Genentech. Not only did my friend Tom let me sleep on his couch, but he was also kind enough to lend me his bicycle. I didn't have any money for groceries, let alone to buy a bike. In fact, I even ate dried nuts and granola from Tom's cupboards when I was hungry. Sorry, Tom. I barely had enough money to ride the subway.

Unfortunately, I also had to ride uphill to get to the Genentech campus, and Tom's bike didn't have any gears. It was a painful commute, especially early in the morning, before the sun came up. Every time I rode that bike, I swore I wouldn't do it again. I had to find a better place in my life. I was 41 years old, making $17 an hour. Every kitchen manager I worked for was younger than me now and made quite a bit more money too. None of it made me feel any better.

One morning, I fell asleep on the subway, and when I woke up, I realized the train wasn't moving. I frantically looked around and realized that I missed my stop. I was at the end of the subway line. *CRAP!* I was going to be late for work. I panicked. I hate being late. *If I'm late, they can fire me,* I thought. Not good. Not good at all.

Wait... the train has to go back the way it came from, I realized. I sat as patiently as I could and waited for the train to start traveling back. I think I only sat there waiting for five minutes, but it seemed like at least 30. Sure enough, the train started heading back toward San Francisco. We arrived back at the Colma Station at 5:50 AM. *Hurry up, hurry up, hurry up!* I yelled in my head. Once the train stopped, I jumped off and rode my bike more furiously than I ever had before. It only took me 15 minutes to get to work that morning. I was completely out of breath and exhausted when I arrived, and luckily, no one even realized I was late.

After just a week of getting up at 4 AM and riding Tom's bicycle, I was ready for payday. Thankfully the agency issued checks every Friday.

TGIF, indeed. I picked up my checks at the office because I needed the money and couldn't wait for them to arrive in the mail. Every time I walked into the office to get my check, I felt ashamed and embarrassed. They knew I was in dire straits, desperate. Something had to change. I had to get out of this hole someday. *No, not someday, soon.*

*****

Since I was determined to stop the painful 4 AM commute, I started looking for a different job. I found an ad for a catering company in Emeryville, just north of Oakland. They were looking for chefs and were closer to where I was staying. I could save subway money.

So, I sent them my resume, and they responded, saying that I had a unique experience. We did a simple phone interview, and they asked me to come in for their employee orientation. I was excited. *Maybe this is it, the change I need.* I thought. Unfortunately, there was little work in the beginning, but it was enough to start saving, saving for a place of my own.

I still don't remember how, but eventually, I saved enough money for my first month's rent, last month's rent, and a security deposit on a $700 per month apartment in Emeryville. I signed a one-year lease and finally moved into my very own, one-bedroom apartment.

My apartment wasn't exactly in a great neighborhood; in fact, many considered it to be in a "bad" neighborhood. There was a lot of drug activity, theft, and vandalism, the "hood," for lack of a better word. My ten-unit apartment complex had a massive metal gate surrounding it, so it was considered safe as long as you didn't go outside of the complex at night. I heard gunshots and police activity almost every night, but I felt pretty safe staying up in my apartment.

Since the catering job wasn't steady, I found a second job at a sushi restaurant in San Francisco. But even that wasn't enough.

A friend then told me about a small firm looking for a graphic designer. I applied and interviewed for the position, and finally got the job: decent pay ($25/hour) and steady, daytime hours. My nights and weekends were still spent working at various restaurants in San Francisco too. I got into a bit of a rhythm. Working multiple jobs finally started to stabilize my income, and I was finally able to focus more on what I wanted to do instead of what I had to do.

Working at a restaurant was fun, but at 41, I started to feel that the long, physical labor at the restaurant kitchen wasn't something I could do for the rest of my life. I didn't want to find myself still working as a chef in a restaurant at the age of 50 or 60 because I had nowhere else to go. I also didn't want to stay in the graphic design business. It just didn't make me happy.

I needed a breakthrough.

Kaz Matsune

BREAKTHROUGH SUSHI

MY FIRST SUSHI CLASS

I wanted to start my own business, but what?

Maybe I could teach a Sushi Class, I thought, *that could bring in some extra money.* I could make my own schedule and offer a class whenever I had time. I decided to give it a try.

But where can I host my classes? That was the biggest question in my mind. I asked the owner of the catering company I worked for if I could use their kitchen. It was a nice size, about 2,000 square feet, and they only used when they had events. The owner agreed, and he was nice enough not to charge me for it. I was beyond thrilled and grateful.

I put a small ad on Craigslist because that was the only place I could think of to advertise. No one registered for the class right away, but I wasn't worried, I had nothing to lose.

One day, the manager of another catering company gave me a call and asked about the class. I explained it was about the basics of sushi – cooking *shari*, sushi vinegar, Inside-Out Rolls, Seaweed-Out Rolls, and Hand Rolls using fish, like Crab and Tuna. She told me about two chefs in her company who needed to learn how to make sushi, and she wanted to make sure I could teach them. I said, "Yes," and hung up the phone. I was excited. It felt great knowing that there were people out there who wanted to learn how to make sushi.

She immediately booked two spots for the class at $100 each.

One additional person also signed up before I held the first class. I told the owner of my catering company that I had three students in my first class, and he simply wished me, "Good luck."

*****

Three people. That was it. Three people signed up for my very first Sushi Class. I thought, *Wow! Three people signed up for my Sushi Class!* No one knew who I was, Chef Kaz Matsune was a nobody, I didn't think anyone would sign up for my class, but they did. Three people paid $100 each to come to a Sushi Class taught by me. In my mind, I was off to a great start.

The catering kitchen had all of the equipment I needed to host the class: cutting boards, knives, pots, and pans. It was very convenient.

All I had to bring in were ingredients. I bought vegetables from the local supermarket, and I found Yellowfin Tuna and Crab at the Tokyo Fish Market in Berkeley, the best retail market for sushi fish in the Bay Area.

I put all of the ingredients in a suitcase because that was the only thing I had available. I looked like I was on my way to the airport. I eagerly hopped on the bus and headed to the catering kitchen, just three miles away.

My friend helped me set up for the class. I was nervous. This was the very first time I was actually teaching other people about sushi. There was so much to think about - *How do I set up the room? Where do I put everything? How much prep should I do?* I knew what I was going to teach, but I wasn't sure what to say or how to explain all of the details. I had a basic class outline, but it simply said *1. Washing rice 2. Cutting vegetables 3. Mixing sushi vinegar 4. Rolling California Roll.*

I was both anxious and excited all at the same time. I had so many ideas about how I wanted to lead the class. I wanted it to be fun, entertaining, and educational all at the same time. It couldn't be boring, like a high school history class boring. I knew I wanted the class to be informative and interactive.

I knew it was a challenge, but I was eager. I wanted to make sure all three participants felt like they were getting their money's worth. I wanted to make my first class a big success.

As it turned out, I probably didn't explain things well enough. During the class, I thought too hard about the best way to describe the techniques, so my explanation wasn't smooth. I didn't choose the proper words. I didn't speak loud enough for such a large kitchen. I didn't smile enough. I was too uptight. The class wasn't as successful as I hoped it would be.

But, at the end of the class, everyone said, "Thank you. It was a great class."

I was thrilled. I was happy. I was content. I had something I could teach. I had something I could share. I could make others happy through sushi.

TEAM–BUILDING

After my first Sushi Class, I did a private Japanese cooking class in Marin County and a birthday Sushi Class for six in San Francisco. All my bookings came from an online class-listing site, TeachStreet.com.

A booking request for six people came in the summer of 2011. The client, Michael, told me to go to a condo at the Ritz-Carlton Residence on Market Street in San Francisco. I assumed it was going to be a private class, just like all of the others. I also assumed that he must be pretty well-off; after all, he lived in one of the most luxurious condominium complexes in the city. I felt intimidated, and maybe a little jealous. I thought, *Why can't I own a luxury condo?* I didn't like it, so I promised myself that one day I'd be successful. I didn't know how long it would take, but I'd get there.

When I arrived at the condo, a woman greeted me at the door and invited me in.

"Hello, my name is Nancy. Pleased to meet you," the woman said in a soft tone. *Wasn't the client's name Michael?,* I thought.

"Nice to meet you as well," I said. "Is Michael here?"

"Oh, no, he is not here yet," she replied. "This is my condo. Michael will be here shortly."

"Oh, it is? It's a very nice condo," I said.

"Well, thank you. It's a timeshare. I am a co-owner along with my colleagues. They will be here soon," Nancy said.

"I see. Is it okay if I start setting up for the class?" I asked.

"Of course. Feel free to use whatever you need in the kitchen," she replied.

I thanked her and started unpacking my things.

We started the class shortly after everyone arrived. I taught the basic rolls, California and Spicy Tuna. The class was great, and everyone told me how much fun they had. While they were enjoying the rolls they made, a woman commented, "This would be a great team-building event."

"Team-building?" I asked.

"Yes, team-building," the woman answered.

"Oh, that's a great idea," Michael agreed.

I had no idea what they meant.

"Hmmm, excuse my ignorance, but what is team-building?" I finally asked.

"You see, this is a company event. We are all from the same office. We work for Oracle," Michael explained.

"Oracle?" I said. I had no idea what that meant either.

"Yes, it's a computer software technology company. I'm the manager for this group, and this is a special gift for them," Michael explained.

"A team-building event is something a whole team or a department would do together to enhance teamwork," Nancy said. "We're saying a Sushi Class like this would be a great team-building event. It will be a bigger event, like twenty or thirty people."

Twenty or thirty at a time, I thought to myself. I tried to calculate how much a twenty-person class would be: two- to three thousand dollars. Wow. Now my mind was all over the place, *How wonderful would it be to have that much money in my bank account?*

Since I only focused on the money, I didn't think much about the team-building part of it. I just wanted to have a bigger class, and I didn't care if it was corporate or private. So, after the Oracle class, I forgot about the whole team-building concept.

A few months passed, and I held a few more private Sushi Classes all over San Francisco. One day a friend of mine asked how they were going.

"I did a class a couple of months ago at the Ritz-Carlton Residences. It was a very nice place," I said.

"That's good," my friend said. "What did they say about your class?"

"They liked the class. They also said something about team-building."

"Team-building?" my friend stopped me. "What is that?"

"It's kind of like a team bonding exercise or event," I explained. "Companies do it to enhance work performance or something like that.".

"You mean the class you did was a company event?"

"Yes, the company paid for it. It was for six people, though," I said.

"That's great," my friend said. "But wait, did you think about what you just told me?"

"What do you mean?" I asked.

"Well, it means that there are companies who are looking for a service like yours," my friend said. "And the best part? They have the money. Companies pay, not individuals. Do you know what that means?"

"I don't..." I said.

"It means you should do team-building classes," my friend said.

"Team-building classes?" I said.

"Yes, that's it! A Team-Building Sushi Class."

LEAP OF FAITH

Just before Thanksgiving in 2011, Dockers, by Levi Strauss & Co., had massive layoffs. They were one of the biggest clients at the graphic design company I was still working for, and consequently, our firm received less and less work. Everyone was abandoning traditional print and shifting into digital, non-print media. I knew that soon, there wouldn't be any work left unless we made the same shift. But the owner of the company showed no interest in leaving traditional print. We didn't design websites or digital online catalogs. When we weren't busy, our boss just sat around, playing video games until it was time to go home.

Feeling uncertain by the lack of leadership, I started to feel like there wasn't a future for me here. The money was decent enough to pay my living expenses, including my credit card debt. Plus, I received a bonus for the very first time in my life. I was forty-two.

After Thanksgiving, it was clear that I needed to find another job. I still had a part-time catering job and took some evening shifts at a sushi restaurant in San Francisco, but I knew they weren't taking me anywhere, either. They were just there to earn some extra cash. I knew that one day, I'd find myself up against a wall. I didn't want to end up like that: old and broke.

My co-worker, Brian, talked about two previous designers, both who quit and started their own successful businesses. Jake was a famous magician who now had a big name, Fortune 500 corporate clients, and a slew of private clients like Robin Williams. Mike opened his own design firm, specializing in political activism. Each time Brian mentioned Jake or Mike, I wished I had something like that. an idea and a talent for a successful business. I was jealous of their success. Here I was, sitting at a small desk in the basement of a 90-year-old building, working at a small graphic design firm most people never heard of, designing catalogs that 99.99% of the population in the U.S. didn't even know existed. The more I thought about it, the more frustrated I became. I'd had enough.

It was time for me to start my own path. My wife helped me start me on a path toward business ownership. It was the only thing that made any sense. It was a leap of faith, I was excited, and I never thought about failure, not even for a moment.

*****

Because of my financial situation, I couldn't just quit all my jobs yet. I figured it would take several months to get things rolling. I had to register my business, build a website, start promoting, and get some clients. I needed some business advice. I contacted Score, a government-run agency offering free business counseling from retired businessmen, and they matched me with Peter. Peter had been in the food business for twenty years. I met him every week, and he gave me some basic, good advice. "Do whatever you can to promote and establish the business. Find some clients. Put up flyers, business cards, and get your website up!" he advised.

More than anything, Peter supported me emotionally. He was there every time I walked into the office in the Financial District of San Francisco.

Peter helped me develop a business plan for Breakthrough Sushi. For the past two years, I'd taught close to a dozen Sushi Classes. I taught the basics, and everyone who came seemed to enjoy it, but I felt that the classes were just too "plain." I wanted to make them more dynamic, more interactive, and more fun. And now, my main target was "team-building." I decided to make it more like a seminar or workshop, bigger classes. This meant I needed a venue that could hold a larger audience.

BREAKTHROUGH SUSHI IS BORN

In 2011, co-working space was just starting to pop up in downtown San Francisco. Hub SF was one of them. They hosted various networking events and had a space large enough to hold fifty people standing. They were also non-profit, so I thought they'd be more open to someone like me, someone with no reputation, no Yelp reviews, no website, not even a Facebook page.

I met Hub's event community manager and shared my ideas. I talked about the "Sushi Challenge," an Iron Chef-like sushi-making competition to promote creativity and team bonding. I mainly wanted to test the class format for future team-building classes for corporate clients.

"We were just thinking, and looking for a community event to invite all of our tenants to," she told me. "This would be perfect. Let's do this on January 25th next year."

Right off the bat, there was one large issue: I planned to charge $100 person for the class, but Hub only wanted to charge $25 per person.

"No one would show up," she said. "Twenty-five is the highest we can go."

Twenty-five dollars per person didn't even cover the cost of ingredients. I told her I could do it only if someone donated all of the ingredients. As luck would have it, Whole Foods Market had a community program that donated produce to non-profits. I sent several emails to their community outreach manager— no answer. I also called the manager many times and left messages— no answer. So, one day, I just walked right into the Whole Food Market in SOMA, the warehouse district in San Francisco, and asked to speak to the outreach manager. He came out, listened to my story, and said, "Okay, email me a list, and we'll donate everything to you. The only thing you have to do is come and pick them up."

To say I was gratified was an understatement, I was ecstatic. It was the very first time in my life that someone was willing to support my business idea. I put together a long list of ingredients: cucumbers, rice, rice vinegar, seaweed, sesame seeds, crab meat, and fish, about $200 worth of groceries.

By mid-January, we had over forty people registered for the Sushi Class. Now I had to find an assistant, preferably a Sushi Chef, who could help me lead the class. Peter at Score told me about a Chef, Adam, who recently came in for business counseling. Adam wanted to start a Sushi Catering business, so I emailed him to ask for his help. He had some experience, worked at a lot of different restaurants doing pop-up events. He sounded like the perfect candidate.

Adam turned out to be available and more than a great help. Initially, I planned to use Hub's kitchen to prep, but there was another event that afternoon. Adam found a kitchen at a Bar in Mission, where he had hosted a pop-up event in the past.

On the day of the class, I picked up the ingredients at Whole Foods and took a cab to Mission to meet Adam. For three hours, we made *shari*, cut Yellowfin Tuna, mixed Crab Mix, and made some appetizers for the group. We packed everything into to-go containers, hopped in a cab, and drove back to Hub SF in SOMA. The cab driver looked unhappy when he saw us carrying the half-plastic wrapped containers of sushi and raw fish.

When we got to Hub, Adam set up the appetizers: Soy Marinated Tuna Temari Ball Sushi, Smoked Salmon Sushi Bites with Cream Cheese, and Vegetable *Chirashi* Sushi in a Cup. I set tables up with cutting boards, knives, bowls, and other equipment, most of which I borrowed from Hub. I didn't have aprons for anyone to wear. I barely had enough cash for the cab.

Peter from Score was there. When he saw almost 40 people, he said, "You have a great turnout!"

He was delighted, watching me taking my very first step, my very first class as Breakthrough Sushi. Honestly, most of the credit should be given to Calgary Brown, the event manager at Hub. She promoted the event and got people to come to the class. I certainly couldn't have gotten that many people to come. I cannot thank her enough.

I imagined the class to have the energy of a Tony Robbins self-help seminar, and the enjoyment of a Millionaire Mind workshop. I had a rough outline, but I didn't include every detail. I knew it would be okay, as long as I trusted the outline.

The first part of the class was a demonstration for the California Roll. I had Adam demonstrate the technique while I talked and took questions from the audience. After the demonstration, I divided everyone up into small groups of four, each tasked to make one California Roll. The second part of the class consisted of what I called "break," an Iron Chef-style Sushi Making competition.

I didn't know if other culinary team-building companies were doing this type of thing. I loved the Iron Chef series so much that I wanted it to be a part of my Sushi Classes. So, I used the same format and adapted it to a Sushi Challenge. Just like the TV show, I introduced the "secret ingredient" (fish) and gave the teams thirty minutes to make a new style of sushi to be judged. In addition to the fish, they had a wide variety of ingredients they could incorporate into their sushi.

When I announced the rules, everyone looked surprised and didn't know what to do. I was puzzled. *Why does everyone look so confused?* When I looked over at Adam, he seemed a bit puzzled too.

"Adam, what do you think is the problem?" I asked. "Everyone looks like they don't know what they are supposed to do."

"I don't know. Maybe it's because it's the first time they are doing something like this. Maybe you need to explain the rules again." Adam said.

"Okay, I will try," I said, a bit agitated.

After my second explanation, a few of the participants seemed to understand, but a lot of them still didn't. Then I overheard someone whisper, "I don't know what sushi to make..."

Then, suddenly, a light bulb went off on in my head.

"Adam, I got it. I got it!" I shouted. "They don't know what sushi is. They don't know what sushi means."

"What do you mean they don't know sushi, Kaz?" Adam looked even more confused.

"They don't know that sushi means 'rice'!" I exclaimed.

I raised my hands in the air excitedly and said, "Can I have everyone's attention, please?"

"I am sorry I forgot to ask you one important question. Does anyone know what the word 'sushi' means?"

Everyone turned around and looked at me, and the whole room was quiet. Their silence was the answer I was looking for. No one knew what sushi was.

"Let me explain what sushi is," I said confidently.

"Sushi is NOT raw fish."

Everyone was still silent.

"It's not fish at all. It's not raw or cooked fish or vegetables," I continued. "So, what does that make you think?" I asked.

More silence.

"The word sushi refers to this," I said, as I lifted a bowl filled with *shari*.

"Sushi, or *Su-meshi*, in Japanese means Seasoned Rice, which is this," I pointed to the rice inside the bowl.

"So, by definition, as long as you use *shari*, you can call it sushi. You don't have to use seaweed and make it a roll. You don't have to cut it into eight pieces. It can be a hundred pieces. It can be one giant piece. It can be any shape or form, like a circle or a triangle, it can stand high or low, it can be big or small, the only thing that matters is that you use this Seasoned Rice," I said.

That moment was the breakthrough.

After thirty minutes, the groups came up with creative sushi that no one had ever seen before. One team placed the *shari* and sliced fish in a small cup of red bell pepper and called it a "Sushi Boat Salad." Another team made a pie-shaped "Sushi Cake" with Smoked Salmon and Cream Cheese inside.

Aside from some of the small details, the class went exactly as I imagined - it was a great success. When I got home, I told my wife about how fantastic the class was and showed her all the pictures I took during the class. It was one of the happiest moments in my life. I thought about starting my own business since I was in my 20s, and now, at 43, I finally made my dream come true.

This was just the beginning of something extraordinary.

EPILOGUE

December 19, 2019

I received an email from Sally James, asking me to do a Live Radio Interview.

We do the shows live every Monday night from 7-8 PM and would love to have you for a half a show early in the new year. How's your schedule?

Cheers

Sally

I was stunned. Sally James is an award-winning Australian author, educator, chef, television presenter, and radio host. Her books and recipes have won international acclaim for food and wine pairing, health, and creativity. Why would someone like Sally James be interested in interviewing me?

Of course, I told her yes, well, more specifically, *I would be delighted.*

The Live Radio Interview took place on January 21, 2019. During the interview, I talked about my early cooking influences, specifically, Graham Kerr, the Galloping Gourmet. I strive to be like him, not only in the way I dress, but also in how I lead my Sushi Classes. I'm always trying to find a new way to entertain my guests. The half an hour interview with Sally went so fast, and it was over before I knew it. It was fun and lovely.

Two days later, Sally emailed me.

I'd like to connect you to my dear friend, Graham Kerr, who was delighted to hear your story and his part in it.

Um, what?! Did Sally just call Graham Kerr a 'dear friend'?? She's going to 'connect' me to him?? What does this mean?? What is happening here?? Am I actually going to be able to speak to the person who had such a significant influence on my career?? The man who influences the way I conduct my business every single day??

"You've got to hear this, " I told my wife. "Guess who Sally James wants to connect me with?? Graham Kerr!!" I exclaimed.

"What? Graham Kerr? Oh, my God. I can't believe it! That is so magical!!" she said.

So I sent an email to the Galloping Gourmet.

Dear Mr. Kerr.

I am delighted to send this email to you.

Ever since I saw you on Japanese TV, you have been my inspiration. You were speaking Japanese back then, so I never knew you had a British accent until I saw your original videos,

Every time I teach a Sushi Class, I feel I carry part of your style - I wear a bowtie, I make jokes, I offer a Hand Roll to a class guest to eat, just as you invited one of your guests to share the meal you cooked with you at the end of your show.

Thank you for showing me how to share the joy of entertaining others through cooking.

I do hope I have an opportunity to meet and talk to you in person.

Sincerely yours,

Kaz Matsune

Breakthrough Sushi.

Then, on February 10, 2019, I received a voicemail.

"Well, Kaz, it's Graham Kerr. You kindly sent me a warm email. Thank you..."

Wait, did that voice just say, Graham Kerr??? It took me a minute to wrap my head around his words.

Graham Kerr just left me a voicemail, and now he was just a phone call away.

When I first started Breakthrough Sushi, I never thought it would fail, but never in a million years did I expect my journey to turn out this way.

ABOUT THE AUTHOR

Kaz Matsune discovered his passion for cooking at a young age. Though he was born and raised in Western Japan, Kaz's inspiration came from watching Graham Kerr cook on the famous TV show "Galloping Gourmet." Kerr's enthusiasm, lightheartedness, and genuine appreciation for food made a lasting impression on young Kaz.

In college, Kaz studied graphic design and excelled in his field, even designing posters for major Hollywood movies, but the kitchen still beckoned him. He continued to cook avidly and learn all he could about the world of food in his own kitchen. When a friend commented that Kaz applied the same artistry and attention to detail to his cooking as he did to his designs, he decided to pursue his passion and become a chef.

Ever eager for a challenge, Kaz decided to tackle one of the most challenging and artful paths a chef can take: sushi. He spent years behind Sushi Bars, at first simply watching ("learning with his eyes"), then practicing tirelessly until he had mastered the skills and nuances. As a Sushi Chef, Kaz developed dishes for San Francisco's first organic Japanese restaurant, Minako, before moving on to Ozumo and then the famed Fort Mason restaurant Greens. In 2008 Kaz started teaching Sushi Classes for professional chefs and private clients, then in 2011, Breakthrough Sushi (www.breakthroughsushi.com) was born - the first and only sustainable team building sushi company in the US.

Since then, Kaz has taught over 10,000 sushi lovers, held lessons at the Culinary Institute of America at Copia, in Napa, California, and led team-building classes for some of the Bay Area's top companies, including Google, Facebook, Oracle, Intel, Hewlett-Packard, Verizon, and Citibank. He's appeared in videos for Survey Monkey and Grammarly, as well as ad campaigns for Adobe and Eventbrite. Kaz's writing is featured on Quora, The Huffington Post, Slate, and Apple News, and he has published three books on sushi.

Kaz is grateful to all our guests, clients, staff, vendors, and everyone who helped Breakthrough Sushi grow. He also states that he could never have achieved any of this without the continued support of his wife, who is the best business partner and adviser he could ever ask for.

Made in USA - Crawfordsville, IN
16545_9781693699283
08.12.2021 1907